CHINESE FOREIGN POLICY

CHINESE FOREIGN POLICY

Developments After Mao

by
Robert G. Sutter

PRAEGER SPECIAL STUDIES • PRAEGER SCIENTIFIC

New York • Philadelphia • Eastbourne, UK
Toronto • Hong Kong • Tokyo • Sydney

Library of Congress Cataloging in Publication Data

Sutter, Robert G.
  Chinese foreign policy.

  Bibliography: p.
  Includes index.
    1. China—Foreign relations—1976–   I. Title.
  DS779.27.S87 1986   327.51   85-6450
  ISBN 0-03-004572-X (alk. paper)

Published in 1986 by Praeger Publishers

CBS Educational and Professional Publishing, a Division of CBS Inc.

521 Fifth Avenue, New York, NY 10175 USA

© 1986 by Praeger Publishers

6789   052   987654321

Printed in the United States of America on acid-free paper

INTERNATIONAL OFFICES

Orders from outside the United States should be sent to the appropriate address listed below. Orders from areas not listed below should be placed through CBS International Publishing, 383 Madison Ave., New York, NY 10175 USA

Australia, New Zealand
Holt Saunders, Pty. Ltd., 9 Waltham St., Artarmon, N.S.W. 2064, Sydney, Australia

Canada
Holt, Rinehart & Winston of Canada, 55 Horner Ave., Toronto, Ontario, Canada M8Z 4X6

Europe, the Middle East, & Africa
Holt Saunders, Ltd., 1 St. Anne's Road, Eastbourne, East Sussex, England BN21 3UN

Japan
Holt Saunders, Ltd., Ichibancho Central Building, 22-1 Ichibancho, 3rd Floor, Chiyodaku, Tokyo, Japan

Hong Kong, Southeast Asia
Holt Saunders Asia, Ltd., 10 Fl, Intercontinental Plaza, 94 Granville Road, Tsim Sha Tsui East, Kowloon, Hong Kong

Manuscript submissions should be sent to the Editorial Director, Praeger Publishers, 521 Fifth Avenue, New York, NY 10175 USA

PREFACE

Since the death of Mao Zedong and the arrest of his more radical followers in 1976, the leadership in China has followed increasingly pragmatic policies focused on a search for economic programs capable of modernizing the country and improving the material standard of living of the Chinese people. Concurrently, Chinese officials have carried out major political reforms designed to bring about a more unified leadership capable of and committed to carrying out the important economic changes.

Chinese foreign policy has been influenced by these domestic policy shifts. It too must serve the primary concern with developing economic modernization. However, realities of international power and influence, seen in China's continued comparative weakness vis-à-vis the two superpowers in Asia, have grounded its foreign policy within the strategic framework developed under the leadership of Premier Zhou Enlai in the late 1960s and early 1970s. Faced with persistently growing Soviet military power and political pressure, but unwilling to mortgage the nation's future to the dictates of the USSR, Chinese leaders have relied on diplomacy as well as on their military power to secure their environment. Relations with the United States and its allies and friends in Asia have remained of key importance in Chinese efforts to secure the stable Asia so essential for national security and development. China's recent focus on economic modernization has strengthened its outreach to the West by adding a growing economic imperative to an existing strategic need. The increase in trade, student exchanges, and technology transfer amply testifies to that.

Within this broad framework, Chinese foreign policy remains capable of significant tactical shifts, which have occurred repeatedly in the post-Mao period. While several scholars have analyzed aspects of these changes in China's foreign policy in articles, compendiums, and shorter monographs, there has not been a comprehensive review of its varied manifestations in recent years. This book attempts to fill that need. It is written for both specialists and students interested in Asian affairs who wish to be brought up to date on the latest developments in Chinese foreign policy and their implications for the strategic framework that has governed China's approach to the world since the late 1960s.

The author has benefited from the publications cited in the notes and in the selected readings. He would particularly like to thank Michael Gibson, Harry Harding, Lee Sands, and Robert Worden, who read an earlier version of the manuscript and offered many helpful comments and suggestions. Of course, they in no way are associated with whatever flaws are seen in the book. Frederick Praeger, president of Westview Press, kindly granted the author permission to use in chapter 5 excerpts from an article the author wrote that was published in David W. P. Elliott, ed., *The Third Indochina Conflict*. (Boulder, Colo.: Westview Press, 1981).

Finally, the views expressed here are those of the author, and do not represent the views of the Congressional Research Service or any part of the U.S. government.

January 1985.

CONTENTS

PREFACE   v
1   DETERMINANTS OF CONTEMPORARY CHINESE
    FOREIGN POLICY   1
2   CHINA'S STRATEGY BETWEEN THE SUPERPOWERS   13
    Concern Over Soviet Intentions   15
    Leadership Debate   16
    The Threat of Soviet Attack   18
    Zhouist Strategy   19
    Sino-Soviet-American Relations   20
    The Tenth Chinese Party Congress, August 1973   24
3   PRC LEADERSHIP DISPUTES, EAST-WEST RELATIONS,
    COMPLICATE FOREIGN POLICY, 1973–76   29
    Fourth National People's Congress, January 1975   33
    Renewed Chinese Concern over the Strategic
    Environment, 1975   36
4   POST-MAO CONSOLIDATION AND REFORM, 1976–78   44
    Domestic Developments   45
    Foreign Affairs—Dealing with Soviet Expansion   48
    Eleventh Party Congress, 1977   50
    View of East-West Relations   52
    Reactive Diplomacy   56
5   CHINESE FOREIGN POLICY UNDER DENG
    XIAOPING—BUILDING A STRONGER ANTI-SOVIET
    FRONT, 1978–79   60
    Building a Stronger Anti-Soviet Front, 1978–79   64
    Foreign Policy Concerns   66
    Confrontation with Vietnam   70
6   TACTICAL ADJUSTMENTS IN THE FACE OF SOVIET
    PRESSURE, 1979–80   87
    Soviet and U.S. Policies   88
    Internal Chinese Complications   91
    Sino-Soviet Relations   93
    Broader Anti-Soviet Efforts   96
    Vice-President Mondale's Visit to China   96
    Southeast Asia   97
    Taiwan and Korea   98
    Signs of Sino-Korean Disagreement   102
    Relations with Other Third World Countries   104
    Relations with Communist Parties   107

7   REACTION TO THE SOVIET INVASION OF
     AFGHANISTAN   113
       Renewed Interest in U.S.-Chinese Strategic Ties   116
       Sino-Soviet Relations   121
       Broader Anti-Soviet Efforts   122
8   DEVELOPING AN INDEPENDENT FOREIGN POLICY,
     1981–83   131
       Domestic Difficulties   133
       Sino-American Relations   139
       Confronting Reagan Administration Policies   146
       Sino-Soviet Thaw   153
       Initiatives in the Third World   156
       Sino-Korean Relations   162
       12th Party Congress, September 1982   164
       National People's Congress, June 1983   168
9   CONSOLIDATING TIES WITH THE WEST AGAINST
     THE USSR, 1983–84   176
       China's Calculus in The Great-Power Triangle   177
       Sino-Japanese Relations   186
       Korea   189
       Vietnam, Kampuchea, ASEAN   191
       Other Foreign Policy Concerns   196
       Sino-British Relations over Hong Kong   204
       International Organizations, Arms Control   211
10   PROSPECTS AND IMPLICATIONS FOR THE UNITED
     STATES   221
SELECTED READINGS   227
INDEX   229
ABOUT THE AUTHOR   241

To "Auntie," Ann L. Beatty

1

DETERMINANTS OF CONTEMPORARY CHINESE FOREIGN POLICY

China has grown in importance to the United States as the two countries have developed a wide range of relations since 1970. Strategically, China's importance is underlined by the fact that it is one of only two world powers that have truly intercontinental ballistic missiles capable of hitting targets throughout the United States. As Beijing and Washington have formed closer ties on the basis of parallel strategic interests against possible Soviet international expansion, especially in Asia, Americans have come to see China as an important international counterweight to Soviet power whose relationship with the West serves to complicate Soviet military planning against U.S. and U.S.-backed forces. China also occupies the central position in the regional balance in Asia, standing among countries along the Asian rim that have longtime close ties to the United States, and provide bases and military facilities to U.S. forces. China's increased focus since 1970 on internal economic development and building closer economic and political relations with the West and with other non-Communist states has allowed the United States to reduce those U.S. deployments in Asia that had in the past been directed against the China "threat." The United States has been able to redesign its strategic plans to take account of Chinese policies considered more likely to help than to hinder U.S. military objectives. Thus, China is often seen as a force of restraint on possible North Korean adventurism against U.S. and South Korean forces, and as supportive of the U.S. alliances and bases in such key countries as Japan and the Philippines.

Politically, China has played a leading role in international forums by virtue of its position as a permanent member of the U.N. Security Council, and its tremendous size and substantial military power. Because of its close identification with the third world, Beijing often sides with

U.S. opponents on sensitive international issues affecting Asian, African, and Latin American countries, but it has increasingly become a more constructive member of the world political community, avoiding disruptive policies of the past. Thus, China has taken a dim view of most forms of international terrorism, has become a staunch supporter of the existing nation state system, has downplayed its past active support for troublesome revolutionary movements, and has even become more moderate on such sensitive issues as nuclear nonproliferation and arms control.

China's indirect influence on U.S. economic interests in Asia is probably more important to the United States than the substantial growth in Sino-American bilateral economic ties. By virtue of its size and geographic location, China exerts a tremendous influence on the entire Asian rim—a critically important area for U.S. economic policy in recent years. Japan and the newly industrialized and developing non-Communist countries of the region have been able to register great economic growth since 1970, in part because China has not followed disruptive policies of the past and has helped to foster a balance of power in the region, allowing these nations to focus more on economic development. Meanwhile, the Sino-American economic relationship has grown to include an annual trade turnover of $6 billion each year, burgeoning transfers of sophisticated U.S. technology to China, Sino-American joint business ventures, and American investments in China, notably the large-scale involvement of American oil firms in China's offshore oil development.

The American people also have had a much greater opportunity than in the past to have tangible experience involving China. Hundreds of thousands of Americans have traveled there as tourists or on business, and the thousands of Chinese studying in the United States have brought home to many Americans a feeling of close identity and empathy with China and its people.

Because China has such widespread and important influence on U.S. interests, Americans require as clear a reading as possible of its current and future course in foreign affairs, especially toward the United States and its allies and friends. Since the start of the Sino-American reconciliation in 1970, Chinese actions in foreign affairs have had an important and often positive impact on the international and domestic concerns of the United States. Americans are particularly alert to any changes in China's posture that could upset U.S. interests or jeopardize important U.S. concerns in Asian affairs and in East-West relations.

Unfortunately, U.S. ability to chart the likely course of Chinese foreign policy has been mixed. In the past, Chinese foreign policy, and Sino-American relations in particular, were subjected to wide swings and sweeping changes, often unanticipated by specialists. Even recently, China's avowed policy regarding the United States has seemed to undergo important adjustments and shifts. Thus, at the time of the Sino-American agreement to establish formal diplomatic relations at the turn of 1978, Chinese leader Deng Xiaoping and other officials impressed their U.S. counterparts with the need for a common Sino-American front against the USSR; but after a period of tension in U.S.-China relations over Taiwan a few years later, the same Chinese leaders publicly disavowed interest in cooperating with the United States against the USSR, and began to pursue a policy ostensibly designed to improve China's relations with the Soviet Union.

If carried to their logical conclusion, such shifts in China's policies could lead to a sharp realignment in Asia that could have very serious negative effects on the United States. Thus, it is important to get behind the ostensible changes, and understand more clearly the motives and goals in China's recent conduct of foreign affairs.

Our understanding and prescience about Chinese foreign policy are limited in large measure because outsiders are not privy to the current thinking of Chinese leaders and are therefore unable to predict how the Chinese decision makers will act under particular circumstances. As in most countries, the factors motivating Chinese foreign policy are a mix of diverse interests. Some are pragmatic considerations readily understood by Americans and other outsiders. Thus, like the leaders of most nations, the Chinese leaders strive to achieve national power, international prestige, and economic prosperity; and in the process they are determined to use foreign policy to enhance their personal reputations and develop their political influence at home.

And yet our appreciation of how the Chinese come to such pragmatic decisions is clouded by the very closed nature of their decision making, and by the massive size and complexity of most developments in China. Moreover, there is a uniquely "Chinese" set of factors that influence foreign policy in ways that sometimes seem to contradict the imperatives of pragmatism, as understood in the West.

China's long history as a grand, basically self-sufficient civilization prompts Beijing officials to assume the nation's greatness, and thereby to be convinced that it deserves a leading world role. It causes them to depend on China's innate capacity to achieve its goals without much assistance from others, to preserve traditional Chinese values, and to avoid possible contamination from outside. China's tradition merges with strong nationalism and revolutionary ideology developed since the 1800s to impel its leaders to strive all out to build a powerful nation-state, independent of outside powers, and to restore fully China's sovereignty over territories "lost" to foreign powers from 1840 to 1945. The trauma of imperialism is still fresh in the minds of Chinese leaders, causing them to work to redress past wrongs and to side with others oppressed by outside forces. It also makes the Chinese especially suspicious of the ultimate intentions of foreign powers.

During the Maoist period of the 1950s and 1960s, Chinese leaders often put forward messianic revolutionary goals designed to free humanity from capitalist imperialist-fostered bondage. China developed a unique brand of Marxism-Leninism that put heavy emphasis on Lenin's theory of imperialism and the inevitability of war to provide a framework for its world view. Although post-Mao leaders moderated the commitment to revolutionary ideology, they remained determined to identify China closely with what they perceived as the progressive forces of the present era: the third world nations, the international Communist and socialist parties, and other groups opposed to power politics and domination by outside forces.

This study reviews the record of China's foreign policy since the nadir of its influence was reached during the most violent and disruptive stage of the Cultural Revolution in the late 1960s. By examining salient trends and significant changes in its behavior abroad and in its leadership's pronouncements and media comment, the study explains what those foreign policy shifts have consisted of and why they have taken place. Against this background, it is hoped that useful perspective will be brought to bear on the current and likely future directions in Chinese foreign policy, thereby increasing our understanding and insight into the underlying factors that have motivated, and are likely to continue to motivate, China's approach to the United States in particular and to foreign policy in general.

From one perspective, Chinese foreign policy shows general continuity throughout this period. The record depicts China emerging from a period of serious dislocation and ideological excess during the violent stage of the Cultural Revolution and its attendant "Red Guard diplomacy." Faced with dangerous international circumstances, Beijing felt compelled to begin a more conventional and rational balance-of-power approach to foreign policy that would shore up its national security and foreign policy interests, while ensuring a more favorable environment for restoring disrupted political order inside China and pursuing the development of national wealth and power. Key determinants of this approach involved the perceived power and policies of the Soviet Union and the United States.

Moscow's persisting military buildup and search for greater political influence around China's periphery became the strategic center of gravity for Chinese foreign policy in the late 1960s. Top-level Chinese leaders of whatever background or ideological inclination were forced by Soviet actions to focus their foreign policy on the fundamental question of how to deal effectively with the Soviet military threat and political intimidation, without compromising Chinese security and sovereignty or mortgaging aspirations for independence and development. Initially, Chinese leaders came up with strikingly different approaches, leading in the late 1960s to the most serious dispute over foreign policy in the history of the People's Republic.

The death of Defense Minister Lin Biao and the purge of a large segment of the Chinese military high command markedly reduced the political importance of Chinese leadership differences over how to handle the Soviet Union. From that time on, China developed a fairly consistent strategy, at first under the leadership of Premier Zhou Enlai and Chairman Mao Zedong, and later under Deng Xiaoping. It attempted to use East-West differences pragmatically to China's advantage. The Chinese leaders recognized that only at tremendous cost and great risk could China confront the Soviet Union on its own. It relied heavily on international counterweights to Soviet power, provided mainly by the United States, and its allies and associates. And as the United States reevaluated its former containment policy directed against China, and no longer posed a serious military threat to Chinese security, Beijing maintained a collaborative relationship with the United States and the West as a key link in its security policy against the USSR.

Meanwhile, Chinese internal policy increasingly focused on economic development and modernization. Chinese leaders, especially in the post-Mao period, saw that these goals would be best achieved through closer economic relations with the West. The United States, Japan, and other non-Communist developed states had the markets, technology, managerial expertise, and financial resources that were crucial in speeding and streamlining China's troubled modernization efforts so as to increase material benefit to the people, and thereby sustain their political loyalty and support.

This simple outline of a framework for recent Chinese foreign policy clearly portrays China as often reactive to the actions of foreign powers, especially the Soviet Union and the United States. It shows Chinese leaders as well aware of the nation's internal weaknesses and desirous to remedy them through a prolonged effort at economic and, eventually, military modernization. In the meantime, they recognized that China needs to secure its international environment in order to focus its energies internally and that while China influences the situation in Asia to some degree, the USSR, the United States, and their friends and allies exert greater influence there. As a result, China repeatedly adjusted to perceived changes in the international situation around it.

Indeed, the record shows that many of the changes in Chinese policy during this period were chiefly reactions to perceived shifts in the international balance of forces and influence affecting Chinese security and development. Salient examples include the following:

- August 1968—The Soviet invasion of Czechoslovakia and Moscow's subsequent announcement of the so-called Brezhnev doctrine of limited sovereignty caused China to view the recently expanded Soviet military presence along the Sino-Soviet border in a more ominous light. It prompted at least some Chinese leaders to advocate a more activist, conventional approach to foreign affairs in order to enhance Chinese international leverage in the face of Soviet power.

- August 1969—Six months of military conflict along the frontier reached a climax as the largest Sino-Soviet border clash on record resulted in a serious Chinese military defeat and was followed by Soviet warnings about possible "preventive strikes" against China. This pressure tipped the scales in the ongoing policy debate in Beijing against those, led by Lin Biao, who held out for uncompromising opposition to both the Soviet Union and the United States. It favored a tactically more flexible posture advocated by Premier Zhou. The fruits of Zhou's efforts were seen in the use of Sino-Soviet talks and Chinese diplomatic maneuvers, along with Chinese defense preparations, to deal with Soviet pressure, and in the start of Sino-American diplomatic contacts focused on the two sides' common opposition to Soviet attempts at dominance in Asia—contacts that led directly to President Nixon's landmark visit to China.

- 1975—The rapid collapse of U.S.-supported governments in Indochina prompted China to adopt a much more active approach throughout East Asia in order to shore up a united front against the perceived danger of Soviet expansion around its periphery as the United States withdrew. Concurrent signs of U.S. weakness seen in the face of growing Soviet military power, and in breakthroughs in negotiating East-West accords over arms control and European security, caused China to state vocal opposition to U.S.-Soviet détente to unprecedented heights. In the process, China underlined its keen suspicion that Western accommodation with Moscow would allow the Soviets a free hand to deal with China.

- 1978—Soviet gains in the third world, especially in areas of direct importance to China (such as Vietnam), enhanced Chinese interest in fostering a common front with the United States, other Western states, and Japan against the USSR. Prospects for such cooperation increased as opinion in the U.S. government gradually shifted from the view advocated by Secretary of State Cyrus Vance that gave priority to U.S.-Soviet arms control, to the view favored by National Security Adviser Zbigniew Brzezinski that advocated confronting Soviet expansion in sensitive third world areas.

- April 1979—China's efforts to confront Soviet expansion focused on Vietnam, leading to direct military intervention that produced mixed results for its interests and left Beijing dangerously exposed in the face of increasing Soviet military pressure. Chinese leaders were compelled to change tactics, to moderate their anti-Soviet stance, and to open a political dialogue with Moscow in order to manage the danger of Soviet military power.

- January 1980—The Soviet invasion of Afghanistan and stiffened Western resolve to combat Soviet expansion prompted China to tack again, reverting to a firmly anti-Soviet posture and suspending talks with the USSR.

- 1981-82—A perceived shift in the international balance of power against the Soviet Union, and a revival of U.S. power and determination against the USSR under the Reagan administration, gave China more freedom for maneuver; it allowed China to distance itself from the Reagan administration over Taiwan, the third world, and other issues; to reopen talks with the Soviet Union; and to adopt an ostensibly more independent posture in foreign affairs.

- Mid-1983—Beijing's growing concern over a projected long-term downturn in Sino-American relations at a time of increasing Soviet pressure on China prompted its leaders to compromise their hard line on sensitive bilateral disputes with the United States in order to solidify relations with the Reagan administration in preparation for a period of difficult relations with the USSR.

Despite such repeated examples of Chinese foreign policy reacting to international events, especially to perceived changes in the international balance of power affecting Chinese interests, there are also instances that vividly demonstrate wellsprings of particular foreign policies within China. For one thing, Chinese views of their surroundings and the international balance of power are filtered through lenses colored by the nation's history, culture, and ideology. The strength and unity of its political leadership has had a profound effect on whether China can take the initiative in foreign policy or merely respond passively to international circumstances. Domestic demands for economic development, military modernization, and political control often have had a vital impact on the course of Chinese foreign policy decision making. Meanwhile, Chinese leaders have demonstrated a desire to manipulate international events and to maneuver more freely among competing outside pressures in order to enhance their particular interests within China, especially their leadership standing.

Key examples of such domestic determinants influencing the course of Chinese foreign policy since the late 1960s include the following:

- February-August 1969—Intense competition for political power in China led to debate over competing approaches to foreign policy, especially concerning relations with the United States and the Soviet Union. Lin Biao and those advocating a tough line toward both powers were able to reverse the opening to the United States initiated by Zhou Enlai and other leaders a few months earlier, which had called for revived political discussions. They succeeded in following their hard-line posture for seven months.

- 1973-74—Leadership conflict over internal political and development questions arose during the intense political campaign against Confucius and Lin Biao. The campaign—pressed by radical political leaders later known as the Gang of Four—spilled over into foreign policy, resulting in an across-the-board toughening in China's approach to the Soviet Union, the United States, and their allies and associates, and a cutback in China's interest in greater economic and cultural contacts with the West.

- 1976-77—Beijing's preoccupation with post-Mao leadership transition and major economic problems resulted in a much less active approach to most foreign issues, even those having a direct bearing on China's security, such as increasing Soviet-Vietnamese collaboration.

- 1979—Some Chinese leaders questioned previous emphasis on establishing close ties with the West in order to better confront the USSR. They stressed China's need for "breathing space" in competition with the USSR, emphasized that defense modernization would have to be postponed in order to speed higher-priority economic modernization, and wished to reestablish China's flagging ties with the developing countries and the international Communist movement. They were successful for a time in easing Chinese confrontation with the USSR and reducing the developing Chinese strategic alignment with the United States and the West.

- 1981-82—These same leadership judgments helped to push China to reassert its policy independence of the United States, in the process adopting a more balanced stance between the superpowers and adhering more closely to nationalistic principles on sensitive issues like Taiwan.

There is no consensus among specialists as to which factors—internal or international—are more important at any given time in determining the course of Chinese foreign policy; thus, there is no agreement as to whether it tends to be more reactive to outside events or to evolve as a result of internal forces. Some analysts have tried to bridge the gap between those specialists who stress foreign determinants and those who stress domestic determinants in Chinese foreign policy. Thus, some point to "policy packages" of mutually reinforcing and compatible foreign and domestic policies advocated by a particular group of leaders, and note how these leaders fare in promoting their approaches in the face of opposition from others with competing foreign-domestic policy arrangements.[1] Others have tried to isolate those aspects of Chinese foreign policy (such as security policy) where Chinese leaders are more likely to be reactive to international pressures from those (such as opening Chinese society to Western economic contact) that are more likely to be affected by Chinese domestic determinants.[2] What is clear from all this work is that domestic and foreign pressures can be mutually reinforcing, but they can also push Chinese decision makers in different directions, at times leading to conflict and contradictions between competing priorities.

The primary objectives of this study are twofold. It attempts to describe the recent course of Chinese foreign policy, especially in the post-Mao period, by reviewing evidence of Chinese developments and international trends. And it endeavors to establish an analytical framework to explain what, in the judgment of the author, appear to be the key factors in determining recent Chinese foreign policy. The key judgments of the study are set forth below.

The objectives of Chinese foreign policy have been determined by a small group of top level leaders who have reflected the broad interests of the Chinese state as well as their own parochial concerns. In the past, Mao Zedong, Zhou Enlai, and other senior leaders exerted overriding control over foreign policy. In recent years, there has been an increase in the number of officials involved in advising on Chinese foreign policy, but key decisions remain the preserve of a small group of leaders, especially Deng Xiaoping.

The primary concerns of these leaders have been to guarantee Chinese national security, maintain internal order, and pursue economic development. Especially since the death of Mao in 1976, the top priority has been to promote successful economic modernization. This development represents the linchpin determining their success or failure. Thus, officials have geared China's foreign policy to help the modernization effort.

But, in order to accomplish economic modernization, as well as to maintain national security and internal order, Chinese leaders recognize the fundamental prerequisite of establishing a relatively stable strategic environment, especially around the nation's periphery in Asia. The alternative would be a highly disruptive situation requiring much greater Chinese expenditures on national defense and posing greater danger to domestic order and tranquillity. China does not control this environment. It has influenced it, but the environment remains controlled more by others, especially the superpowers and their allies and associates. As a result, China's leaders have been required repeatedly to assess their surroundings for changes that could affect Chinese security and development interests. And they have been compelled repeatedly to adjust foreign policy to take account of such changes.

At the same time, Chinese leaders have nationalistic and ideological objectives regarding irridentist claims (such as Taiwan) and a desire to stand independently in foreign affairs as a leading force among "progressive" nations of the third world. These goals have struck a responsive chord politically inside China. Occasional leadership discussion and debate over these and other questions regarding foreign affairs have sometimes had an effect on the course of Chinese foreign policy. In the Maoist period, for example, leaders sometimes allowed these nationalistic and ideological objectives, and other questions of political debate, to jeopardize seriously the basic security and development interests of the nation. China's move toward greater pragmatism in foreign and domestic policy since the late 1960s did not develop smoothly; it was accompanied by often very serious leadership debates over which foreign policy goals should receive priority. However, since the early 1970s, the debates have become progressively less serious, and the foreign policy differences raised in them have become more moderate and less of a challenge to the recent dominant objectives of national development and security.

Thus, China's top foreign policy priority has remained the pragmatic quest for the stable environment needed for effective modernization and development. Chinese leaders since 1969 have seen the main danger of negative change in the surrounding environment posed by the Soviet Union. At first, China perceived Soviet power as an immediate threat to its national security. Over time, it came to see the USSR as more of a long-term threat, determined to use its growing military power and other sources of influence to encircle and pressure China into accepting a balance of influence in an Asia dominated by the USSR and contrary to PRC interests.

China's strategy against the Soviet threat has been both bilateral and global. Bilaterally, China has used a mix of military preparations and tactical political moves to keep the Soviets from attacking it. Globally, China's strategy has focused on developing—either implicitly or explicitly—an international united front designed to halt Soviet expansion and prevent the consolidation of Soviet dominance abroad.

As the most important international counterweight to Soviet power, the United States has loomed large in Chinese calculations. Once the United States, under terms of the Nixon Doctrine announced in 1969, seemed determined to withdraw from its past policy of containing China in Asia, and thereby ended a perceived threat to China's national security, the PRC was prepared to start the process of Sino-American normalization. The process has been complemented in recent years by China's enhanced interest in pragmatic economic modernization, which has emphasized the importance of technical and financial help from the West and access to Western markets.

Closer Chinese ties with the United States continue to be complicated by Chinese nationalistic and ideological concerns over Taiwan and third world questions, as well as by fundamental differences between the social-political and economic systems of the United States and the PRC. Most notably, U.S. support for Taiwan is seen as a continued affront to China's national sovereignty. But Chinese leaders have differentiated between substantive threats to their security, posed by the USSR, and threats to their sense of national sovereignty, posed by U.S. support for Taiwan.

In short, China has worked hard, and continues to work hard, to ensure that its strategic environment, threatened mainly by Soviet expansion, remains stable, so that it can focus on economic modernization. The USSR is seen as having a strategy of expansion that uses military power relentlessly but cautiously in order to achieve political influence and dominance throughout its periphery. China has long held that the focus of Soviet attention is in Europe, but that NATO's strength requires Moscow to work in other areas, notably the Middle East, Southwest Asia, Africa, and East Asia, in order to outflank the Western defenses. China is seen as relatively low on Moscow's list of military priorities, although Chinese leaders clearly appreciate the dire consequences for the PRC should the USSR be able to consolidate its position elsewhere and then focus its strength to intimidate China.

China's strategy of deterrence and defense, therefore, aims basically to exacerbate Soviet defense problems by enhancing the worldwide opposition to Soviet expansion in general, and by raising the possibility of the Soviet Union confronting a multifront conflict in the event it attempted to attack or intimidate China in particular. Chinese leaders see their nation's cooperation with the United States as especially important in strengthening deterrence of the Soviet Union and in aggravating Soviet strategic vulnerabilities. Beijing also encourages anti-Soviet efforts by so-called second world, developed countries—most of whom are formal allies of the United States—and by developing countries of the third world. At the same time, Beijing uses a mix of political talks, bilateral exchanges, and other forms of dialogue to help manage the danger posed by the USSR.

Within this overall strategy to establish a stable environment in Asia, Chinese leaders have employed a varying mix of tactics to secure their interests, depending on international variables, such as the perceived strength and intentions of the superpowers, and Chinese domestic variables, such as leadership cohesion or disarray. For example, when Chinese leaders have judged that their strategic surroundings to be at least temporarily stable, they have seen less immediate need for close ties with the United States, and thus have felt more free to adopt strident policies on Taiwan and other nationalistic issues that appeal to domestic constituencies but offend the United States. (This type of logic was in part responsible for China's tougher approach to the United States over Taiwan and other issues in 1981-83.) But, when the Chinese leaders have judged that such tactics could seriously alienate the United States and thereby endanger the stability of China's environment, they have put them aside in the interest of preserving peaceful surroundings. (Such reasoning undergirded much of China's moderation in approach to the United States in 1983-84.)

This study also will carefully review Chinese domestic developments and signs of leadership debate over foreign policy, not because the author believes that these are the main determining factors in China's foreign policy but because they, along with altered international circumstances, help to explain recent tactical shifts in China's approach to foreign affairs. In particular, it is noted that some leaders in China may prefer a foreign policy truly independent of both the Soviet Union and the United States, and circumstances at home and abroad at times may push foreign policy tactics in this direction. But such temporary and marginal shifts are unlikely to lead to a basic change in China's overall foreign strategy, at least for some time to come. China's weakness in influencing its Asian surroundings, the steady buildup of Soviet pressure in Asia, and the implicitly positive role the United States continues to play in basic Chinese security and development interests have continued to require a Chinese strategy of tilting closer to the West against the USSR.

NOTES

1. See, for example, Carol Hamrin, "Emergence of an 'Independent' Chinese Foreign Policy and Shifts in Sino-U.S. Relations," in James Hsiung, ed., *U.S.-Asian Relations* (New York: Praeger, 1983). See also Kenneth Lieberthal, "Sources of China's Foreign Policy," paper presented at the U.S. Department of State, Washington, D.C., 4 November 1983.

2. See, for instance, Michael Yahuda, *Towards the End of Isolationism: China's Foreign Policy After Mao* (New York: St. Martin's Press, 1983).

2

CHINA'S STRATEGY BETWEEN
THE SUPERPOWERS

In mid-1968, Chinese foreign affairs were marked by acute isolation, stemming from the negative impact of the Cultural Revolution on the conduct of foreign policy. Beijing's provocative diplomatic behavior, particularly during 1967 and early 1968, severely weakened China's international stature and isolated it from most of an already limited number of foreign friends. Toward many neighboring states in Asia, for example, Beijing adopted an attitude of self-righteous hostility and disdain. Red Guards in Beijing launched poster attacks in early 1967 against Korean Communist Party leader Kim Il-song, triggering an official Korean protest and further exacerbating already strained relations.[1] Moreover, obnoxious Chinese diplomatic behavior in Beijing and abroad alienated the previously friendly neighboring states of Cambodia, Nepal, Ceylon, and Burma. Red Guard demonstrations in southern China during mid-1968 resulted in the interruption of vital war shipments to North Vietnam, exacerbating tensions in Sino-Vietnamese relations, which had begun with Hanoi's decision to enter the Paris peace talks with the United States in May 1968.[2] Elsewhere, China's proselytizing efforts and shrill polemics alienated a number of nonaligned states, including Kenya, Tunisia, Algeria, the United Arab Republic, and many European states.

The diplomacy of the Cultural Revolution also affected China's posture toward the Soviet Union and the United States, resulting in a markedly more uncompromising approach to both superpowers. Chinese demonstrations in front of the Soviet embassy in Beijing and abrasive anti-Soviet activity by Chinese representatives abroad were only the most visible Chinese actions serving to widen the Sino-Soviet rift during this period. At the same time, in May 1968 Chinese officials underlined an anti-American stance by suspending the Sino-American ambassadorial discussions, which were taking place in Warsaw. Beijing called off the talks for at least six months, ostensibly because it judged that "there was nothing to talk about" with the U.S. representatives. Thus, by mid-1968 the Chinese had pared their international contacts to the point that Beijing's circle of foreign influence was limited to a small handful of states, such as Albania, Pakistan, and a few African states.[3]

Prospects for a return to a more effective Chinese international policy appeared less than promising in 1968. The Foreign Ministry apparatus, seriously disrupted during the Cultural Revolution, had only begun to show tentative signs of a return to more normal functioning. Foreign Minister Chen I, a number of vice-ministers of foreign affairs, and other high-ranking Foreign Ministry officials had come under strong Red Guard attack. Many no longer appeared in public, though their positions were not filled by others. Beijing had also recalled all but one of its ambassdors abroad, in many cases leaving only extremely junior and inexperienced officials at foreign diplomatic posts.

Beginning in late 1967, the government attempted to restore a veneer of normality to Chinese foreign affairs. Red Guard demonstrations against foreign embassies in China were halted, and Chinese officials were once more attending some diplomatic functions in Beijing. In May 1968, for example, the Chinese gave an enthusiastic welcome to a visiting joint delegation from Guinea and Mali, which had come to China to conclude initial agreements for Chinese assistance to a highly ambitious railway project to join the two African states.[4] In June, President Julius Nyerere of Tanzania was warmly received by the Chinese during a goodwill visit, and he conferred at length with Zhou Enlai.[5]

More significantly, the Chinese demonstrated willingness to overlook recent disagreements with some states in order to rebuild China's international influence. In May, for example, the Chinese improved relations with Nepal by warmly receiving the visiting Nepalese foreign minister.[6] In July, *Xinhua* reported that a Chinese vice-minister of foreign affairs had attended a Cuban anniversary reception in Beijing—a noticeably more amicable attitude toward the event than China had expressed in 1967.[7] Also in July, China began to clear up one of its many outstanding disagreements with Great Britain stemming from the Cultural Revolution, permitting a senior British diplomat to leave China, the first such occurrence since restrictions had been imposed on the British mission in August 1967.[8]

However, Beijing's efforts to establish a more conventional approach to foreign affairs were extremely slow and halting. There was little change in China's state of international isolation. Moreover, there were signs that some of the efforts to mend relations with certain states were halfhearted. In the case of Burma, for example, the Chinese gradually moderated their public criticism of the Ne Win government during the first half of 1968, and they gave several signs of a more positive approach toward Rangoon. These included a donation of 10,000 yuan by the Chinese Red Cross to the Burmese Red Cross to assist relief operations for hurricane victims in May 1968; participation of the Chinese chargé d'affaires in a 19 July ceremony honoring Burmese independence leaders; and a 1 August PRC Army Day reception at the Chinese embassy in Rangoon, which *Xinhua* reported was attended by Burmese officals.[9] In mid-August, however, the Chinese unexpectedly reversed course, issuing a series of strong statements attacking the "reactionary Ne Win government" and supporting the dissident Burmese Communist Party.[10] By late 1968, relations had once again become severely strained and there was little prospect for rapprochement.

The Chinese leadership continued to reveal its preoccupation with matters other than foreign affairs. The volume of Beijing's media coverage of diplomatic events and foreign issues was still far below what it had been before the Cultural Revolution. Such reports were more than overshadowed by public attention to domestic affairs, and to pronouncements on such ideological matters as the thought of Mao Zedong. In addition, the Chinese leadership was preoccupied with a number of crucial developments in domestic affairs. Beijing at this time was striving to complete the formation of provincial administrative structures and was encouraging the army to end civilian disorders, dissolve factions, and restore internal peace in preparation for a number of strong domestic reforms.[11] In this context, Beijing's concern over a restoration of Chinese influence in foreign affairs remained secondary.

CONCERN OVER SOVIET INTENTIONS

Beijing's lack of attention to foreign affairs was not substantially altered until the Soviet Union invaded Czechoslovakia on 20 August 1968 and formulated the so-called Brezhnev Doctrine of limited sovereignty within the socialist community. As a result, the Chinese focused much more on the potential Soviet threat, showing increased concern over the buildup and conduct of Soviet forces along the Sino-Soviet frontier. Beijing demonstrated greater public conviction that the United States was collaborating and colluding with the USSR on a number of important international issues contrary to Chinese interests, and increased concern over what was seen as a tightening U.S.-Soviet military-political "ring of encirclement" established by the two superpowers in order to contain and stifle China in Asia. Against this background, the Chinese demonstrated more interest in improving relations with several countries of critical importance in the Sino-Soviet dispute, and a greater willingness to overlook past disagreements with certain nations, in order to improve China's diplomatic position vis-à-vis the Soviet Union and to reduce Beijing's international isolation. Thus, Chinese leaders began to highlight publicly the danger posed to China by the buildup of Soviet forces along the Sino-Soviet and Sino-Mongolian borders that had begun in the mid-1960s. Beijing saw Moscow as taking the lead in forming an anti-China alignment with the United States, and as promoting ties with Japan, India, and other Asian states to serve as a counter to Chinese interests.

Pulling back from the extremism of Cultural Revolution diplomacy, Chinese leaders tried through more effective, convential diplomacy to offset Soviet influence with a number of nations of importance in the Sino-Soviet rivalry, including Romania, North Korea, and North Vietnam. At the same time, the Chinese showed greater willingness to overlook past disagreements and to improve ties with a number of important countries—including even the United States—in order to enhance Chinese leverage in the face of Soviet pressure.[12]

LEADERSHIP DEBATE

China's overture to the United States came in a late November 1968 Foreign Ministry spokesman's statement calling for renewed ambassorial talks with the United States once the Nixon administration had taken power in 1969. The Chinese overture was influenced both by Beijing's need for leverage against the USSR and by the possibility that, in the wake of U.S. setbacks in Vietnam, the new administration might be more willing than past U.S. governments to pull back from its military "containment" of China. The demarche had a major effect inside China, bringing leadership conflict over foreign policy to its highest level in the history of the People's Republic. Over the next three years, until the death of Defense Minister Lin Biao in September 1971, foreign policy became one of the most salient issues in the ongoing leadership struggle for power.[13]

The perceived change for the worse in the balance of forces around China had compelled its leaders to address foreign affairs more directly. They could continue the self-righteous isolation of the past few years only at great risk to China's basic security, and possibly its survival. The implications of the new situation affected, and in turn were influenced by, differing political, economic, and defense priorities of competing groups in the Chinese leadership.

While the leadership situation was often confused, it is possible to isolate differing policy approaches of competing leaders under Mao. At this time, Mao did little that showed distinct policy preferences; he appeared receptive to diverse recommendations. Only by late 1970 did Mao appear to link himself solidly with the opening to the United States.

One group of leaders, headed by Premier Zhou Enlai, China's de facto foreign minister, stressed China's need to use more pragmatic diplomatic approaches in order to buy time and deal more effectively with its dangerous predicament. In general this group argued as follows:

- The Soviet buildup in Asia and invasion of Czechoslovakia had demonstrated that the expanding power of the USSR represented China's most dangerous threat. The escalating Sino-Soviet border clashes of March-August 1969 appeared to support this view.

- The United States was less aggressive, and therefore a less dangerous adversary. It had not threatened China's security directly in many years. China and the United States had even managed to work out an understanding to avoid direct military confrontation during the Vietnam War. Moreover, following the Tet offensive and U.S. presidential election of 1968, there was a distinct possibility that the United States might begin at least a tactical withdrawal from its long-standing military containment of China in Asia.

- China's internal administrative structure was only beginning to be rebuilt following the disruptions of the Cultural Revolution. The army was bogged down in running state affairs. China's defenses were weak and ill prepared to confront one major adversary, not to mention two superpowers in Asia.

- In these circumstances, China's interests would be well served by a gradual buildup of its military forces, complemented by active diplomacy designed to offset Soviet pressure, to encourage U.S. withdrawal from around China's periphery and to split the United States from the USSR so as to increase China's leverage within the triangular relationship.

Not surprisingly, Zhou's foreign approach was designed to reinforce many of the internal objectives of his group inside China: to reduce the share of government spending going to the military; to restore civilian control over the People's Liberation Army (PLA); to rebuild China's party and government structure with civilian rather than military veterans, many of whom had been purged during the Cultural Revolution; to limit disruptions of China's restoration of order and pursuit of economic development that would be caused by provocative Chinese international behavior, especially confrontation with the two superpowers.

At the same time, Zhou almost certainly recognized that success in these areas would enhance his political prestige and reduce the power of those leaders associated with the radical disruptive policies of the recent past, notably his two chief political rivals, Lin Biao and Jiang Qing.

Zhou's opponents nonetheless represented potent political forces opposed to moderation in Chinese foreign policy. They viewed successful implementation of a Zhouist approach to foreign affairs not only as adverse to their ideals but also as having important negative implications for their struggle for power. Thus, they worked during this period to undercut some of the more controversial aspects of Zhou's efforts at moderation, notably his more reasonable approaches to the United States and the USSR.

They argued that the USSR and the United States were implacably hostile to China; both were determined to cooperate to contain Chinese influence in Asia; moderate diplomacy designed to split the two powers, using one against the other, would only reveal Chinese weakness and encourage both to pressure China even harder; China must rely on its own efforts, spending more on defense and preparing the masses for protracted people's war.

In large measure because of the opposition of political forces led by Lin Biao and Jiang Qing, early Zhouist diplomatic initiatives were obstructed and reversed. Most notably, the November 1968 overture to the new Nixon administration, calling for revived ambassadorial talks with the United States, was attacked almost immediately in allegorical articles linked with Jiang Qing. The subsequent defection of a Chinese diplomat to the United States tipped the scales in the leadership debate, and China reversed the initiative in February 1969. For the next six months, Beijing followed a truculent foreign approach toward both superpowers favored by Lin, Jiang, and their supporters. This was seen notably in China's tough military confrontation of the USSR during the Sino-Soviet border clashes of March-August 1969. While there was some restoration of normality along the margins of its foreign policy, China remained unrelenting in strident opposition to both Moscow and Washington.

THE THREAT OF SOVIET ATTACK

The hold of these leaders over Chinese foreign policy was broken only by a sharply altered perception of Soviet military intentions. In mid-August, Soviet forces badly mauled Chinese units in the largest border clash ever, along the western frontier. The battle lasted all day and reportedly involved tanks and combat planes. Moscow then began warning of an imminent Soviet military attack deep into China, to annihilate nuclear weapons installations. This was backed by a rapid buildup of Soviet forces all along the frontier that the PLA appeared powerless to deter or stop.[14]

Beijing was now compelled to give ground. Premier Zhou was given another chance to demonstrate the efficacy of diplomacy in managing outside pressure. During talks with Premier Aleksei Kosygin at the Beijing airport on 11 September, Kosygin proposed that talks begin immediately between Chinese and Soviet officials, at the level of vice-minister of foreign affairs, to deal with the border situation. He also proposed that Sino-Soviet ambassadorial relations be restored and that trade ties be resumed. Ideological and party matters were to be put aside for consideration later. The Chinese apparently remained noncommittal at the meeting, and Beijing did not respond publicly to the Soviet initiative until a month later.

The Chinese finally dropped previous preconditions and agreed to start talks with Moscow on 20 October. But Beijing was not prepared to make any further compromises with Moscow, and it began to structure a more effective international posture centered on the need to offset the Soviet threat. Thus, following his talks with Kosygin, Zhou in rapid succession moved to improve China's relations with North Korea, North Vietnam, and Cambodia; backed off from China's past opposition to the Paris peace talks; improved relations with Algeria; and restored ambassadorial relations with Yugoslavia after a hiatus of over a decade.[15]

Recognizing that the United States represented the main international counterweight to Soviet pressure, Zhou was interested in stronger ties with the United States. The Nixon administration had improved prospects for better ties by starting the massive withdrawal of U.S. forces from around China's periphery under terms of the Nixon Doctrine, thereby strengthening the Zhouist point that the United States was not necessarily implacably opposed to China. Nixon also made repeated calls for better U.S.-China ties.

But a revival of Sino-American ties remained controversial in China. Thus, the associates of Zhou Enlai awaited an American initiative, which came in December, in the form of a demarche by the U.S. ambassador to the Chinese chargé in Warsaw. Beijing responded positively, agreeing to meet in the secure conference rooms of the Chinese and U.S. embassies, rather than the meeting room provided by the Poles in the past. The decision was clearly designed to preclude Soviet bloc eavesdropping and to enhance an already evident Soviet concern about Sino-American cooperation against the USSR.

ZHOUIST STRATEGY

When the U.S. and Chinese sides met in Warsaw in January and February 1970, the broad outlines of the Zhouist approach to Chinese foreign policy were already beginning to emerge:

- Soviet military pressure and political intimidation, especially around China's periphery in Asia, would remain the predominant Chinese foreign policy concern for the foreseeable future.

- China would try to manage the Soviet threat by building its defense forces and through adroit use of diplomacy. China was not prepared to compromise on important issues with the USSR.

- The United States represented less of a military threat as it pulled back forces from around China's eastern and southern borders. As long as it remained strongly opposed to the USSR, the United States would be an effective source of international leverage helping China to offset Soviet pressure. The United States and China thus had common ground on their fundamental opposition to the Brezhnev Doctrine and broadly compatible views concerning the balance of power in Asia.

- China's previous self-righteous ideological approach to foreign affairs had left it diplomatically isolated and weak in the face of Soviet pressure. China was now more prepared to overlook past grievances, ideological disputes, and other difficulties in order to spread its influence.

- Past support for revolutionary movements was generally ineffective or counterproductive in spreading Chinese influence. China attempted to work more closely with existing governments and international organizations, even if they were not deemed ideologically progressive.

SINO-SOVIET-AMERICAN RELATIONS

The implications of China's altered approach to foreign affairs became apparent during the next few years. The policy focused, fundamentally, on an increasingly differentiated approach to the United States and the Soviet Union. Thus, even though China was willing to ease border tensions and enter talks with the USSR, it soon became apparent that it was using such exchanges mainly to buy time as it prepared for a long-term struggle with its dominating neighbor.

Beijing appeared to welcome the limited easing of tensions that accompanied the start of the Sino-Soviet border talks in October 1969 and the concurrent measures undertaken by both sides to reduce border friction. But it used this opportunity to focus even greater attention on what it now clearly saw as the overriding security problem of dealing with the Soviet threat. On the one hand, China pursued a large-scale defense buildup and war preparations campaign, and on the other, it worked to end its international isolation and to build links with world powers potentially useful against the USSR, notably the United States. The differences of opinion within the Chinese leadership on how strong a stance Beijing should take in favor of the United States and against the USSR became less important once Mao endorsed the opening to the United States, and Lin Biao and many of his military and political lieutenants were eliminated in 1971.

Recognizing that it faced a long-term strategic problem in China,, Moscow attempted to deal with the People's Republic mainly by means of military pressure and by political moves in Asia and elsewhere that could be carefully regulated. The Soviet Union continued its buildup of forces along China's northern border, improved ties with some Asian states useful in helping contain Chinese influence in the region, and attempted to apply political pressure to other states that were in the process of developing closer ties with China.

The Soviet Union supplemented this approach with a series of gestures to China in order to ensure that Sino-Soviet tensions would not get out of hand, to give China an incentive to deal more moderately with the Soviet Union over time, and to reduce the perceived advantage the United States and other adversaries had gained as a result of Soviet preoccupation with China.

Significant Soviet overtures during the first four years of the Sino-Soviet talks included the following:[16]

- Proposals to limit forward patroling and curb propaganda exchanges along the frontier

- Soviet troop adjustments along the border, including a pullback from some disputed border river islands, notably Zhen Bao (Damansky) Island, the site of the March 1969 border clashes

- Soviet willingness to accept the main channel as the boundary along the eastern frontier rivers (earlier Soviet statements had said that the border should run along the Chinese bank of these rivers; the new Soviet position, in effect, would have recognized China's claim to Zhen Bao and other disputed islands, though the USSR reportedly remained firm regarding its hold on Heixiazi/Big Ussuri Island, opposite Khabarovsk)

- A cutback in Soviet propaganda criticism of China in late 1969 and early 1970

- Proposals for a Soviet nonaggression pact with China

- An offer for a nonuse-of-force agreement with China

- Soviet offers to restore ambassadorial relations, to improve trade relations—including the sale of whole Soviet plants—and to resume scientific, technical, sports, and cultural exchanges

- Soviet willingness to follow Beijing's lead and base Sino-Soviet relations on the Chinese-proposed five principles of peaceful coexistence

- Soviet offers for summit meetings, and hints at possible interest in restoration of Sino-Soviet Communist Party ties.

China signaled its limited interest in improved relations with Moscow by responding positively to only a few of these Soviet overtures and by offering an occasional gesture of its own. In particular it did the following:

- China responded positively to proposals designed to reduce the chances of conflict between border patrols.

- It agreed to restore ambassadorial relations and to resume negotiations on bilateral trade.

- China returned to the border river navigation talks, but did so in order to press territorial claims, with the result that those talks made no progress.

- Beijing reciprocated Moscow's propaganda standdown for a few weeks in late 1979. But by the end of the year, Chinese comment was again virulently attacking Brezhnev by name, and Chinese-supported media in Hong Kong were disclosing to the world China's version of the first sessions of the supposedly secret border talks. By the spring of 1970, Soviet media were reciprocating Chinese media attacks.

In short, Beijing kept its foot on the brake, allowing only very slow forward movement in Sino-Soviet relations. The Chinese implied that no serious improvement in relations could take place until the border dispute was settled, and that such a settlement required the USSR first to withdraw its forces from Chinese-defined "disputed territory" along the frontier. The USSR was unwilling to give in to this demand, which would have opened up the border to full discussion on Chinese terms and would have reduced Soviet military leverage against China. As a result, the two sides remained at an impasse on most issues.

Meanwhile, Beijing put aside its past appraisal of U.S.-Soviet "collusion" against Chinese interests. The Zhouist approach to foreign affairs differentiated increasingly sharply between the superpowers, as Chinese leaders portrayed the Soviet Union as the enemy of both China and the United States, and viewed Washington as increasingly less of a threat to Chinese interests. This public posture served implicitly to justify a pragmatic Chinese effort to seek closer ties with Washington in order to offset the USSR.

The implications of China's reorientation in foreign policy were seen in its defense programs. In the late 1960s, the Chinese had followed an "all-azimuth" policy aimed at developing ballistic missiles that would provide a powerful capability against both the Soviet Union and the United States. At the same time, they had stressed the mobilization of numerous, lightly armed ground forces to defend against possible attack by better-armed American or Soviet forces through the use of Maoist "people's war." Following Beijing's recognition of the Soviet Union as its primary adversary and its opening to the United States in the early 1970s, the Chinese put aside their "all-azimuth" policy in strategic weapons development and deployment, and realigned their entire defense strategy to focus against the USSR. At the same time, there was an overall decline in China's military spending. Both developments were related to Chinese domestic leadership politics, particularly the 1971 demise of Defense Minister Lin Biao and much of the Chinese military high command.[17]

President Nixon's visit to China and the signing of the joint Sino-American communiqué at Shanghai in February 1972 solidified China's new approach to the superpowers.[18]

The communiqué had two major features. On the one hand, it noted that the two countries had reached general agreement about the international order in East Asia. In particular, they pledged to cooperate to ensure that the region would not become subject to international "hegemony"—code word used especially by China to denote Soviet expansion.

On the other hand, the communiqué noted that the Taiwan issue was the mjaor stumbling block in the normalization of Sino-American relations. For example, the PRC declared that Taiwan was the crucial question obstructing the normalization of relations. It claimed that Taiwan is a province of China, that its "liberation" is China's internal affair, and that all U.S. military forces must be withdrawn from Taiwan. The United States acknowledged that all Chinese on either side of the Taiwan Strait maintain that "there is but one China and Taiwan is a part of China." The United States did not challenge that position and reaffirmed its interest in a "peaceful settlement of the Taiwan question by the Chinese themselves." With this in mind, the United States declared that its ultimate objective was to withdraw all of its forces and military installations from Taiwan. Both sides pledged to continue negotiations on the normalization of relations.

The Shanghai communiqué thus showed that at the time, the United States and China were willing to defer problems of diplomatic relations and Taiwan in order to work together on the basis of their common strategic interests in East Asia. Prospects for such cooperation had been enhanced during the Nixon administration by the reduction of the U.S. military role in Vietnam and by the scaling down of the U.S. military pressure along China's periphery in East Asia. Apart from opening relations with a major nuclear power and the largest power in Asia, the Nixon administration apparently judged that its new move in regard to China would assist the United States in finding a compromise solution to the Vietnam conflict. At the same time, the administration also seemed to judge that improved relations with China might serve to make the Soviet Union more accommodating in negotiations with the United States over strategic arms limitation and European disarmament. Beijing, for its part, was actively searching for international support against the Soviet Union. The Chinese had been facing heavy Soviet military pressure since the Sino-Soviet border clashes of 1969. They now viewed the Soviet Union as their major adversary and saw the United States as a secondary enemy that could provide useful leverage against the Soviet Union.

In response, Beijing began to report favorably on the strengthening of the U.S. nuclear arsenal and of U.S. forces in Europe, the Middle East, and Asia as a means to counteract Soviet power in these areas. Chinese leaders sometimes noted the implications of U.S. strength for China, asserting that U.S. power served to preoccupy the USSR so that Moscow could not easily increase its military pressure on China.

Beijing duly acknowledged U.S.-Soviet negotiations and agreements on strategic arms and other issues. But, in line with the prevailing Zhouist approach to foreign affairs, Chinese comment tended to belittle the "collusive" aspects of U.S.-Soviet relations and to emphasize the two superpowers' continuing intense rivalry. A prime example was seen in Premier Zhou's first comment on the Salt I accords, signed during President Nixon's May 1972 visit to the USSR:

> The agreements they reached not long ago on the so-called limitation of strategic nuclear weapons were by no means "a step" toward curbing the arms race as they boasted, but marked the beginning of a new stage of their arms race. The fact is that the ink on the agreements was hardly dry before one announced an increase of billions of dollars for military expenditure and the other hastened to test new-type weapons clamoring for seizing nuclear superiority. "Disarmament" is out of the question, let alone "international peace and security," in circumstances when the superpowers continue to intensify their arms expansion and war preparation, to set up military bases of all descriptions and to station armed forces in other countries.[19]

THE TENTH CHINESE PARTY CONGRESS, AUGUST 1973

A milestone in the development of Beijing's more conventional approach in foreign affairs was reached at the Tenth Chinese Communist Party Congress in August 1973. In his 24 August report to the congress, Zhou Enlai showed increased confidence in China's strategic position, portraying the Soviet danger as now focused against the West in Europe rather than against China. He offered a lengthy rationale for China's rapprochement with the United States and its continued opposition to the

Soviet Union, and he implied that Beijing was now feeling more secure in international affairs, and would focus its attention and resources more on dealing with internal questions of political order and economic development.[20] Zhou's lengthy rationale did not prevent other Chinese leaders at the congress, notably members of the Gang of Four, from offering statements somewhat less supportive of his opening to the United States. While such differences caused some problems in the implementation of Zhou's approach during the next three years, they had little lasting effect.

Zhou's treatment of foreign affairs reflected the transformed triangular relationship and Beijing's recent trend toward more conventional geopolitical and diplomatic approaches to foreign policy. Zhou's report to the congress pressed the line, familiar since 1970, of forming the "broadest united front" against the "hegemonism of the two superpowers," but it did so in a way that clearly sanctioned the moves toward Sino-American détente in the interest of counterbalancing Soviet influence. Zhou's report also served as an authoritative rebuttal of a recent Soviet polemical offensive against Beijing. Observing that the "Brezhnev renegade clique" had recently "talked a lot of nonsense" about Sino-Soviet relations, Zhou stated that Moscow had been playing up to monopoly capitalists by accusing Beijing of opposing détente and refusing to improve Sino-Soviet relations.

Zhou sharpened the formula of great-power rivalry that had served as his major premise in foreign policy in recent years. While noting that the superpowers "contend as well as collude" with each other, Zhou advanced a clear-cut formulation of where the balance lay: "Their collusion serves the purpose of more intensified contention. Contention is absolute and protracted, whereas collusion is relative and temporary." In the context of analyzing superpower contention, Zhou cited Europe as "strategically the key point" in their rivalry. According to Zhou's analysis, the West always sought to divert the "Soviet peril" toward China, and the Soviets were now feinting to the east while thrusting toward the west.

Consistent with the emphasis on geopolitical considerations, Zhou all but ignored revolutionary movements and armed struggles. In contrast, Lin Biao's Ninth Congress report in April 1969 had given pride of place to this subject in its discussion of foreign affairs. In the interim, Beijing had stopped or reduced support to anti-government movements in several third world countries, notably stopping support for anti-government insurgencies in Oman and Ethiopia.[21] China continued support for anti-colonial, anti-apartheid groups in Africa and for the pro-China Communist insurgencies in Southeast Asia. Typifying Beijing's current approach, Zhou's report hailed the awakening of the third world as "a major event in contemporary international relations," and Chinese efforts to cultivate Western Europe and Japan were reflected in his reference to resentment in these areas of superpower dominance.

Zhou's report pulled few punches in its attack on the Soviets, likening Brezhnev to Hitler and all but writing off any hope for an improvement in Sino-Soviet relations. He recited a familiar litany of charges, accusing the Kremlin of enforcing a fascist dictatorship at home and practicing "social imperialism" around the globe. He reiterated Beijing's position that disputes over "matters of principle" should not hinder normalization of state relations on the basis of peaceful coexistence, and that the border question should be settled peacefully, through negotiations "free from any threat"—a formulation reflecting Beijing's consistent demand for a Soviet troop withdrawal from the disputed regions along the frontier. But that Zhou made these points merely for the record seemed to be indicated by a sarcastic rhetorical question: "Must China give away all the territory north of the Great Wall to the Soviet revisionists" in order to demonstrate a willingness to improve Sino-Soviet relations?

Zhou made a passing reference to Soviet troops massed along the Chinese border, but the most direct portrayal of a threat to China's security came in the course of an appeal for vigilance against "any war of aggression that imperialism may launch and particularly against surprise attack on our country by Soviet revisionist social imperialism." The warning against surprise attack, which was new, also appeared in the congress communiqué. Taken as a whole, however, the congress' discussion of foreign affairs did not evoke a sense of imminent threat, and Zhou's report put a more optimistic gloss on Mao's 20 May 1970 dictum on the danger of a new world war by asserting that it was possible "to prevent such a war."

Zhou's tough approach to Moscow was based on China's calculation that its defense programs, its remarkably successful diplomatic offensive in the early 1970s, and the establishment of closer ties with the United States had managed to offset the steadily building Soviet military and political power in Asia. China appeared to judge that it had little need for any further compromise with the USSR, and would use continued talks with the USSR mainly as a safety valve to prevent tensions from getting out of hand. Moscow also saw the futility of further gestures toward China at this time. It judged that Mao's obviously declining health raised the possibility that Soviet efforts to improve relations might meet with a more positive Chinese response in a few years, after Mao's death.

On 19 July 1973, Moscow announced the departure of the chief Soviet negotiator, Deputy Foreign Minister Leonid Ilichev, from the Beijing border talks, ostensibly to carry out official duties.[22] He was not to return to China for almost a year. Prior to his departure, Ilichev had offered what would turn out to be the last major Soviet proposal on the border problem for three years—an offer involving an agreement on mutual nonaggression.[23] He was rebuffed by the Chinese. In August, authoritative Soviet commentary in *Pravda* and a speech by Brezhnev on 15 August placed full blame on China for the stalemate in relations,[24] prompting Zhou to respond in his congress report on 24 August.

In contrast with his attack on Moscow, Zhou offered a positive assessment of the Sino-American rapprochement. In the course of listing Beijing's successes in foreign affairs, he observed that "Sino-U.S. relations have been improved to some extent." The upturn in these relations could be measured against Lin's Ninth Congress report, which had called the United States "the most ferocious enemy" of the world's people and had criticized the U.S. president for employing "counterrevolutionary dual tactics."

In a notable passage, Zhou's report justified Beijing's moves to improve Sino-American relations while denigrating Soviet-American détente. Distinguishing "necessary compromises between revolutionary countries and imperialist countries" from "collusion and compromise" between Moscow and Washington, Zhou cited Leninist scripture for the observation that "there are compromises and compromises." He drove his point home by invoking Lenin's conclusion of the Brest-Litovsk Treaty and contrasted it with "the doings of Khrushchev and Brezhnev" as "betrayers of Lenin."

In another justification for Sino-American détente, Zhou said the United States had "openly admitted that it is increasingly on the decline" and that it "could not but pull out of Vietnam" under terms of the January 1973 Paris peace agreement. This portrayal of receding U.S. power contrasted with his catalog of the "evil and foul things" perpetrated by an expansionist Soviet Union. His report also echoed Beijing's conciliatory approach on the Taiwan issue during the previous year, appealing to compatriots on the mainland and in Taiwan to "strive together" to liberate Taiwan and unify the country.

NOTES

1. Washington *Post*, 29 January 1968.

2. Harold Hinton, *China's Turbulent Quest* (New York: Macmillian, 1970), pp. 157–58.

3. For a general discussion of this period in Chinese foreign affairs, see Melvin Gurtov, "The Foreign Ministry and Foreign Affairs During the Cultural Revolution," *The China Quarterly* 40 (1969): 65–102. See also Hinton, *Quest*, pp. 127–64; and Robert G. Sutter, *China-Watch: Toward Sino-American Reconciliation* (Baltimore: Johns Hopkins University Press, 1978), pp. 63–82.

4. *Xinhua*, 18 May 1968, in U.S. Foreign Broadcast Information Service, *Daily Report* (hereafter *DR*) *China*, 20 May 1968.

5. *Xinhua*, 17 and 18 June 1968, in *DR China*, 19 June 1968.

6. *Xinhua*, 24 and 25 May 1968, in *DR China*, 27 May 1968.

7. *Xinhua*, 26 July 1968, in *DR China*, 30 July 1968.

8. Agence France Presse (AFP), 31 July 1968.

9. Gurtov, "The Foreign Ministry," p. 93.

10. *Xinhua*, 11 August 1968, in *DR China*, 13 August 1968; *Xinhua*, 15 August 1968, in *DR China*, 16 August 1968.

11. Philip Bridgham, "Mao's Cultural Revolution: The Struggle to Seize Power," *The China Quarterly* 41 (1970): 1–25.

12. For background and varied analytical approaches to this crisis, see Harold Hinton, *Bear at the Gate* (Washington, D.C.: American Enterprise Institute, 1971); Richard Wich, *Sino-Soviet Crisis Politics* (Cambridge, Mass.: Harvard University Press, 1980); Thomas Gottlieb, *Chinese Foreign Policy Factionalism and the Origins of the Strategic Triangle* (Santa Monica, Calif.: Rand Corp, 1977).

13. This section draws heavily on the analytical framework in Gottlieb, *Chinese Foreign Policy*, and on data in Sutter, *China-Watch*, pp. 83–93.

14. For background, see Sutter, *China-Watch*, pp. 93–102.

15. Ibid.

16. Many of these overtures and China's responses are reviewed in Kenneth Lieberthal, *Sino-Soviet Conflict in the 1970s: Its Evolution and Implications for the Strategic Triangle* (Santa Monica, Calif.: Rand Corp, 1978). Supplementary information is provided notably in a series of commentaries on Sino-Soviet relations in *DR USSR*, 3, 4, and 10 March 1982.

17. For background, see Michael Pillsbury, *SALT on the Dragon: Chinese Views of the Soviet-American Balance* (Santa Monica, Calif.: Rand Corp., 1975); BDM Corp., *China and SALT* (Vienna, Va.: BDM Corp., 1976); Harlan Jencks, *From Muskets to Missiles* (Boulder, Colo.: Westview press, 1982).

18. The communiqué is published in *DR China*, 28 February 1972.

19. *Xinhua*, 17 July 1972, in *DR China*, 18 July 1972.

20. The text of Zhou's report at the congress appeared in *DR China*, 31 August 1973. It is analyzed in Foreign Broadcast Information Service, *Trends in Communist Propaganda* (hereafter *FBIS Trends*), 6 September 1973. For background see Robert Sutter, *Chinese Foreign Policy After the Cultural Revolution* (Boulder, Colo.: Westview Press, 1978).

21. See the discussion of this issue in Yitzhak Shichor, *The Middle East in China's Foreign Policy* (London: Cambridge University Press, 1979).

22. Tass, 19 July 1973.

23. See Lieberthal, *Sino-Soviet Conflict*.

24. Ibid.

3

PRC LEADERSHIP DISPUTES, EAST-WEST RELATIONS, COMPLICATE FOREIGN POLICY, 1973-76

By the end of 1973, it was clear that Beijing's more pragmatic approach in foreign affairs had greatly enhanced China's international position and had gone far toward securing its interests around its periphery in Asia. In little more than four years, Beijing had marked the following major achievements:

- Beijing had managed to use the Sino-Soviet border talks to help reduce the Soviet threat against China. And it had used active international diplomacy to block suspected Soviet efforts to keep China isolated in Asia and elsewhere. Meanwhile, by this time the Chinese had deployed significant numbers of nuclear-tipped ballistic missiles, so hidden or maneuverable that they represented a credible nuclear deterrent to Soviet attack.[1]

- Beijing had gained entry into the United Nations, normalized diplomatic relations with such major capitalist powers as West Germany, Japan, and Great Britain, and reestablished its traditionally favorable position among independent Communist-ruled states like Romania, North Korea, and North Vietnam. The most significant advance involved Beijing's beginning of what promised to be a fruitful reconciliation with the United States.

- On the basis of its strengthened international position and Taiwan's growing diplomatic isolation, Beijing attempted to elicit Taipei's interest in eased tensions and political reunification. This involved calls for peace talks and exchanges with Taipei, and a lessening of polemics with the Chinese Nationalists that had not been seen in over a decade.

- Beijing had put aside some of its ideological bias against increasing trade with capitalist states and had begun to open more of its markets to the advanced technology and resources available in the West, hoping thereby to build its strength with equipment purchased abroad. China revived larger-scale imports of machinery from capitalist countries—dormant since the Cultural Revolution—and it began to use oil and other resources as significant export commodities.

- Beijing was pursuing programs of cultural and technical exchange with an increasingly large number of countries, thereby greatly strengthening China's appeal internationally.

Thus, the Beijing leadership appeared more sanguine about its security concerns in the Asian environment and the overall international balance of power against the USSR. In particular, as a result of the Nixon Doctrine and the Sino-American reconciliation, China increasingly saw the United States as a friendly strategic partner; it provided an effective counterweight capable of checking Soviet global expansion and of sustaining a balance of influence against the USSR in Asia that would allow China to focus more on its internal development. Accordingly, the Beijing leadership intensified efforts to build its domestic political order and to develop economically. In late 1973, for example, Beijing finally addressed the issue posed by the presence of inordinately strong military leaders maintaining a controlling influence in certain civilian administrative posts in the Chinese provinces. This problem was a holdover from the era of Lin Biao, when military leaders exerted great influence in newly rebuilt organs of political power following the violent stage of the Cultural Revolution of the late 1960s. Chinese civilian leaders now managed to reassert control by carrying out a long overdue transfer of military regional commanders.

The wholesale transfer of China's military commanders, many of whom were also provincial party chiefs, was revealed in a 1 January 1974 *Xinhua* report of army-people gatherings on the occasion of the new year. The moves reflected a general pattern, evident since the death of Lin in 1971, to reduce the independent power of the PLA, which had grown to control China's political life during the turmoil of the Cultural Revolution. While none of the military commanders were purged, the transfers from areas where many had years of experience and personal loyalties effectively reduced their power.[2]

Nevertheless, Chinese leaders harbored deep differences on a range of important issues, including several involving foreign policy. Because of the political leadership vacuum created by the steady decline in the health of both Mao and Zhou in the mid-1970s, the struggle for power and succession to the leadership among other Chinese officials intensified and spilled over to affect foreign policy in several key areas. Most notably, more radical officials led by the four Chinese Politburo members (Jiang Qing, Zhang Chunqiao, Yao Wenyuan, and Wang Hongwen, later labeled the Gang of Four) made clear through speeches and media comment their doubts about basic precepts of the Zhouist approach to foreign affairs employed since 1970. In particular, they questioned whether:[3]

- The principal international contradiction was between the superpowers and the rest of the world, rather than between socialism and capitalism-imperialism

- China should reduce contacts with like-minded but generally ineffective revolutionary movements in favor of forming closer ties with existing governments—even those considered "reactionary" or capitalist—of the developed and developing world

- The Soviet Union alone was the principal threat to China and should be dealt with by a combination of negotiations, gradually increasing defense preparations, and closer ties with the United States

- The United States could serve as an implicit counterweight to the USSR because it was less of a threat to China and remained fundamentally opposed to the USSR

- China, relying on U.S.-Soviet contention and bilateral talks with the USSR, could afford to reduce and streamline its armed forces, using the savings for economic modernization

- China should increase trade with capitalist countries and purchases of advanced industrial equipment from abroad—on short-term credit if necessary—in order to advance economic modernization

- China should use savings from defense and earnings from increased sales of its resources to developed countries to finance purchases of equipment from those states

- China could exploit its diplomatic success, especially closer ties with the United States, to encourage Taipei to begin the process of political reunification.

Had the Chinese leadership not been relatively relaxed about the stability of their surroundings in Asia, it is questionable whether the Gang of Four would have been as free to raise such skeptical questions about the pragmatic Zhouist approach to foreign affairs. Indeed, the success of Zhou's program seems to have increased Chinese room for maneuver in foreign affairs, to a point where dissidents in China could air alternative policies without running a strong risk of being accused of endangering national security at a time of international crisis.

In any event, the radical challenge of the mid-1970s had potentially broad implications for Chinese foreign policy only if the policy approaches of those leaders were followed to their logical conclusion. Under those circumstances, they pointed to a return to the rigidly orthodox foreign policy of the mid-1960s. In fact, however, the radicals appeared more interested merely in using orthodox Maoist critiques of certain pragmatic policies of Zhou and his chief aide, Deng Xiaoping, for broader political gain in the struggle for succession in China. Moreover, the dissidents did not have a strong base of power, nor did they have a viable foreign policy program with which to challenge the status quo. As a result, their attacks temporarily disrupted or halted progress in certain foreign policy areas, but had no lasting or longer-term effect.

Critical of the use of negotiations to deal with the Soviet threat, the radicals called for a more uncompromising approach based ultimately on China's ability to defend itself and confront the USSR through people's war. They exploited the highly charged atmosphere surrounding the anti-Confucius, anti-Lin Biao campaign of 1973-74 to prompt a sharp increase in polemics against the Soviet Union. At this time, the Chinese also took the highly unusual step of arresting as spies a number of Soviet diplomats and three Soviet border guards. The arrest and prolonged detention of the latter, who landed in China by helicopter and were captured in March 1974, resulted in an exchange of strong protests and the most serious crisis along the Sino-Soviet border since the clashes of 1969.[4]

Regarding Taiwan, Beijing's approach stiffened noticeably from the more moderate theme that Sino-American reconciliation and growing Chinese international stature would eventually compel Taiwan to open negotiations with Beijing. Instead, Chinese media stressed that Taiwan's reunion with the mainland would result from China's determination and military preparedness. This tougher line was in evidence during the February 1974 Chinese comment marking the anniversary of the Taiwan uprising of February 1947, a sharp contrast with the more moderate comment of the year before.[5]

Chinese media became more explicit in condemning the "rotten capitalist system." It also revived sharp criticism of U.S. culture, thereby serving to dampen Chinese interest in cultural exchanges with the United States and other "bourgeois" countries. Media comment in July 1974 was particularly virulent in condemning the sex and violence in U.S. films and literature.[6]

Beijing also began sharp criticism of trade with capitalist countries and reaffirmation of Chinese interest in economic self-reliance, thereby helping to reduce Chinese interest in trade with the West—an interest already dampened by serious trade deficits. It was later disclosed that the Gang of Four had opposed China selling its oil and other resources to the "exploitative" capitalist countries and using the proceeds of such sales to purchase the "outdated" Western technology that would always keep China in an economically "subservient" position vis-à-vis the West, "trailing behind at a snail's pace" in the race for economic modernization and development. To them, only the policy of economic self-reliance provided China with the means to control its economic destiny and to achieve the technological breakthroughs that would allow it to catch up with the developed world.[7] More broadly, radical-influenced comment harshly criticized foreign music, films, and other cultural works.[8]

These episodes of radical-inspired challenge to the Zhouist course in foreign policy recurred periodically until the death of Mao and the arrest of the Gang of Four in 1976. Nevertheless, the broad outlines of Zhou's approach remained clear and provided the foundation for China's continued development. The radical approach in particular provided no adequate response to the continued, potentially dangerous shifts in the international strategic environment affecting China's security and development. These changes were dealt with in a more pragmatic way, under the leadership of Zhou's chief deputy, Deng Xiaoping, with an eye toward stabilizing China's strategic environment in order to safeguard national security and development needs, even at the expense of past ideological and political positions or of offending the sensibilities of some Chinese leaders.

FOURTH NATIONAL PEOPLE'S CONGRESS, JANUARY 1975[9]

Zhou Enlai's 13 January 1975 report to the Fourth National People's Congress represented a particularly useful benchmark that allowed outside observers to chart the evolution of China's progress toward a more pragmatic, geopolitical approach to foreign affairs. Generally echoing the views he had presented in his report to the Tenth Party Congress in August 1973, his last comprehensive discussion of foreign affairs, Zhou portrayed a world situation favorable for China. He suggested that Beijing felt reasonably confident that its foreign approach was dealing effectively with the problems posed by Soviet pressure and other sources of instability in the Asian region. He did give more credence to the possibility that contention between the superpowers could lead to world war, but his remarks were couched in a theoretical framework and did not picture China as threatened. Rather, the emphasis on world war seemed designed to attempt to disparage and undermine future U.S.-Soviet détente that China would increasingly come to see as complicating its security balance with the USSR. He assessed Sino-American relations in positive terms, but he bluntly characterized Sino-Soviet relations as at a standstill.

In departing from the PRC line on world war and revolution that had been standard for almost five years, Zhou said that the "fierce contention" between the United States and the Soviet Union "is bound to lead to world war some day," and he was equivocal as to whether war or revolution was more likely, saying that "the factors for both war and revolution are increasing." By contrast, at the Tenth Party Congress Zhou had quoted the passage in Mao Zedong's 20 May 1970 statement that while "the danger of new world war exists," revolution against imperialism was the "main trend" in the world today.[10]

Zhou's remark on the inevitability at some future time of a military confrontation between the two superpowers seemed to be aimed primarily at undermining the notion of a possible relaxation of U.S.-Soviet tensions under the cover of détente. Referring to recent talk of détente and peace around the world, Zhou maintained that all the talk merely proved that "there is no détente, let alone lasting peace, in this world." Assessing what he saw as progressively increasing U.S.-Soviet contention for world control, Zhou indicated that the developing "economic crisis in the capitalist world"—a reference to the recession at that time—had served to intensify U.S.-Soviet competition, and he repeated his judgment at the Tenth Party Congress that Europe was the focus of U.S.-Soviet rivalry.

Zhou was more sanguine about China's national security than he had been in 1973. He repeated his 1973 slogan playing down the Soviet Union's threat to China, noting that Moscow merely "makes a feint to the east while attacking in the west," and he dropped his 1973 allegation that the West had always sought to divert the Soviet threat eastward, toward China. Zhou also dropped his 1973 warning against the possible launching of an imperialist war against China and his special warning against "suprise attack" from the USSR. His routine instructions on national defense included calls for the people to maintain "vigilance" and to be "prepared" against war. (In 1973 Zhou had enjoined the people to maintain "high vigilance" and to be "fully prepared" against war.)

Zhou voiced continued support for Beijing's flexible foreign policy approach under the banner of Mao's "revolutionary line in foreign affairs," and he gave special attention to improving ties with the developed countries of the so-called second world. The ideological rationale for such ties had been presented by Deng Xiaoping in a major address to the U.N. General Assembly in April 1974.[11] He announced and explained Mao Zedong's "three worlds theory," which sanctioned China establishing closer ties with developing and developed countries of various political and ideological orientations in the interest of forming a broad international front against the "hegemonism of the two superpowers," especially the Soviet Union. In any event, Zhou went on to offer Beijing's highest-level endorsement for West European unity against superpower threats and bullying, and voiced Chinese readiness to promote friendly relations with Japan on the basis of the 1972 Sino-Japanese statements on diplomatic normalization. He routinely reaffirmed China's intention never to be a superpower, its solidarity with the third world, and its intention to uphold proletarian internationalism. He also promised to enhance ties with "socialist countries."

Zhou echoed his assessment at the Tenth Party Congress that Sino-American relations "have improved to some extent." However, he added a phrase giving credit to the United States as well as to the PRC, stating that improvement had been achieved through "joint efforts of both sides." Though Zhou noted that "there exist fundamental differences between China and the United States," he expressed confidence that bilateral relations would continue to improve so long as the two countries carried out "in earnest" the principles of the Shanghai communiqué.

Zhou's assurance reflected the progress made in China's pragmatic approach to the United States and stood in contrast with his defensive 1973 assessment of PRC ties with Washington, in which he had gone to great lengths to rationalize the need for "necessary compromises between revolutionary countries and imperialist countries." Suggesting that at that time he was having some difficulty justifying Sino-American détente to more rigid ideologues at home and abroad, Zhou at the Tenth Party Congress had cited Leninist scripture to distinguish Beijing's new policy from Soviet collaboration with Washington.

Zhou did not repeat his 1973 references to U.S. "defeats" in Korea and Vietnam and to the "decline" of U.S. power over the past generation. And, although he continued to list the United States ahead of the Soviet Union in commenting on the superpowers, he dropped all reference to "U.S. imperialism," which had been cited frequently in his 1973 report. By contrast, he continued to refer to "Soviet social imperialism." The premier gave only routine attention to Taiwan, reaffirming determination to "liberate" the island while calling on "fellow countrymen" on Taiwan to join the liberation struggle.

Though his discussion of the USSR was shorter and less polemical than his anti-Soviet diatribe at the 1973 Tenth Party Congress, Zhou characterized Sino-Soviet relations as at a standstill, openly attacked Soviet "deception" on the border issue, and challenged Moscow to meet Chinese demands concerning the frontier. He accused the "Soviet leading clique" of having betrayed Marxism-Leninism and of having taken a series of actions—including subversion and the provoking of armed clashes along the frontier—to worsen state relations with China. Zhou repeated recent lower-level Chinese charges concerning the Sino-Soviet border and the Beijing border talks that had previously been put forth in a Chinese message to the USSR on 6 November 1974, the anniversary of the October Revolution, and in an article in December 1974 in a Chinese historical publication.[12] Zhou's charges represented his first public discussion of the supposedly confidential Sino-Soviet border talks, as well as Beijing's first authoritative comment on the substance of the negotiations since they had begun in October 1969.

Zhou claimed that Moscow was totally responsible for the lack of progress because it had refused to adhere to the understanding China said was reached during the September 1969 meeting between Zhou and Premier Kosygin at the Beijing airport that led to the decision to start the talks. Zhou said that the understanding—which Moscow later denied had ever been made—included an accord on mutual nonaggression and nonuse of force, as well as an agreement to withdraw forces from disputed border regions. Zhou said that Moscow had refused to withdraw from, and had even denied the existence of, the disputed border areas. He accused the Soviets of talking profusely about "empty treaties" on nonuse of force and nonaggression in order to deceive Soviet and world opinion, and advised Moscow to stop its "deceitful tricks," negotiate honestly, and "do something" to solve "a bit" of the border problem. Zhou's statement served notice on the Soviet Union that it must make the next move to improve relations.

RENEWED CHINESE CONCERN OVER THE STRATEGIC ENVIRONMENT, 1975

As 1975 wore on, Chinese leaders perceived fundamental challenges to their vital security and development interests emanating from two foreign developments. The first concerned the altered perception of the East Asian balance as a result of the collapse of U.S.-backed governments in Indochina in the spring of 1975. The second involved the altered Chinese view of the East-West balance of power following the end of the Nixon administration. In both cases Beijing adjusted its foreign posture to take account of these perceived shifts and thereby to foster better Chinese ability to maintain the stable strategic environment needed for top-priority Chinese security and development concerns.

East Asia[13]

In 1975 Beijing's primary foreign policy worry was over what it saw as a major shift in the balance of power in East Asia. Geopolitical concerns stemming particularly from the rapid collapse of the U.S. position in Indochina in the spring of 1975 prompted stepped-up efforts in pragmatic, conventional diplomacy designed to stabilize the East Asian balance of influence to prevent further Soviet gains.

The Sino-American relationship had remained the centerpiece of Chinese strategy in the region since the early 1970s. In general accord with Beijing's interests, Washington continued to implement the Nixon Doctrine, gradually withdrawing from forward positions in Southeast Asia, Taiwan, Japan, and Korea. At the same time, the United States repeatedly made it clear that its withdrawal should not be interpreted as a sign of weakness, and that Washington remained fully opposed to any other power's attempts to gain a dominant position in East Asia—this applied especially to the Soviet Union. The Nixon administration kept sufficient force on hand to back up its stance, thereby reassuring Beijing that provisions in the 1972 Shanghai communiqué against any one power's establishment of "hegemony" in East Asia would be fulfilled.

Events surrounding the rapid collapse of U.S.-backed regimes in Cambodia and South Vietnam in the spring of 1975 upset the steady development of an East Asian balance favorable to Chinese interests. From Beijing's viewpoint, the stability of the newly emerging East Asian order had met with a significant setback. While Beijing had expected the United States to withdraw eventually from Indochina, the precipitous U.S. pullback held serious implications for China's interests. The United States had suffered a serious defeat at a time when its leadership and resolve abroad, particularly in East Asia, had already been called into question as a result of the Watergate affair and the 1974-75 economic recession. (Beijing media had noted the debilitating impact of the economic "crisis" on U.S. internal and international strength from the outset of the recession. The Chinese leaders were also reported by the Western press to have been seriously concerned over the fall of the Nixon administration, though Beijing media discreetly remained virtually silent on the matter.)

Against this backdrop, the U.S. defeats in Indochina cast some doubt on a key premise in Beijing's plan for stability in East Asia. In particular, was the United States now strong enough—and, more important, was it resolute enough—to continue to serve as the main strategic block against Soviet encroachment and advances in East Asia? Beijing judged that the United States had indeed been weakened by the Indochina events, and that U.S. strength and resolve in East Asia had been significantly affected. The Chinese signaled that they had an altered perception of the balance of forces in the area—they saw the United States as less influential in Asia, and thus viewed Washington's utility as a bulwark against future Soviet expansion as somewhat compromised.

The Chinese responded to their perception of the altered East Asian balance in several ways:

- Beijing demonstrated that it continued to adhere to a Sino-American-supported East Asian order as articulated in the antihegemony clause of the Shanghai communiqué. But, whereas in the past Beijing had relied mainly on U.S. strength to sustain the favorable balance, the Chinese began to take greater responsibility in their own right for shoring up East Asian positions against Soviet expansion. In particular, Beijing moved adroitly to solidify China's relations with, and to cement anti-Soviet feelings in, the two non-Communist states in East Asia most affected by the collapse of the U.S. positions in Indochina: the Philippines and Thailand. Beijing's establishment of diplomatic relations with these states—employing in each instance a joint communiqué testifying to both sides' opposition to international "hegemony"[14]—was intended to reassure Manila and Bangkok of their security and stability in the wake of the U.S. defeat. In particular, China's reassurances to both governments had precluded the possibility that Manila and Bangkok, in a hasty search for big-power support in the new Southeast Asian situation, might have moved into a one-sided relationship with the USSR. Chinese support was particularly important for Thailand, which now lacked a credible international backer in the face of possible Vietnamese military pressure. China, of course, had long wished to normalize relations with these states, if possible on the basis of principles inimical to the USSR. But the speed with which Beijing exploited these governments' new interest in relations with China after the Indochina events, and the unusually blunt Chinese stress on anti-Soviet invective during negotiations, showed heightened PRC concern to offset what was seen as growing possibilities of Soviet expansion in the face of the U.S. withdrawal.

- Beijing acknowledged that the United States had been "beaten black and blue" in Indochina, and noted that the Asian people, especially those in Southeast Asia, were increasingly successful in efforts to drive the "wolf"—the United States—from the "front gate." But the Chinese made it plain that they were opposed to any unilateral, rapid U.S. withdrawal from international involvement as a result of this setback. They clearly indicated that they wished the United States to remain heavily involved abroad, and strategically vigilant against the USSR in Europe, the Middle East, and Asia. Beijing went so far as to stress a propaganda line that its defeats in Indochina had actually presented the United States with an "opportunity" to pull back from "secondary" areas where it had been overextended, in order to serve more effectively as a strategic bulwark against Soviet expansion into more "vital" areas abroad.[15] In this vein, Beijing reduced past criticism of U.S. military presence and political influence in Asia, and gave unusually favorable notice to U.S. statements of resolve to retain strong ties with Japan and selected non-Communist Asian states, and to maintain a strong naval presence in the western Pacific and the Indian Ocean.

- Beijing viewed the USSR as a more immediate and serious threat to China's aspirations in East and Southeast Asia than it had in the early 1970s. Accordingly, the Chinese adopted a more active policy against the USSR, focused on blocking Moscow's attempts to advance along China's flanks as the United States withdrew. In particular, they launched a major propaganda campaign to warn Asian states of the danger posed by the ravenous "tiger"—the USSR—lurking at the rear door as the Asians pushed the "wolf" out the front gate. Beijing also laid special stress on criticizing Moscow's plan for a collective security system in Asia as a thinly veiled Soviet effort to achieve political "hegemony" in Asia, portraying it as the direct antithesis of the "antihegemony front" fostered by China and its friends. Beijing's higher profile against the USSR caused the Chinese to view with increased suspicion Asian states that maintained cordial relations with Moscow, notably Communist Vietnam.

By late 1975, Beijing began to see the situation in East Asia in a more optimistic light. Even though its power and influence in the region had been weakened, the United States continued to demonstrate an active interest and involvement in maintaining an East Asian balance of power that would preclude heavy Soviet penetration into the region. This was underlined by President Ford in late 1975 when he announced the so-called Pacific Doctrine. This strategic policy in East Asia following the defeat in Indochina was based on U.S. air and naval power in the region, and on close ties with traditional allies, such as Japan, and with the PRC. It significantly avoided mentioning any major role that the Soviet Union might play in the area.

Meanwhile, Beijing had achieved considerable success over the past few months in broadening its influence among non-Communist Southeast Asian states. The Chinese propaganda line warning against the danger of Soviet expansion as the United States withdrew also was winning new adherents in the region. At the end of 1975, the only nations in East Asia where the Soviet Union maintained considerable influence were Vietnam and Laos.

U.S.-Soviet Détente

Beijing, however, still could not afford to be overly optimistic about the broad international trends in East-West relations, which China saw as having ominous implications for stability in Asia and China's ability to deal with the Soviet presence in particular. The Chinese showed new alarm over signs in late 1975 concerning what they viewed as a less resolute Western posture vis-à-vis the Soviet Union. In particular, the August 1975 East-West summit meeting of the European Security Conference in Helsinki was viewed by China as evidence of a growing trend in the United States and the West to "appease" the Soviet Union in order to direct the Soviet menace away from Europe and toward China. Beijing responded with warnings to the West against "appeasement" of Soviet "expansionism" under the cover of détente. It stepped up propaganda concerning the danger of a new world war that, it charged, would be started by the Soviet Union. It also became more critical of what it viewed as Western attempts to capitulate to the USSR.[16]

Beijing depicted the Soviet Union as rapidly building up its armed strength to a point where it was equal to, and in some respects surpassed, the power of the United States. China noted in particular alleged Soviet "advantages" regarding the size of its conventional forces, and the size and superior "throw weight" capability of its nuclear rocket forces. It warned that Moscow was also endeavoring to catch up with and surpass the United States in accuracy and technical capability of strategic weapons—an area where the United States was seen as still having the edge over the USSR.

In general, the United States was said to have been weakened as a result of the 1974-75 economic recession, the political disruption caused by the Watergate affair, and the collapse of the U.S.-supported governments in Indochina. Not only was the United States seen as failing to keep pace with Soviet power, but it was said to have shown an alarming tendency to "appease" the USSR over such issues as strategic arms limitation, détente in Europe, East-West trade, and Soviet involvement in conflicts in Africa.

The Chinese were frank in explaining why they wanted the United States to be less accommodating to the Soviet Union in SALT negotiations and elsewhere. Beijing was well aware that if the United States did not offset Soviet strength in areas away from China, Moscow might be more inclined to focus greater force against China. Chinese media repeatedly criticized leaders in the West who were allegedly reducing its strength against Moscow and "appeasing" the Soviet Union.

Typical of Beijing's stepped-up rhetoric against détente following the European Security Conference summit, Foreign Minister Qiao Guanhua's address to the U.N. General Assembly on 26 September 1975 emphasized the growing danger to the world of superpower-initiated war—especially war started by the Soviet Union.[17] Qiao showed concern over possible gains for Soviet-sponsored détente following the Helsinki summit meeting.

Sharply rebutting superpower claims of an "irreversible process of détente," Qiao stressed the enhanced danger of a "new world war" stemming from the U.S.-Soviet world rivalry, stating that "whether war gives rise to revolution or revolution prevents war," the future would be "bright." In 1974, by contrast, Qiao had stressed the view that revolution, not superpower war, was the "main" international trend, and he had been more sanguine that world popular opinion had successfully "seen through" the "smokescreen" of superpower détente. The foreign minister showed special concern over "deceptive" Soviet détente propaganda following the Helsinki summit, bluntly warning that "it would be dangerous indeed" to "be so naive as to believe in the Soviet propaganda." Qiao designated the Soviet Union as the major threat to peace, asserting that "the danger of war comes mainly from the wildly ambitious social imperialism"—the first time this charge was made in authoritative Chinese comment.[18]

Chinese criticism of Western "appeasement" of the "wildly expansionist" Soviet Union under the cover of détente received new impetus in response to the dismissal of U.S. Secretary of Defense James Schlesinger in late 1975.[19] From Beijing's perspective, the dismissal capped a trend of declining U.S. resolve against the Soviet Union. *Xinhua* depicted Schlesinger's dismissal as a deliberate step by President Ford and Secretary of State Henry Kissinger to sacrifice the defense secretary for the sake of reaching a new SALT accord and improving relations with the USSR. It said that Schlesinger was an advocate of a "prudent" U.S. defense posture, and it noted a British press report that his dismissal showed that Ford and Kissinger were determined to ease tensions with Moscow even at the expense of important U.S. security interests.

On the same day, Beijing media began to call attention to the "policy of appeasement" followed by British Prime Minister Neville Chamberlain during negotiations with Adolf Hiltler at Munich in 1938.[20] Chinese comment noted that the policy of appeasement followed by the West at that time had been designed "to divert the spearhead of fascist aggression toward the east," but in fact had only succeeded in whetting Hitler's appetite for further expansion in the west, leading to the start of World War II. Concurrent Chinese comment equated Brezhnev and Hitler, and made clear the implication that the Ford administration's dismissal of Schlesinger represented part of an attempt to appease the USSR and divert the threat of Soviet power eastward, toward China.

Beijing's criticism of U.S. appeasement and its encouragement of a more resolute U.S. position against the USSR received an authoritiative endorsement from Vice-Premier Deng Xiaoping in remarks at a banquet for President Ford at Beijing in December 1975.[21] Deng took the unusual step of clearly indicating that the PRC was less concerned at that time over U.S. policy on bilateral Sino-American problems such as Taiwan than it was over U.S. policy toward the Soviet Union. After routinely discussing U.S.-PRC bilateral relations, Deng stressed what he called "a more important question"—the need for a firmer U.S. policy toward the Soviet Union on SALT and other issues. He dismissed the possibility of meaningful compromise with the Soviet Union, which he labeled the "most dangerous source of war." Deng told President Ford that Beijing saw "the crucial point" in Sino-American relations to be the policy the United States would follow in relations with Moscow. He exhorted the president to follow Beijing's example and to wage a "tit-for-tat struggle" against the USSR, noting that such a stand was sure to succeed, inasmuch as the USSR "fears the tough but bullies the weak."

NOTES

1. See Harlan Jencks, *From Muskets to Missiles* (Boulder, Colo.: Westview Press, 1982), pp. 158–59.

2. For a review of these military changes, see *FBIS Trends*, 3 January 1974.

3. Harry Harding and Ann Fenwick provide excellent assessments of these leadership differences in their articles in Thomas Fingar, ed., *China's Quest for Independence: Policy Evolution in the 1970s* (Boulder, Colo.: Westview Press, 1980).

4. For background, see *FBIS Trends*, 30 May 1974.

5. See, for instance, discussion of the Taiwan issue in Robert Sutter, *Chinese Foreign Policy After the Cultural Revolution* (Boulder, Colo.: Westview Press, 1978).

6. See *DR China*, 30 July 1974.

7. See article by Richard Batsavage and John Davie in U.S. Congress, Joint Economic Committee, *Chinese Economy Post-Mao* (Washington, D.C.: U.S. Government Printing Office, 1978).

8. Reviewed in Sutter, *Chinese Foreign Policy*.

9. This section relies heavily on analysis in *FBIS Trends*, 22 January 1975. The text of Zhou's report was printed in *DR China*, 20 January 1975. For background, see coverage of this issue in Sutter, *Chinese Foreign Policy*.

10. The Mao formulation had been frequently quoted in authoritative Chinese comment up to that time. Reflecting his balanced view of war and revolution, Zhou appeared sanguine about the strength of the third world, and he declared that "whether war gives rise to revolution or revolution prevents war, in either case the international situation will develop in a direction favorable to the people . . . ." This assertion was similar to Lin Biao's remark at the Ninth CCP Congress in April 1969, when he had cited a quotation from Mao to the effect that either world war would give rise to revolution or revolution would prevent war.

11. Deng's speech appeared in *DR China*, 11 April 1974.

12. The message appeared in *DR China*, 7 November 1974. The article appeared in *DR China*, 6 January 1975.

13. This section is based on Robert Sutter, "China's Strategy in Asia Following the U.S. Defeat in Indochina," *Issues and Studies* (Taipei), 1978, and on relevant sections of his *Chinese Foreign Policy*.

14. The Thai-Chinese communiqué appeared in *DR China*, 1 July 1975. The Philippines-China communiqué appeared in *DR China*, 9 June 1975.

15. See, for instance, a Radio Beijing review of U.S. foreign strategy in *DR China*, 19 June 1975.

16. For background, see relevant section in Sutter, *Chinese Foreign Policy*. See also U.S. Library of Congress, Congressional Research Service, *Foreign Perceptions of SALT*, report no. 79–115F (Washington, D.C.: 1979), pp. 56–60; and BDM Corp., *China and SALT* (Vienna, Va.: BDM Corp., 1976).

17. The text of the address appeared in *DR China*, 29 September 1975. For an analysis see *FBIS Trends*, 1 October 1975.

18. Though Qiao had ignored Moscow's Asian security plan in his 1974 speech, this time he accused Moscow of drumming up support for the plan so as to "fill the vacuum" left by the United States in Asia—a charge in line with other recent Chinese comment. Linking Soviet designs in Europe and Asia, Qiao added a unique charge that Moscow was using propaganda on Asian security to conceal its prime objective of gaining control of Europe. Underlining this point, he reaffirmed the past Chinese judgment that Moscow was making a "feint to the east while attacking in the west."

Without mentioning Asian states by name, Qiao lauded Asian resistance to superpower "hegemony," hailing particularly the Southeast Asian states' efforts to create a regional zone of peace, "new progress" against hegemonism in South Asia (an apparent allusion to the rise of an anti-Soviet government in Bangladesh during August 1975), and the Iran-Iraq accord in early 1975 assisting the growth of the Persian Gulf states' unity against outside interference. Qiao claimed that the Soviet Asian security plan's alleged provision for recognition of existing frontiers was designed to legalize Soviet occupation of the territory of "some Asian countries" and to support "one Asian country"—meaning India—in violating its neighbors' boundaries.

19. See analysis in *FBIS Trends*, 12 November 1975.

20. See *DR China*, 10 November 1975.

21. Deng's remarks appeared in *DR China*, 2 December 1975.

4

POST-MAO CONSOLIDATION
AND REFORM, 1976-78

Beijing's preoccupation with internal affairs placed China in a relatively passive position in the two years immediately following the deaths
of Zhou Enlai and Mao Zedong in 1976. The arrest of the Gang of Four
in October 1976, one month after Mao's death, eliminated those in the
top leadership who had advocated a return to the more strident
diplomacy of the 1960s. China's leaders, though divided on many issues,
were able to achieve a consensus in broadly supporting the differentiated
policy toward the superpowers seen in the "three worlds theory"—the
theoretical underpinning of Chinese foreign policy officially unveiled by
Deng Xiaoping at the United Nations in April 1974.[1]

While the Chinese leadership softened some of Beijing's ideologically
based antipathy toward the Soviet Union and resumed some more conventional Sino-Soviet interchange, Beijing was prompt in reacting critically to what it saw as Soviet international expansion. And China remained sharply critical of perceived Western weakness or appeasement
in the face of the Soviet threat. At bottom, the Chinese leadership saw
such unchecked Soviet expansion as having potentially serious negative
implications for the stability of China's surroundings in Asia, and it attempted to do what it could in order to foster international resolve to
check the Soviet pressure. But because of the serious domestic political,
economic, and other complications in the immediate post-Mao period,
Beijing judged that it was in no position—militarily or otherwise—to employ provocative tactics designed to confront the USSR directly. Rather,
it retreated to a second-line postion vis-à-vis the USSR while strongly encouraging the United States and the West to stand firm in bearing the
brunt of Soviet power; China reacted with tough words but few deeds

to perceived signs of weakness in the international front that it was attempting to nurture in opposition to Soviet expansion.

DOMESTIC DEVELOPMENTS

Serious domestic problems influenced China's decision to alter foreign policy tactics as Beijing attempted to secure important interests in the unsteady international and Asian balance threatened by Soviet expansion. Following the death of Mao Zedong and the arrest of the Gang of Four in late 1976, China's leaders faced a host of internal problems, including a stagnant economy, a highly factionalized and cumbersome administrative structure, widespread public dissatisfaction with Maoist rule, and a cultural and intellectual life stunted by the dictates of Mao's ideology. Chinese foreign policy remained centered on a united-front strategy focused against the Soviet Union, in which China stressed good relations with third world countries and attempted improvement in strategic, economic, and political relations with developed nations, including the United States. However, ties with the United States and other capitalist countries were still explained more as a temporary expedient than as part of a longer-term strategy. Close economic, cultural, and intellectual exchanges with them were limited by ideological restrictions held over from the Maoist period.

Chinese officials focused on grappling with internal problems in order to lay a firmer foundation for Chinese economic development and political stability. At the same time, they attempted to capitalize on improved relations with powerful developed countries like the United States in order to solidify international resistance to the Soviet Union and gain the financial, material, and technical support needed for China's push toward the "four modernizations" (in agriculture, industry, science and technology, and national defense).

Economic progress increasingly became the litmus test of success or failure for the post-Mao Chinese leaders. PRC officials repeatedly emphasized the need to end the economic dislocations of the past and to foster programs that would improve the welfare of the people while advancing the nation toward the goal of becoming a modern and powerful socialist country.[2]

Despite a respectable average level of national growth in the past, post-Mao leaders faced very serious problems in industry and agriculture. By 1977, it was becoming apparent that poor planning, growing inefficiencies, and severe sectoral imbalances had resulted in such failures as heavy investments in unneeded industrial infrastructure, wasteful use of energy and other raw materials, inadequate transportation, poor coordination of production activities, and flat agricultural growth.

Economic policies and reforms adopted by post-Mao leaders did not represent a clear-cut, coherent program; rather, they were the result of continuous institutional and policy changes to deal with specific problems as they emerged.

PRC leaders attempted to solve economic problems in the ten-year draft plan (1976-85) unveiled belatedly in February 1978.[3] Although the plan gave more prominence to agricultural development than in the past, its central focus was on heavy industrial growth. The most innovative element in the plan was China's greater willingness to use large-scale imports of Western equipment and technology in the development effort.

Between the announcement of the plan in February and the watershed Third Plenum of the Eleventh Chinese Communist Party Central Committee in December 1978, the leadership came to a new and more sober appraisal of the size and nature of the gap between China's existing capabilities and its ambitions.[4] As a result, the leadership shelved the ten-year plan and embarked on a three-year (1979-81) readjustment program. The underlying theme of Chinese domestic policy then centered on the judgment that economic productivity and consumer welfare were closely related. The many changes in economic policy after the Third Plenum in late 1978—increasing the material incentives for production, and hence incomes of workers and peasants; installing new systems of rewards and penalties for individual managers and economic entities; and experimenting with new and more efficient forms of industrial organization—were aimed at productivity increases.

Resource allocation policies were shifted to support the new policy. Investment in heavy industry, particularly iron and steel, was cut back while the allocations to agriculture, light industry, and the building materials industry were increased. While maintaining its interest in acquiring foreign equipment and technology, and continuing to enter into selected undertakings on favorable credit terms, the leadership suspended or postponed a number of planned purchases abroad. The domestic construction program was also cut back, eliminating poorly planned projects and those requiring long lead times. A drive to alleviate long-standing constraints on industrial production—electric power, coal, building materials, and transportation—was put among the first priorities of China's economic managers.

Effective economic development and pursuit of the "four modernizations" required reform of China's political system. The reforms included changes in laws, institutions, and administrative practices, but at their heart were leadership changes. Following the death of Mao and the arrest of the Gang of Four, Chinese leaders inherited a massive administrative structure staffed by cadres seriously divided along ideological, generational, institutional, and factional lines. Decision making on economic development and other programs continued to be disrupted by such divisions, thus barring the establishment of a more unified and competent group at the top levels of the party, government, and army. Leadership unity was needed to rally the support of frequently hesitant and indecisive cadres at lower levels in the administration, and to win the backing of the people for the modernization programs. Without a more unified leadership, factional, ideological, and policy differences among senior leaders would cause indecisiveness and vacillation over modernization policies and other programs. Officials at lower levels would be inclined to hedge their bets in this uncertain atmosphere, and would avoid the full commitment needed to carry out modernization programs effectively.[5]

Beijing's initial steps in political change were slow and incremental. Maoist loyalists were gradually removed from power, and more pragmatic and technically competent managers were appointed to direct day-to-day affairs. Provincial-level posts changed hands, as many leaders removed during the Cultural Revolution were returned to power. A variety of other past injustices were redressed, and the rule of law in society and the use of more democratic practices within the Communist Party were established as goals of the new administration.

Maoist dogma, the cult of personality, disruptive mass political campaigns, and other features of the Cultural Revolution were discredited as Chinese leaders began to emphasize a new approach that "seeks truth from facts" and to cite "practice as the sole criterion for truth." Excessive revolutionary fervor—a hallmark of the Maoist era—was labeled an impediment to development and the main cause of China's economic shortcomings over the previous 20 years. Intellectuals and scientific personnel were freed from many of the ideological shackles that had prevented them from working to their full potential. Science and technology were viewed as key elements in the modernization process and their practitioners basked in new prestige. Economic development rather than ideological purity was established as the main source of legitimacy of the Chinese administration.

Nonetheless, while leaders at top levels agreed on the need to reduce the influence of Maoist policies, they differed strongly on how far they should go in this regard and how rigorously they should attempt to remove officials who were closely associated with the past radical policies. They debated over the need for decentralized economic decision making, as opposed to strong adminstrative control of economic planning. Other issues included how much adminstrative control should be exerted on public opinion, the workings of supply and demand in the consumer market, and the freedom of intellectuals and scientists to pursue their work.

Other differences centered on defense issues.[6] Reformers stressed the need to give priority to economic over military modernization, to streamline and professionalize the large Chinese ground forces, to modernize their training and tactics, and gradually to improve military equipment. This ran up against past emphasis on large field forces imbued with Maoist ideology, and the hopes of many in the military that they would receive a greater share of resources under the new modernization programs.

In foreign affairs, Chinese leaders appeared to hold different views on the wisdom of large-scale investments and other foreign involvement in China. Some called into question compromises China was required to make in order to reach a modus vivendi with the West. This was particularly the case over the sensitive Taiwan issue in Sino-American relations.

Slow progress toward reform generated confusion and uncertainty among cadres in China. Faced with rapidly changing and sometimes conflicting signals from the top, working-level cadres were reluctant to commit themselves fully. They sometimes reverted to a low profile and tried to avoid individual responsibility—a practice that was widely reported as a major factor undermining many changes China tried in support of the "four modernizations." Some commentaries even referred to a "crisis of confidence" in China—a belief on the part of some officials that the system as it existed was not capable of successfully achieving the "four modernizations."

FOREIGN AFFAIRS—DEALING WITH SOVIET EXPANSION

Given these domestic preoccupations, it was not surprising that Beijing's posture in foreign affairs received only secondary attention. Thus, Chinese leaders continued past emphasis on dealing with the Soviet challenge in Asia and elsewhere by means of an international anti-hegemony front supported by China, but Beijing's ability to make tactical probes that would take the lead in this endeavor was limited by domestic constraints. Meanwhile, the passing of the Maoist legacy in foreign affairs allowed China to begin loosening the ideological shackles that had blocked more effective collaboration with the West and with "nonprogressive" regimes elsewhere in the developing and developed worlds; reduced China's incentive to offer foreign economic and military aid, and to give assistance to revolutionary movements abroad; and broadened

China's room for maneuver as it attempted to use conventional diplomacy less impeded by ideological concerns to deal with the Soviet threat.

Mao's death on 9 September 1976 presented the Soviet Union with a possible new opportunity. Having consistently viewed Mao as the main instigator of Beijing's anti-Sovietism, Moscow responded to his death with a series of public gestures ostensibly designed to show the post-Mao leaders that the Soviet Union was prepared to seek an accommodation of Sino-Soviet differences:

- Moscow media stopped criticism of China. The closest Moscow came to criticizing China in the next four months was to note disapprovingly that Beijing propaganda continued to criticize Soviet policies.

- Brezhnev sent a Soviet Communist Party message of condolence on Mao's death, the first such Communist Party message to be sent to China in a decade. Brezhnev followed with a message congratulating Hua Guofeng on his appointment as the new Chinese Communist Party chairman in October.[7]

- Soviet media gave unusually prominent attention to China's 1 October 1976 National Day celebrations. *Pravda* articles on the anniversary had previously been written by ordinary commentators, but this time the article appeared under the authoritative byline I. Aleksandrov. It echoed prevailing Soviet comment in recalling Soviet aid to China during the 1950s, and Soviet efforts to normalize relations and ease Sino-Soviet border tensions since the start of the Beijing border talks in 1969.[8]

- In late November, the Soviets sent Deputy Foreign Minister Ilichev back to China to resume the border talks after a hiatus of 18 months.

Beijing formally disavowed any interest in the Soviet gestures, but it also demonstrated that China's approach to the USSR would not be as ideologically strident as it had been during the previous three years, when the Gang of Four influenced the tone of Chinese foreign policy. For example, the volume of Chinese criticism of the Soviet Union was significantly reduced for four months following Mao's death; Beijing did not formally reject the Soviet gestures toward China until mid-November 1976;[9] and for several weeks following Ilichev's late November return to Beijing, Chinese comment on the USSR remained moderate.

At the turn of the year, Chinese spokesmen once again reaffirmed a hard line against Moscow and the volume of anti-Soviet polemics began to increase. Beijing nonetheless was willing to demonstrate a very limited improvement in Sino-Soviet state relations. In mid-1977, China compromised on its past insistence that territorial issues be discussed at the annual border river navigation talks; as a result, for the first time in over a decade, the two sides were able to announce that some agreement had been reached in these talks.[10] China also agreed to increase Sino-Soviet trade, which grew from $377 million in 1977 to $499 million in 1978,[11] and it sent the Chinese foreign minister to the Soviet National Day reception in Beijing on 7 November 1977—the first time the Chinese minister had attended the Soviet party since 1966.[12]

Against this backdrop, Moscow attempted to move the relationship foward with a major initiative in February 1978 that called for Sino-Soviet talks to negotiate a joint statement of principles to govern Sino-Soviet relations. The Soviet demarche came in the form of greetings from the Supreme Soviet of the USSR to China's National People's Congress and appeared to be timed to influence the foreign policy deliberations of the Fifth National People's Congress, which met in February 1978. Chinese Premier Hua Guofeng rebuffed the overture. In his report to the congress, Hua avoided mentioning past ideological requirements for improved Sino-Soviet relations, but he pointedly linked any further progress in those relations to a firm Chinese demand that the USSR implement the Zhou-Kosygin understanding involving troop withdrawals from "disputed" regions along the border. He added demands that Moscow withdraw Soviet forces from Mongolia, and reduce forces along the Sino-Soviet frontier to the level that existed prior to the build-up of Soviet forces that began in the mid-1960s. Hua said that these Soviet "deeds" were necessary "if the Soviet leading clique really desired to improve state relations."[13]

Pravda responded with an editorial on 1 April refuting Beijing's view of the Zhou-Kosygin meeting and denying that any such understanding about withdrawing troops from disputed border regions had ever been reached.[14] Soviet leaders nonetheless sent Ilichev back to the border talks on 26 April. By June, however, the Soviet negotiator left the border negotiations for the last time.[15]

ELEVENTH PARTY CONGRESS, 1977

In their broader foreign policy pronouncements, Chinese leaders repeatedly made clear their sharply anti-Soviet policy orientation and their strong concern with perceived Western weakness in the East-West balance. In the foreign policy section of his political report to the Eleventh Chinese Communist Party (CCP) Congress in August 1977, Party Chairman Hua Guofeng adhered to positions Zhou Enlai had outlined at the Tenth CCP Congress in 1973 and at the Fourth National People's Congress in 1975. However, Hua went further in differentiating between the superpowers more sharply than Zhou had, specified that the Soviet Union presented the "greatest danger" to the world, and listed the USSR ahead of the United States—reversing the order that Zhou had used in referring to the two superpowers in 1973 and in 1975.[16]

Hua's remarks on the possibilities for world war and for revolution reflected Beijing's growing concern over the evolution of the world balance of power in the years since the Tenth CCP Congress, culminating in a view that was more pessimistic on the inevitability of world war and that accommodated Beijing's perceptions of the growth during the 1970s of Soviet power in the world at the expense of the United States. While declaring that "factors" for both war and revolution had increased in recent years, he dwelt on the former, observing that superpower contention would "lead to a conflagration someday," and cited a newly publicized Mao statement, made in early 1976, on war as a natural continuation of international politics.

Hua reaffirmed Zhou's 1973 analysis that Europe represented the focus of Soviet-American contention and, as Zhou had, he denounced U.S. and Soviet pretensions of détente, disarmament, and peace. Also following Zhou, Hua attacked a "trend toward appeasement" in the West in dealing with the Soviet threat and attempts to "divert the peril of the new tsars toward the East," actions that Hua said will only "abet" Moscow's ambitions and "hasten the outbreak of war." Although Hua, unlike Zhou in 1973, did not explicitly warn of a Soviet "surprise attack" against China, he did mention Moscow's "wild ambition to subjugate China," a reference that had become common in Chinese comment since early 1977 to justify more rapid modernization of China into a "powerful, socialist country before the turn of the century."

Hua strongly reaffirmed Mao's strategic division of the globe into three worlds, a concept that Beijing had used regularly since 1974 to rationalize its more flexible foreign policy launched earlier. The "three-worlds" theory, Hua declared, had provided the "correct strategic and tactical formations for the world proletariat in the present era and its class line in the international struggle."[17]

Hua's brief remarks on Beijing's relations with Washington constituted an authoritative reaffirmation of all fundamental aspects of the Sino-American relationship defined in the 1972 Shanghai communiqué. Regarding the coincidence of strategic interests underlying the Sino-American relationship, Hua recalled the Shanghai communiqué's commitment of both sides to opposition to "hegemony." On bilateral relations, Hua spelled out the three conditions posed by Beijing for complete normalization of relations: withdrawal of U.S. troops from Taiwan, severance of diplomatic relations with Taipei, and abrogation of the 1954 mutual defense treaty. He went on to say that "when and how" Taiwan was liberated was "entirely China's internal affair"—language apparently calculated to make more explicit Beijing's unwillingness to provide formal guarantees against the use of force in resolving the Taiwan issue.

This was only the second time that Beijing media on an authoritative level had spelled out the conditions for normalized Sino-American relations. The first such assertion was in early July 1977, when Beijing media reported Vice-Premier Li Xiannian as citing the conditions in a conversation with visiting U.S. Admiral Elmo Zumwalt.[18]

Hua was suitably downbeat on Sino-Soviet relations, accusing Moscow of showing not "one iota of good faith" about improving state relations with China. Instead, Hua declared, Moscow attempted to coerce China into abandoning its Marxist-Leninist principles, "whipped up one anti-China wave after another" to divert world attention from its own expansionist ambitions, and "made it impossible to achieve anything" in the Sino-Soviet border talks.

VIEW OF EAST-WEST RELATIONS

Elsewhere, China underlined its keen concern over developments in East-West relations having potential consequences adverse to Chinese interests with a steady stream of media commentary. In particular, Chinese expressions of concern over U.S. "appeasement" of the USSR concerning SALT and other issues were a feature of Beijing media coverage of the policies of the Carter administration, especially in 1977 and 1978. However, Beijing comment was sometimes contradictory in its assessment of the administration's position. On the one hand, it frequently criticized what it saw as the administration's willingness to make "unwarranted" concessions to the Soviets in order to reach agreement. On the other hand, Beijing media frequently portrayed the administration as standing firm vis-à-vis the USSR on arms control and other important matters. These contradictory assessments coincided with, and probably reflected, Chinese reactions to conflicting reports emanating from the United States; but they could also have been a sign of disagreement in Beijing as to whether the Carter administration was maintaining a stance vis-à-vis the Soviet Union strong enough to preclude a substantial increase in Soviet pressure against China.

Chinese media comment depicted three schools of thought in the United States concerning SALT and détente with the Soviet Union. Some U.S. officials were said to favor a policy of appeasement toward the Soviet Union. Beijing comment claimed that these leaders "pinned their hopes" on the possibility of the Soviet Union acting with restraint in international affairs, and opposed an expansion of U.S. armed strength for fear of antagonizing Moscow and undercutting the SALT talks. While never so identified by Chinese media, Beijing may have seen Secretary of State Cyrus Vance as a leading advocate of this school of thought.

Beijing saw mustered against these "proponents of appeasement" a group of U.S. leaders who actively opposed concessions to the USSR. National Security Adviser Brzezinski was clearly seen by China in this light. Between these groups were other U.S. leaders, including President Carter, and the bulk of the American people, who were seen as still undecided regarding U.S. policy toward the USSR. Chinese media implied that pro-appeasement forces in the United States—although a clear minority—might be able to gain the upper hand in leadership councils and push through a SALT II agreement or other U.S.-Soviet accord detrimental to U.S. and Western—and, by implication, Chinese—security interests.[19]

By the end of 1977, for example, Beijing had become seriously alarmed by what it saw as widespread influence of pro-appeasement thinkers in the United States and other Western countries. Its concerns over such appeasement were initially reflected in September, in reporting and comment on U.S. strategy in Western Europe, focused on Presidential Review Memorandum (PRM)-10. Media criticism later expanded to include the administration's approach to U.S.-Soviet relations in connection with SALT, the Middle East, and the Soviet-Cuban "aggression" in Africa. The negative reporting and comment were primarily reactive, responding to events. Criticism of specific administration policies and leaders was conveyed by citation of attacks by U.S. and foreign public figures and press, rather than by direct Beijing denunciations on its own authority.

Typically, a strongly worded *People's Daily* article warning the United States and Western Europe against appeasement of Soviet expansionism underscored Beijing's concern over what it saw as emerging U.S.-Soviet rapprochement. The article appeared in the 26 November 1977 issue of the paper under the byline of Ren Gubing, a prominent Chinese press commentator on foreign affairs. While Ren adhered to familiar propaganda themes, his article was China's lengthiest and most comprehensive attack on alleged U.S. weakness against Moscow in many months.[20]

Warning that the "shadow of a new Munich looms ahead," the Ren Gubing article made a point-by-point comparison between the policies aimed at appeasing Hitler before World War II and the programs advocated by exponents of détente in the 1970s. It cited historical parallels for policies that minimized the danger of the Soviet threat, placed undue faith in arms control talks at the expense of national security, promoted the export of capital and technology to the USSR, and attempted to divert the "Soviet peril" eastward toward China.

The article was addressed to "some Western political figures" who had "forgotten the bitter lessons of the Munich tragedy 40 years ago"; it did not attack current U.S. or West European leaders by name. But it did denounce "certain representatives of the U.S. monopoly bourgeoisie" who advocated "appeasement" of Moscow to "preserve U.S. global interests" as U.S. power declined, and it noted that "under the influence" of U.S. policies, the "appeasement mentality" was spreading in Western Europe. The article warned that "no one knows how the United States would react" to a Soviet attack on Western Europe, pointing out that "some Washington strategists" argued that the United States should not deplete its forces in Europe in such an event, and recalling the controversy over alleged provision in PRM-10 for abandonment of forward defense in West Germany.

While contending that "world war is inevitable so long as imperialism exists," the article repeated the position, pressed in PRC comment since the Eleventh CCP Congress in August 1977, that the outbreak of war might be "put off." The best tactics for achieving this, according to Ren, were not those of appeasement but, rather, the formation of an "international anti-hegemony united front" of all positive forces, including the Soviet and American peoples.

Meanwhile, one of the most detailed Chinese critiques of U.S. concessions in the SALT II negotiations came in a 19 January 1978 *Guangming Daily* article pegged to the resumption of the SALT negotiations in Geneva ten days earlier. The article criticized three reported U.S. concessions in a proposed SALT II accord:

> ...in the new agreement: 1) The United States will no longer insist on restricting the original number of heavy Soviet land-based missiles; 2) the Soviet Backfire bomber has not been included on the list of the total number of strategic weapons; 3) a restriction will be imposed on the range of the U.S. cruise missile which will deprive or reduce its ability to make a surprise attack on the Soviet mainland.[21]

The article alleged that U.S. concessions to the Soviet Union in past SALT agreements had allowed the Soviet Union "to gradually overtake the United States and contend for nuclear supremacy," and it pointed out that many people in the West felt that "the United States has received the short end of the bargain and would be placed in an unfavorable position in the armaments race" by the proposed SALT II accord. The article made known its preferred policy by highlighting comment of Western spokesmen who strongly opposed the reported SALT agreement:

> Paul Nitze, who was the assistant U.S. secretary of defense and a delegate to the nuclear disarmament talks, held that the concessions made by the United States will put it in an adverse position. He strongly criticized the government for giving up the demand for imposing a limita-

tion on the heavy Soviet ICBMs and the Backfire bomber. *Die Welt am Sonntag* of West Germany pointed out: For the sake of the success of "SALT II," the United States has made concessions regarding the weaponry system of great strategic significance to the NATO Western alliance. *Die Presse* of Austria said that the important concessions made by the United States to the Soviet Union caused Europe to worry about its safety. The *Los Angeles Times* of the United States said that the United States, in concluding this treaty, will lose far more than it gains.

Reflecting possible confusion or disagreement in Beijing on U.S. policy toward SALT and détente with the Soviet Union, a length *Xinhua* commentary two days earlier had offered a very different assessment of the SALT II negotiations.[22] In particular, it claimed to see no evidence that the United States intended to make significant concessions to the Soviet Union. Reviewing the setting of the current round of talks, the commentary said:

> The five-year Soviet-U.S. accord expired on October 3 last year, yet a long-term agreement is still nowhere in sight. Stranded for six months, the Geneva talks were resumed on May 21. The 218th meeting of the five-year-old talks was held on December 13. In an effort to arrive at something before October 3, the two parties talked matters over in Moscow in March, Geneva in May and Washington in September, but without positive results. They had to make verbal pledges to continue to observe the expired accord.

Portraying the United States and the Soviet Union as standing firm in the talks, it added:

> The main reason for the failure of the talks last year is that each of the two superpowers was out to gain military superiority at the expense of the other. While one pushes on, the other refuses to yield.

Xinhua went on to dismiss reports of recent U.S. weakness or concessions in the talks:

> Since last October, much has been said about Moscow and Washington agreeing to make major concessions each in its own way and conlude an eight-year agreement and a three-year protocol. It was, however, disclosed that the Soviet Union had not yielded to the American desire to limit its missiles carrying heavier warheads. On the other hand, Washington had contemplated accommodations to the Soviet demand concerning cruise missiles. But news leaks to this effect touched off a wave of criticism and objection at home and abroad and the White House had to think it over before making an ultimate compromise. Con-

sequently, only assurances in vague terms were made concerning the cruise missiles and Backfire bombers in a temporary protocol.

This is not all. Both sides have already found pretexts for a new round of arms race when a SALT accord is still a rather remote possibility. U.S. President Carter was reported by UPI on December 10 to have said, "We have shown them that we are firm and can't be pushed around."

REACTIVE DIPLOMACY

China's policy toward the developed and developing countries of the second and third worlds also was largely reactive. Beijing basically stood aside as Soviet-backed Cuban troops helped to install a pro-Soviet government in Angola, undermining years of Chinese support for anti-Portuguese liberation movements there. China backed President Anwar Sadat of Egypt and President Barre of Somalia when they broke with the USSR in 1976 and 1977, respectively, but it did little to try to stop the spread of Soviet influence in Ethiopia or to alter Arab efforts to isolate Sadat's Egypt following his opening to Israel.

Chinese leverage in the third world was reduced further by the sharp decline in Chinese economic and military aid commitments, beginning in 1976. Faced with serious economic problems at home, reduced ideological commitment to the third world in the post-Mao period, and mixed results from past large-scale aid efforts, Chinese aid commitments dropped from $366 million in 1975 to under $200 million for each of the next three years.[23]

Relying mainly on diplomacy and propaganda, China bitterly condemned perceived signs of Soviet-backed expansion while encouraging the formation of the broadest international anti-hegemony front of third world and second world countries, and also implicitly including the United States, to confront the Soviet Union. From Beijing's perspective, the USSR was on the offensive and making substantial gains in the third world, while the West in general and the United States in particular were often portrayed as on the defensive and ineffective in the face of the Soviet "threat."

Typically, the Chinese responded to Soviet support for Angolan-based Katangan forces invading Zaire in early 1977 by castigating the USSR and its Cuban "hirelings," and by supporting efforts by the West to back Zaire President Mobutu.[24] That Beijing viewed the United States as less than resolute against the Soviet-Cuban challenge in Africa was seen in a 17 October 1977 *Xinhua* report that criticized both President Carter and U.S. Ambassador to the United Nations Andrew Young for viewing

Cuban troops in Angola as a "stabilizing force" in the region. It said this view reflected "the attitude of appeasement toward Soviet aggressiveness."[25]

The decline of ideology as a determing factor in Chinese foreign policy was signaled by Beijing's revival of formal Communist Party relations with Yugoslavia. The agreement came during President Tito's landmark visit to China in September 1977.[26] Nevertheless, the post-Mao leaders continued on occasion to justify their foreign policies on the basis of elaborate constructs grounded in Leninist ideology. In particular, they carried on a polemic with Albania concerning the appropriateness of Mao's "three worlds" theory and China's sharply differentiated posture toward the two superpowers.[27]

Xinhua articles in August 1977 responded indirectly but clearly to a major Albanian polemic against China in a 7 July *Zeri i Popullit* editorial. The Albanian critique had claimed that China had betrayed Marxism-Leninism by allying with the United States against the USSR, by promoting ties with developed industrial countries of the second world, and by neglecting class struggle in the third world countries for the sake of rallying a united front, including governments of whatever political stripe, against the USSR. One Chinese article reprinted comment by China's longtime ally, Australian Comunist Party (Marxist-Leninist) Chairman E. F. Hill, who declared that Mao's "three worlds" theory correctly stressed the fundamental contradictions between the two superpowers and pointed out the greater danger from Soviet social imperialism.[28] Noting that Lenin himself had ridiculed Trotsky's opposition to tactical compromise with imperialism, Hill cited Stalin's conclusion of the 1939 Nazi-Soviet nonaggression pact as a good example of Lenin's principles in practice. According to *Xinhua*, Hill labeled "absurd" the criticism that Beijing had ignored class struggle in the third world in rallying an anti-Soviet united front, and claimed that all third world countries—even those with "fascist" governments—share a fundamental "trend of anti-imperialism." Ridiculing those who would refuse to unite such forces and those who would attack the wisdom of using one imperialism against another, Hill asked rhetorically, "If everyone is the enemy and there are no allies, no main enemy, is this not akin objectively to Trotsky's position?"

The other *Xinhua* report[29] likened arguments against differentiation between the two superpowers and between progressive and reactionary forces in the developed countries of the second world to arguments by the "renegade" Kautsky that the imperialist world is a "monolithic bloc" and to Trotsky's "abuse" of Lenin over the 1918 Treaty of Brest-Litovsk. Refusal to distinguish "major" and "minor" enemies, the article concluded, would only "give help to the enemy in weakening the revolutionary forces and lead the revolution to failure."

NOTES

1. The text of Deng's report appeared in *DR China*, 11 April 1974.

2. For background on the domestic developments in this period, see U.S. Congress, Joint Economic Committee, *China Under the Four Modernizations* (Washington, D.C.: U.S. Government Printing Office, 1982); U.S. Central Intelligence Agency, *China: The Continuing Search for a Modernization Strategy*, ER80–10248 (Washington, D.C.: 1980).

3. See Hua Guofeng's report dealing with the plan in *DR China*, 7 March 1978.

4. An authoritative overview of the economic policies of this period is in Robert Dernberger, "The Chinese Search for the Path of Self-Sustained Growth in the 1980s," in U.S. Congress, Joint Economic Committee, *China Under the Four Modernizations*, pp. 19–76.

5. The assessment here of political dynamics in China benefited greatly from insights provided by H. Lyman Miller, Carol Hamrin, and Kenneth Lieberthal. See especially H. Lyman Miller, "China's Administrative Revolution," *Current History*, September 1983; Carol Hamrin, "Competing 'Policy Packages' and Chinese Foreign Policy," *Asian Survey*, May 1984; Kenneth Lieberthal, "Domestic Politics and Foreign Policy," in Harry Harding, ed., *China's Foreign Relations in the 1980s* (New Haven: Yale University Press, 1984).

6. For background, see Thomas Robinson, "China's Military Modernization in the 1980s," in U.S. Congress, Joint Economic Committee, *China Under the Four Modernizations*, pp. 578–96.

7. See the review of the Brezhnev messages and other Soviet actions at this time in Robert Sutter, *Chinese Foreign Policy After the Cultural Revolution* (Boulder, Colo.: Westview Press, 1978).

8. Ibid.

9. See Li Xiannian's rebuff of the USSR in *DR China*, 16 November 1976.

10. The accord is reported in *DR China*, 7 October 1977.

11. Sino-Soviet trade figures are based on Central Intelligence Agency, *China's International Trade* (periodically updated).

12. *DR China*, 7 and 8 November 1977.

13. Hua's report appeared in *DR China*, 7 March 1978. The Soviet message was reviewed in *FBIS Trends*, 22 March 1978, pp. 10–11.

14. See *FBIS Trends*, , 5 April 1978, pp. 4–6.

15. Ilichev's comings and goings were reported by Soviet media and reprinted in *DR USSR*, April–June, 1978.

16. Hua's report appeared in *DR China*, 22 August 1977. This assessment of his remarks is based on analysis in *FBIS Trends*, 24 August 1977.

17. In the first Beijing-originated, albeit still indirect, criticism of recent Albanian public attacks against the three-world thesis, Hua also cited Lenin's statements that the proletariat must use to its own advantage all allies—no matter how "temporary, vacillating, unstable, unreliable or conditional"—and that "those who fail to understand this fail to understand even a particle of Marxism."

18. Li's statement seemed more notable coming as it did in the wake of Secretary of State Cyrus Vance's 29 June New York address, in which he said that during his August visit to China he wanted to explore ways to normalize relations. See *New York Times*, 30 June 1977.

19. For background, see U.S. Library of Congress, Congressional Research Service, *Foreign Perceptions of SALT*, report no. 79–115F (Washington, D.C.: 1979); pp. 60–64.

20. The article appeared in *DR China*, 29 November 1977. It is analyzed in detail in *FBIS Trends*, 30 November 1977, pp. 8–10.

21. *Guangming Daily*, 19 January 1978. Reviewed in U.S. Library of Congress, Congressional Research Service, *Foreign Perceptions of SALT*, p. 61.

22. The commentary appeared in *DR China*, 17 January 1978.

23. See in particular Harry Harding, "China and the Third World," in Richard Solomon, ed., *The China Factor* (Englewood Cliffs, N.J.: Prentice-Hall, 1981), p. 274.

24. See Chinese media coverage in *DR China*, 18 and 22 April 1977.

25. Reprinted in *DR China*, 18 October 1977.

26. See *DR China*, 30 August-9 September, for coverage of Tito's visit.

27. A detailed review of the polemic is in *FBIS Trends*, August 1977, pp. 19–20.

28. *Xinhua*, 9 July 1977.

29. *Xinhua*, 11 July 1977.

5

CHINESE FOREIGN POLICY UNDER DENG XIAOPING—BUILDING A STRONGER ANTI-SOVIET FRONT, 1978-79

Beijing proved unable to resume more active tactics to secure its interests abroad until Deng Xiaoping began to consolidate his power, in the year following his return to leading positions in 1977, and to endeavor to restore more unified direction to Chinese policy by 1978. Most immediately, Deng's political leadership was clearly instrumental in crafting the more activist approach to foreign affairs that, by the end of 1978, had seen several major successes, notably the signing of the Sino-Japanese peace treaty and the establishment of Sino-American diplomatic relations, as well as a major setback, the Vietnamese invasion of Chinese-backed Kampuchea.

It is widely held that Deng's return to power ushered in a new era in Chinese domestic policy that put unprecedented emphasis on the need for pragmatic efforts at economic modernization and sweeping political reform. But there was no comparable sea change in China's basic strategy in foreign affairs. Because of its continued relatively weak influence in Asian affairs, and the constantly growing Soviet pressure along its periphery, Beijing had little alternative but to continue to focus its foreign efforts fundamentally on effectively managing the Soviet pressure in order to stabilize a reasonably favorable balance of influence on its borders. If anything, the more pragmatic, development-oriented domestic policies under Deng Xiaoping's leadership reinforced China's awareness that its interests required the use of effective diplomacy—and closer ties with the West in particular—to secure its environment. Of course, interest in economic modernization added a growing imperative to China's strategic need for closer ties with the West. Thus, the various shifts in foreign approach carried out during the period of Deng Xiaoping's leadership since 1978 represented largely tactical adjustments to altered domestic and international conditions, within a broader strategic framework still basically defined by Chinese vulnerability vis-á-vis the USSR.

Deng Xiaoping did not establish himself as a leading influence in Chinese foreign policy until two years after the death of Mao and the fall of the Gang of Four. Although he was a prime victim of the Gang's political attacks, Deng had to wait one year after their arrest before he was restored to the leadership ranks during the 11th CCP Congress in August 1977. That conclave reflected more the influence of Hua Guofeng and other Maoist loyalists, who called for a continuation of many previous policies and programs, avoided or soft-pedaled political and economic reforms, and advocated the maintenance of the status quo among competing leadership groups. In the ensuing months, Deng gradually gained power but was still relegated to second-echelon duties in foreign affairs, as was shown in the relatively low level of protocol and media treatment that accompanied his visit to Burma and Nepal in early 1978.[1]

But as the year wore on, Chinese political and economic reformers led by Deng grew in strength, and took repeated initiatives in Chinese domestic affairs and in foreign policy. They successfully pushed a series of important programs in both areas that often were mutually reinforcing and were generally supportive of a more pragmatic and pro-Western orientation in Chinese foreign policy. By year's end, Deng was established as the preeminent Chinese political leader and by far its most important strategic thinker.

The overall thrust of domestic policies followed by reform advocates under Deng centered on economic development and modernization. They followed an unprecedentedly pragmatic, often trial-and-error approach to raise the level of production and productivity, and to improve the material standard of living of the Chinese people. Unlike Mao, who could base his leadership claim on the success of the Chinese Communist revolution and the perceived appropriateness of his ideology to Chinese conditions for much of the 20th century, Deng and his lieutenants had no such historical or ideological legacy. For them, economic modernization became the linchpin of their success or failure as leaders.

Several major policies flowed from this task:

- A thorough leadership purge to ensure that competent and responsive officials were in place to carry out development efforts effectively

- Streamlining and modernizing of Chinese armed forces. At first this involved curbing waste and excessive spending, using the savings for economic modernization, and relying on economic modernization to lay the groundwork for substantial modernization of China's obsolete military equipment later on. Meanwhile, the military was encouraged to modernize its organization and training in anticipation of getting better equipment in the future.

- Removal of ideological strictures on economic and political change. This involved a major revision of past belief in Mao's infallibility; allowed for the large-scale rehabilitation of leaders, managers, and experts who had been discredited in the mass campaigns of the Maoist period; gave new prominence to competence over political reliability in managing and promoting progress; allowed for the greater separation of the party from economic decision making, at least at lower levels; opened the way for greater use of material incentives to encourage worker productivity; and increased interchange with the West—seeking more advanced training and technology, greater amounts of credit, foreign aid, and investments, and improved access to markets.

The changes also clearly showed that China's foreign policy would have to be geared to help the all-important modernization effort. Nevertheless, strategic factors continued to play the predominant role in foreign policy, just as they had throughout the 1970s. They did so in large measure because Deng and the reformers recognized that a successful modernization effort required a relatively stable strategic environment, especially around China's periphery. Unfortunately for Chinese interests, this environment was not controlled by China. Beijing was able to exert some influence there, but its surroundings remained controlled more by others, especially the superpowers and their associates. As a result, Deng and his colleagues saw—just as Zhou Enlai and his moderate aides had seen earlier in the 1970s—that the chief foreign policy requirement for Chinese leaders was to review repeatedly the often fluid international environment for changes that would affect Chinese basic security and development goals. They recognized that China, in response, would often have to adjust its policy.

The Chinese leaders were well aware of their nation's relative weakness, especially when compared with the United States and the Soviet Union, which so heavily influenced developments in Asia. And now Beijing had embarked on a protracted effort focused on steady but gradual economic development—a course that precluded a major increase in military power for some time to come. Thus, the Chinese leaders saw that the nation's weakness would remain a fact for the foreseeable future. Accordingly, they employed their highly perceptive and sophisticated assessment of world politics and the international balance of influence in order to determine, adjust to, and influence trends that could help or hurt Chinese security or development concerns. They did not look only at the balance of military forces surrounding China; they assessed evidence of economic, political, and social strength in their existing and potential enemies and friends, and considered such factors as leadership ability and national will in making their net assessments and in deciding how China could best survive and prosper in this environment.[2]

Of course, Chinese leaders under Deng Xiaoping retained nationalistic and ideological objectives regarding irredentist claims (such as Taiwan and Hong Kong) and a desire to stand independently as a leading force among "progressive" developing nations of the third world and the international Communist movement. These goals continued to strike a responsive chord in China, even with the decline of Maoism by late 1978; and they represented issues of discussion and debate in the leadership,[3] although the significance of such disagreements was small in comparison with the differences over similar issues earlier in the 1970s.

The import of leadership differences over foreign policy was kept in check because there was no viable alternative for a relatively weak China other than to develop further the Zhouist differentiation between the superpowers. The Soviet Union continued to present the main danger of negative change in the environment around China. While Beijing came to see the USSR as less of an immediate military threat, it also saw Moscow as determined to use its growing military power and other sources of influence to encircle China and pressure it into accepting a balance of influence in Asia dominated by the USSR and contrary to Chinese interests in indendent development and progress.

China's strategy against the Soviet threat remained divided into bilateral and international approaches. Bilaterally, China used a mix of military preparations and tactical political moves to keep the Soviets from attacking, without compromising its basic security interests or political and economic goals. Internationally, China's strategy continued to focus on encouraging world resistance to Soviet expansion in order to prevent the consolidation of Soviet dominance elsewhere that would allow the USSR a freer hand to deal with China.

As the most important international counterweight to Soviet power, the United States remained prominent in Chinese calculations. Since the United States was no longer seen as a threat to its security, the PRC was prepared to develop the process of Sino-American reconciliation. The process was reinforced by China's enhanced interest in pursuing economic modernization, which increased the importance of technical and financial help from the West and access to Western markets.

Of course, closer ties with the United States continued to be complicated by Chinese nationalistic and ideological concerns over such issues as Taiwan and third world policies, as well as by fundamental differences between the two nations' systems. But Chinese leaders were realistic enough to differentiate between substantive threats to their security and development, posed by the USSR, and threats to their ideological sense of national sovereignty, posed, for example, by U.S. support for Taiwan.

Chinese leaders under Deng Xiaoping thus continued past practice in working hard to ensure that China's strategic environment, threatened mainly by Soviet expansion, remained stable, so that the PRC could focus on internal development and economic modernization. China saw the USSR as having a strategy of expansion that used military power cautiously but relentlessly in order to achieve political influence and dominance. While it continued to hold that the focus of Soviet attention was in Europe, Beijing maintained that NATO's strength required Moscow to work in other areas, including East Asia, in order to outflank the Western defenses. While China thus was seen as relatively low on Moscow's list of immediate military priorities, its leaders clearly perceived dire consequences for the PRC should the USSR succeed in consolidating its position elsewhere and then focus its strength on intimidating China.

China's strategy of deterrence and defense, therefore, continued to aim basically at exacerbating Soviet defense problems by enhancing worldwide opposition to Soviet expansion in general, and by raising the possibility of the Soviet Union confronting a multifront conflict if it attempted to attack or intimidate China in particular. This gave cooperation with the United States special importance in Chinese eyes as a means of strengthening deterrence of the Soviet Union and aggravating its strategic vulnerabilities.[4]

BUILDING A STRONGER ANTI-SOVIET FRONT, 1978-79

Deng began to reestablish his leadership in the Beijing hierarchy by pushing domestic political reforms that fundamentally challenged the prevailing balance of influence in the official structure. The first major initiative by the reformers led by Deng came in early 1978 and focused on the need for change in domestic political priorities.[5] Media comment on a campaign to rectify and modernize the army showed that Chinese leaders disagreed over the extent to which the party and state apparatus should be cleansed of sympathizers of the Gang of Four. The intense army rectification campaign, fueled by a series of Liberation Army Daily commentaries, was designed to lead to a more thorough purge of Gang of Four followers throughout the institutional structure. Opposition to such a course of action was apparent, however, in the erratic treatment of the Liberation Army Daily comment in People's Daily, and the failure of the official party newspaper to endorse the army campaign.

The army campaign attacked three kinds of cadres that, it said, continued to pose serious danger to China's future development: persons who "follow the wind" by shaping their political convictions and principles to prevailing circumstances; persons who "slip away" from responsibility for political error; and persons who "create earthquakes" politically and hope to profit from the disorder.

The campaign marked a sharp turnaround from the previous Chinese line, seen at the 11th CCP Congress in mid-1977, which maintained that investigations and purges of the leadership since the arrest of the Gang of Four had been largely completed.[6]

CCP Chairman Hua Guofeng reaffirmed his opposition to further leadership changes in an address at the Fifth National People's Congress in February 1978. He reiterated the line that the rectification of official ranks since the arrest of the Gang of Four had "in the main been completed."[7] But other comments at the congress were insistent that more sweeping political changes were needed to smooth the way for effective modernization. Thus, the 6 March joint editorial marking the close of the congress said that "We can...take big strides on the road of the new Long March [toward modernization] only when we strip away the gang's 'leftist' cloak, uncover their ultrarightist essence and clarify right and wrong with regard to theory and line."[8]

Renewed signs of debate over leadership issues were seen at the March 1978 national science conference. Deng Xiaoping advocated that China's scientific elite be freed from past political controls to pursue their professional work, while Hua Guofeng reaffirmed the continued importance of politics and Maoist egalitarian ideology, even in the scientific world.[9] At an army political conference in May, Hua and CCP Vice-Chairman Ye Jianying advocated such mild political methods as ideological training based on Mao Zedong's military writings in order to rectify the army's work style, whereas Deng Xiaoping was less inclined to treat Mao's legacy with reverence and implied that an expanded purge of army officers was called for.[10]

The CCP work conference and the Third Plenum of the its 11th Central Committee were held in late 1978 and represented a major benchmark in the strengthening of the power of Deng Xiaoping and other officials interested in broad rectification and reform of the Chinese leadership. New appointments to the Central Committee and its Politburo widened support for reformist policies in those bodies. The selection of Hu Yaobang—a close associate of Deng—as CCP secretary general and propaganda chief augmented Deng's ability to implement these policies and enhanced the likelihood of their long-term survival.[11]

The Third Plenum also endorsed efforts to transform the basic style and character of Chinese politics along lines favored by reformers. It dismantled the personality cult surrounding Mao and promoted intraparty democracy; it reduced the authority of Mao's legacy by suggesting the late chairman's fallibility and limitations; and it reasserted the ultimate authority of the party organization. As a result, the plenum fostered an atmosphere of leadership collectivity and cast off ideological bonds that had hobbled Chinese efforts to modernize. The moves also served to dilute the authority of Hua Guofeng, whose status as Mao's heir and arbiter of the Maoist ideological legacy was substantially diminished.

In economic policy, the plenum launched a prolonged adjustment program; emphasized the link between economic productivity and consumer welfare; and promoted increased wages and other material incentives for greater production, as well as new incentives for effective managers and more efficient industrial organizations—all with an eye to increasing production. Resource allocation priorities were shifted to light industry in order to enhance productivity and consumer welfare.[12]

Although reformers won important gains at the Third Plenum, the long deliberations required an accommodation with other leaders holding differing views, particularly those who had profited from the Cultural Revolution and its subsequent struggles. Thus, some high-ranking leaders who had opposed political change lost their bases of power but retained their seats on the Politburo for the time being. More important, the plenum decided to shelve for a time such potentially divisive issues as an assessment of the Cultural Revolution, in the interest of getting on with the modernization drive.

FOREIGN POLICY CONCERNS

Coincident with his growing political control over domestic policies in 1978, Deng was able to play a greater role in the conduct of foreign policy. His initial efforts in foreign affairs centered on establishing a more assertive, less reactive approach to foreign affairs, designed chiefly to check the expansion of Soviet power and influence, especially in key third world areas. Altered economic and political priorities at home added to Chinese reluctance to engage in a foreign policy that would have led to direct military confrontation with the USSR or to intense competition with Moscow in granting economic and military aid in order to garner influence in the third world. Instead, Beijing attempted to use greater political maneuver and stronger propaganda efforts to encourage firmer international opposition to the spread of Soviet power and influence.

China's approach at this time had several important features:

- Beijing was relatively undiscriminating—even downright expedient—in seeking international support against the USSR. Chinese officials put aside past ideological concerns and identified closely even with strongly conservative regimes, so long as they were appropriately anti-Soviet. A salient example was China's strong association with the Shah of Iran until almost the last days of the regime at the turn of 1978.[13]

- Chinese officials repeatedly highlighted "anti-hegemonism" (opposition to Soviet expansion) as the centerpiece of Beijing's developing relations with the West, especially the United States and Japan. This was most notable in Chinese treatment of the conclusion of the Sino-Japanese peace treaty in August 1978,[14] and in the Sino-American communiqué announcing the normalization of diplomatic relations in December 1978.[15]

- Beijing voiced greater support than in the past for Western and pro-Western international groupings and other efforts that it saw as useful in countering the USSR. Chinese leaders gave stronger endorsements of the Association of Southeast Asian Nations (ASEAN), supported Japanese defense efforts against the USSR, and expressed understanding of the U.S.-Japanese security treaty.[16]

- Beijing linked its stepped-up efforts to achieve Sino-American normalization with a softer approach to Taiwan designed to encourage peaceful reunification of the island with the mainland.

- Chinese activism in the third world had a strongly anti-Soviet thrust. On the one hand, Beijing sharply condemned Cuba and Vietnam as proxies of Soviet expansion; on the other, China aligned itself with anti-Soviet policies of such disparate anti-Soviet governments as Zaire, Chile, Egypt, and Somalia. Beijing also encouraged third world nations to cooperate more with the West in order to preclude the opening of opportunities for Soviet expansion.[17]

- China kept stringent limits on its foreign aid outlays,[18] and cut off Vietnam and Albania.

- China's interest in developing closer economic relations with the United States and other capitalist countries was demonstrated in its greatly increased willingness to develop more trade, investment, and financial ties with developed countries that would assist its modernization.

During 1978, Beijing remained seriously concerned about what it continued to see as a trend toward appeasing the USSR in U.S. strategy. Foreign Minister Huang Hua noted the dangers of Soviet "expansion and aggression" when he welcomed U.S. National Security Adviser Brzezinski to Beijing on 20 May 1978. Huang warned that the "shadow of social imperialism" was visible "in every part of the world," and charged that Moscow was exploiting the cover of "détente" in its drive for "world hegemony." He pointedly cautioned against "illusions of peace" and tactics of "appeasement" in dealing with Soviet power—a warning other Chinese comment had directed specifically at the Carter administration when criticizing U.S. conduct of relations with Moscow.[19]

Although the Chinese subsequently were encouraged by the Carter administration's determination to push ahead with secret discussions on normalizing Sino-American relations, they remained wary of U.S. intentions toward the USSR. Beijing tailored its comment in order to encourage U.S. policy to move in strongly anti-Soviet directions. For example, Xinhua on 2 October 1978 critically assessed Secretary Vance's talks with Soviet Foreign Minister Gromyko by portraying the administration as "overly eager" for a new SALT agreement. On 14 October Xinhua followed up with an account critical of the administration's "accommodating attitude" toward Moscow. But when Secretary Vance showed he was unwilling to make further concessions during talks at Moscow in late October, Beijing hailed this show of U.S. resolve.[20]

The announcement of the establishment of U.S.-PRC diplomatic relations prompted a massive Chinese media campaign that focused on the joint communiqúe's anti-hegemony clause as of vital significance in the international struggle against the expansion of the Soviet Union and its proxies. The People's Daily editorial of 17 December 1978 said that Beijing and Washington's "reaffirmation of the principle of antihegemony helps opposition to major hegemonism as well as minor hegemonism, to global hegemonism as well as regional hegemonism"—allusions to the USSR and Vietnam in particular.[21]

The Sino-American accord was designed to put an end to the Taiwan issue as an impediment to normal diplomatic relations. The Taiwan question had remained the major stumbling block between Washington and Beijing following President Nixon's visit to the PRC in February 1972. At that time, Nixon and Chinese leaders signed the Shanghai communiqué, which deferred problems of diplomatic relations and Taiwan for the sake of working together on the basis of common strategic interests in Asian and world affairs. In particular, the two sides had pledged to cooperate to ensure that the East Asian region would not become subject to international "hegemony"— a code word used by China to denote Soviet expansion.

Beijing leaders had long demanded that the United States meet three conditions for the normalization of Sino-American diplomatic relations: the United States must withdraw all military forces from Taiwan, break diplomatic relations with the government on Taiwan, and terminate the U.S.-Taiwan defense treaty. At the same time, the leaders had urged the United States to follow the example of Japan's normalization of relations with the PRC in September 1972. The "Japanese formula" required the

United States to end diplomatic relations with the Taipei government, recognize Beijing as the sole legal government of China, and acknowledge Beijing's claim that Taiwan is part of China. This approach foretold the ending of the U.S.-Taiwan defense treaty, but U.S. economic relations with Taiwan would continue unhindered and political relations were to be maintained through private offices staffed by career foreign service officers who were officially "retired," "separated," or "on leave."

President Carter's 15 December 1978 speech announcing the establishment of U.S.-PRC relations made it clear that the United States would meet Beijing's three conditions and that it would follow the Japanese formula with few modifications. The United States did not immediately terminate the U.S.-Taiwan defense treaty, but notified Taiwan that it was to be terminated one year from 1 January 1979, in accord with the provisions of the treaty. Administration spokesmen told the press after the president's announcement that the United States would continue during 1979 to deliver military equipment already contracted for by Taiwan, and that even after formal military ties ended, the United States would make available to Taiwan "selected defense weaponry" on a "restricted basis."

China's interest in closer economic and technical ties with the United States was signaled even before the announcement of diplomatic normalization. Vice-Premier Li Xiannian gave the first authoritative endorsement of such ties when he told U.S. investors on 11 November that "China could use advanced technology and funds from developed countries like the United States."[22] Deng Xiaoping's visit to Japan in October had underlined the strategic and economic imperatives in China's outreach to the West. Deng went to Tokyo to attend ratification ceremonies of the recently concluded Sino-Japanese peace treaty. The conclusion had long been delayed by Chinese insistence on inclusion of an anti-hegemony clause, and Deng repeatedly called attention to the importance of the clause in remarks at a 25 October press conference at Tokyo, in which he referred to anti-hegemonism as the "nucleus" of the treaty.[23] Deng also gave constant attention to China's need for economic, technological, and scientific help, and his tour's heavy emphasis on visits to industrial plants reflected the hope that improved relations would yield a high economic return.[24]

Deng soft-pedaled past disputes with Japan over the Senkaku Islands, claimed by both China and Japan. He said that the issue had been put aside for a time because "our generation is not wise enough to find common language on this question."[25] In the National People's Congress (NPC) deliberations concerning the results of Deng's trip, there was a notably explicit and authoritative statement of the policy on key Japanese defense issues that heretofore had been treated only indirectly or implicitly. In particular, on 4 November, *Xinhua* reported that the NPC standing committee "now found it possible to understand" the need for the Japan-U.S. security pact and "appreciates" Japan's need for defense forces.[26]

Beijing's more assertive approach to the USSR and its allies in the third world included a forceful campaign at midyear against Soviet-backed Cuban activities in Africa. China sent Foreign Minister Huang Hua to Zaire to support the Mobutu government, under attack from Soviet- and Cuban-supported insurgents in Angola,[27] and it strongly pressed its case for Cuban expulsion from the Nonaligned Movement.[28] Beijing reaffirmed its indictment of Cuba as a Soviet proxy at the time of the July 1978 Nonaligned Movement ministerial conference,[29] while Politburo Member Geng Biao stressed the anti-Cuban theme during his tour of three Caribbean nations.[30] Vice-Premier Li Xiannian used his tour of Tanzania, Mozambique, Zambia, and Zaire at the turn of the year to remind his hosts of the constant danger of outside interference, particularly by the Soviets.[31] Li's visit capped a series of trips by Chinese officials to some 20 African countries in late 1978, visits that reflected greater Chinese activism in checking Soviet-backed expansion in the third world.

CONFRONTATION WITH VIETNAM[32]

Perhaps the most striking example of China's more assertive anti-Soviet policy at this time concerned Soviet-backed Vietnam. Following the collapse of the U.S.-supported governments in South Vietnam and Cambodia in 1975, China was concerned by the growing closeness of Soviet-Vietnamese relations and by its inability to influence Hanoi to follow policies more consistent with Chinese interests. Vietnam's relations with the USSR and its persistent conflict with Chinese interests in Cambodia (now called Kampuchea) and over the Sino-Vietnamese border, continued to present the most serious problem in China's Asian strategy. But Beijing maintained its past practice of sustaining correct party and state ties with the Vietnamese leaders and restricting signs of disagreement largely to oblique signs in the Chinese media. Even after the Vietnamese engaged in a reportedly large-scale military action against Kampuchea in late 1977, Chinese leaders carefully avoided criticizing their actions. The Chinese followed a low-key public posture designed to keep channels of communication open and to encourage the Vietnamese to dissociate themselves from the USSR while the Chinese tried to contain the possible spread of pro-Soviet influence from Vietnam to other parts of Southeast Asia.

China's restrained approach toward Vietnam was also seen in its treatment of high-level Vietnamese visitors during the latter half of 1977. Chinese leaders gave a "cordial and friendly" welcome to Socialist Republic of Vietnam (SRV) Defense Minister Giap on his arrival in early June,[33] offered standard celebrations marking Vietnam's National Day in September,[34] and provided "cordial and friendly" greetings for Le Duan on his visit to China during November.[35] The latter visit demonstrated a continuation of strains between China and Vietnam, but it produced no evidence of a deterioration in relations.

The cordial welcome for the Vietnamese was particularly remarkable inasmuch as the visit came at a time when the same Vietnamese leaders were actively solidifying their nation's relations with the USSR and were consolidating its strategic power at home and in Laos, in apparent preparation for an attack on Kampuchea. (Kampuchea later reported a major Vietnamese assault against it during September 1977.) For example, both Giap and Le Duan traveled to China after extensive visits and negotiations in the Soviet Union. Giap followed his trip to China by touring several Vietnamese provinces bordering Kampuchea, presumably in preparation for the assault in September. Le Duan had consolidated Vietnamese power in Laos during his visit there in July 1977.[36]

In the wake of the Vietnamese attack on Kampuchea during September (which was not made public until Kampuchea broke relations with Vietnam in early 1978), Beijing gave an extremely warm welcome to the Kampuchean Communist Party leader Pol Pot in October 1977, and the Chinese media at that time announced the development of the previously clandestine Kampuchean Communist Party.[37] Beijing sent high-level delegates to Kampuchea in December 1977 and January 1978, led respectively by a vice premier and by Zhou Enlai's widow, Deng Yingchao.

Although these steps clearly underlined strong Chinese support for Kampuchea and reportedly coincided with increased military aid to the country, the Chinese officials carefully eschewed criticism of Vietnam. For example, Deng Yingchao's 19 January 1978 speech in Phnom Penh avoided specifically mentioning the Kampuchean-Vietnamese border problem, instead merely expressing the conviction that the Kampucheans "will win more brilliant victories in the sacred cause of defending the motherland." And while *Xinhua* carried most of the text of Deng's speech, it omitted the portion of the speech of her Kampuchean host that referred to the border conflict with Vietnam.[38] Two weeks earlier, Beijing had appeared to show continued goodwill toward Vietnam when it announced, only a few days after Kampuchea's public break with Vietnam, that the agreement with Vietnam on mutual supply of goods and payments for 1978 had just been signed in Beijing. The

Chinese could have delayed the agreement if they had wished to demonstrate displeasure with Hanoi. The Vietnamese trade delegation had been in Beijing only 18 days; the previous year's negotiations on the annual trade agreement had kept the Vietnamese in Beijing for almost six weeks.[39]

Sino-Vietnamese relations hit a major new snag as a result of apparently unrelated policy changes in both nations that affected the ethnic Chinese minority in Vietnam. In January 1978, Beijing launched its first major campaign in over ten years to win the allegiance and support of overseas Chinese throughout the world. The campaign seemed designed primarily to improve China's access to their considerable technical and financial resources—especially those in Southeast Asia and the West—as part of the broader effort to improve foreign contacts in order to facilitate the modernization of its economy. The campaign did not appear to be directed specifically at Vietnam. Even though the Chinese continued to repeat standard disavowals of any interest in using overseas Chinese as a source of political influence in foreign countries, the new effort reportedly alarmed a number of Southeast Asian nations, including Vietnam, that China might become more assertive in defending the interests of the large ethnic Chinese populations in the area.[40]

Vietnam, meanwhile, faced bleak economic prospects in early 1978, with high unemployment in urban areas and vacant land in the countryside. A major element in the planned solution was a new emphasis on the ongoing campaign to move many urban dwellers to primitive "new economic zones" in the countryside and to confiscate much of their wealth in the process. Since a large portion of the urban population was Chinese, the campaign fell heavily on the Chinese minority in Vietnam. At the same time, Hanoi moved to exert greater political and economic control in urban areas of the south, and it viewed the ethnic Chinese merchants there with particular distrust. In March 1978, the government took control of trade in the south. The effects of these new policies on the ethnic Chinese may have been made worse by traditional Vietnamese prejudices against them—prejudices exacerbated by the generally widening Sino-Vietnamese rift. In any event, their effect was to promote a large exodus of ethnic Chinese from the country.[41]

The Break in Relations

The turning point in Sino-Vietnamese relations came in the spring of 1978. China and Vietnam began to exchange public charges regarding mistreatment of ethnic Chinese in Vietnam—a propaganda volley that soon escalated to accusations involving Sino-Vietnamese party, economic, territorial, and security issues. China took the offensive against

Vietnam, repeatedly upping the ante, with the presumed objective of forcing Hanoi to back away from its policies opposed to Chinese interests. The Vietnamese rebuffed the Chinese pressure tactics, and they tried to counter the newly apparent Chinese threat in a variety of ways involving the USSR to a considerable degree.

China's precise motives for changing its approach toward Vietnam are not completely clear. Its overall objective in the region remained the development of a favorable balance of influence that would reduce or preclude the expansion of Soviet power and the power of countries seen by China as Soviet surrogates. In this regard, it appeared to outsiders that the overall situation in Asia was generally good for China in mid-1978, with only Vietnam, Laos, and Afghanistan representing significant trouble spots. Nonetheless, the Chinese apparently judged that their past policy of restraint toward Vietnam did not represent a satisfactory approach in the current situation.

The new, more forceful approach to Vietnam was closely associated with Deng Xiaoping, whose influence in Chinese leadership councils grew tremendously during 1978. Deng was especially outspoken in his criticism of Vietnam and of Vietnamese-Soviet relations during conversations with Western visitors to China in mid-1978.[42] He charged, among other things, that Vietnam was already a de facto ally of the Soviet Union and had allowed the Soviet Union to establish military bases on its territory. (Deng was able to offer no proof of this charge, and Western intelligence sources at the time reportedly were unable to detect any solid indication that Soviet forces in fact had bases in Vietnam.)

The new Chinese attitude toward Vietnam coincided with a generally more assertive foreign policy against suspected Soviet "expansion" abroad—a policy also strongly pushed by Deng. For instance, beginning in mid-1978, the Chinese sent several high-level envoys to areas of Africa experiencing Soviet-backed pressure;[43] began taking a markedly more active role against Soviet programs in international disarmament forums;[44] demonstrated unprecedented interest in Eastern Europe by sending CCP Chairman Hua Guofeng to Romania and Yugoslavia; and signed a peace treaty with Japan and a normalization agreement with the United States—both on the basis of the principle of "anti-hegemony."

Beijing's new pressure tactics against Vietnam began with a 24 May 1978 *Xinhua* interview with a spokesman for the Overseas Chinese Affairs Office of the PRC State Council; he accused the Vietnamese of instituting a massive program to persecute and deport Chinese residents in Vietnam. The initial protest was buttressed with a carefully orchestrated propaganda campaign, using national and provincial radio, television, press, and newsreels to dramatize that Vietnam was brutally mistreating overseas Chinese. On 26 May, Beijing unilaterally escalated the conflict by announcing that the Chinese government had decided to send ships to Vietnam to "bring home the persecuted Chinese residents."[45]

Reflecting the implications of these moves for broader Sino-Vietnamese relations, the 24 May interview failed to note that Vietnam was a socialist country. In repeating an otherwise standard Chinese litany, the spokesman left out the word "socialist" in noting that "China and Vietnam are neighboring [socialist] countries linked by common mountains and rivers." At the same time, articles in the Hong Kong Communist press signaled Beijing's fundamental concern with Vietnam's close relationship with the USSR, charging that Vietnam, as a tool of Moscow, was seeking to dominate Indochina and Southeast Asia. Several Hong Kong articles in the week after the 24 May statement portrayed Hanoi as carrying out Moscow's designs, referring to Vietnam as a "second Cuba." They also warned that Hanoi might turn over naval facilities in Vietnam to the Soviet Union.

Although Vietnam announced grudging acceptance of Beijing's plan to send ships to evacuate the resident Chinese and called for negotiations on the problem, the polemics between China and Vietnam escalated during the second week in June. Beijing charged that Vietnam was adopting anti-Chinese actions at the behest of the Soviet Union, and Hanoi responded by identifying Beijing as Kampuchea's patron. Beijing began this round of polemics with a PRC Foreign Ministry statement on 9 June that repeated criticism of the Vietnamese policies toward overseas Chinese, rejected Hanoi's request for negotiations, announced that the burden of caring for refugees from Vietnam necessitated a cut in PRC aid to Vietnam, and implied that Hanoi was acting in response to a foreign backer. On 10 June 1978, the *People's Daily* "Commentator" spelled out the charge that the Soviet Union was "the behind-the-scenes provocateur and supporter of Vietnamese authorities in ostracizing Chinese residents and attacking China." The Foreign Ministry statement urged a change in Hanoi's policies without threatening any consequences but, by turning down the Vietnamese request for negotiations, failing to mention Hanoi's offer to accommodate the Chinese ships, and raising the Soviet connection, Beijing appeared to have deliberately mapped out a collision course with Hanoi.[46]

Added Chinese pressure against Vietnam appeared in a sharply worded *People's Daily* "Commentator" article of 17 June, along with the announced closing of Vietnamese consulates in China the day before. Vietnam responded by refusing to allow overseas Chinese to leave in Chinese ships under terms set by Beijing; and on 28 June, five weeks after the start of the Chinese pressure, Hanoi announced that it had asked to join the Soviet bloc's economic organization, the Council for Mutual Economic Assistance.[47]

Beijing subsequently took several steps against Vietnam. On 3 July, the Chinese declared an end to all economic and technical assistance to Vietnam; on 11 July, Beijing closed its borders to the thousands of overseas Chinese trying to flee across the land frontier with China; and on 12 July, Beijing for the first time condemned Hanoi's policies toward Kampuchea. Vietnam rebuffed the Chinese pressure and escalated charges against China for allegedly threatening Vietnam along their frontier and through Chinese support for Kampuchean attacks against Vietnam.

It was clear by midsummer that Beijing's moves had yet to prompt any softening of Vietnamese opposition to Chinese interests in Southeast Asia. The Chinese at this time began to show sensitivity over, and to alter, some of their recent actions. For example, a 3 July *People's Daily* editorial exhibited considerable concern that the dispute over Chinese residents in Vietnam might have a negative impact on PRC relations with other Southeast Asian countries that have large overseas Chinese populations. The editorial strongly condemned alleged Soviet attempts to create anxiety in Southeast Asian countries about Chinese policies toward overseas Chinese. The editorial stressed that the problem with Vietnam was unique, growing out of Vietnam's "persecution" of Chinese nationals, and that China was concerned only with protecting the "justifiable rights and interests" of its citizens abroad.[48]

At the same time, Beijing probably had mixed feelings over two steps that it had taken in the face of Vietnamese intransigence. The closing of the border with Vietnam on 11 July had put pressure on the Vietnamese for a change in policy toward overseas Chinese there, but it had also shown the Chinese leaders to be unfeeling in regard to the plight of the overseas Chinese in Vietnam—Beijing had first encouraged these people to return to China, then abruptly halted their return when they had left their homes in Vietnam but had not yet crossed the Chinese border. Moreover, Vietnam refused to allow the Chinese ships—sent in late spring—to land in Vietnam, forcing the Chinese to order the ships to return empty to China.

In mid-July, Beijing briefly tried a more conciliatory approach, in an apparent effort to break its deadlock with Hanoi, or at least to avoid being perceived as the intransigent party in the dispute. A 19 July PRC Foreign Ministery note offered to start talks with Vietnam at the vice-foreign minister level; an accompanying *Xinhua* commentary called the proposal "an important step in defense of traditional Sino-Vietnamese friendship," and predicted that both sides could reach a settlement and achieve "unity and friendship." This element of conciliation was not carried over into other Chinese commentary, however; and even though the talks began at Hanoi in August, they quickly bogged down in strong polemics.[49] The talks broke off in September, amid heated Sino-Vietnamese charges of mounting tension along the frontier and Chinese accusations that Hanoi was using its dispute with China to divert international attention from the Vietnamese military preparations against Kampuchea.

In the fall, the Vietnamese took a long step forward in relations with the USSR and successfully outmaneuvered China's power—at least for a time—by signing a friendship treaty with the Soviet Union during a visit to Moscow in early November by an SRV delegation led by Le Duan. The treaty implicitly reassured the Vietnamese against Chinese pressure and allowed Hanoi to focus attention on preparing for a military attack against Kampuchea. Beijing's initial response did little to offset Hanoi's advantage. The Chinese dispatched a delegation led by CCP Vice-Chairman Wang Dongxing to Phnom Penh, but Chinese leaders remained restrained in their expressions of support for the Kampuchean government and avoided reference to possible assistance to the Kampucheans. Deng Xiaoping tried but failed to elicit strong statements from Southeast Asian leaders against Vietnam during his tour of several nations there in November.

Leadership Differences Over Policy Toward Vietnam

Chinese leadership considerations of what steps should be taken in the face of the new Soviet-Vietnamese treaty and in anticipation of Hanoi's apparent intention to launch a major military assault on China's ally, Kampuchea, coincided with the most important Chinese leadership meetings since the death of Mao and the arrest of the Gang of Four in 1976. The leadership sessions during November and December 1978 culminated in the Third Plenum of the 11th Central Committee. According to a variety of sources and reports in the Hong Kong media, the meetings were marked by strong debate at the highest levels of the leadership over a wide variety of sensitive political and economic issues.[50]

Although there were no reports of Chinese leaders sharply disagreeing over foreign policy at this time, an analysis of Chinese media pronouncements strongly suggests that they were not in agreement over how to handle their relations with Soviet-backed Vietnam and the related issue of Chinese support for Kampuchea against Vietnam. Some leaders, notably Vice-Premier Li Xiannian, pointedly associated themselves with the argument that Vietnam, backed by the Soviet Union, represented a direct threat to China and that China should adopt strong measures to deal with the threat. Others, including—curiously—Deng Xiaoping, associated themselves, at least for a time, with an argument that stressed that the threat of aggression against China came from the "north," and implicitly played down the threat to China emanating from Vietnam in the south.

There also appeared to be differences in the leadership over how far China should go in backing Pol Pot's government in Kampuchea after it came under heavy attack from Vietnam in December 1978. Some leaders, notably Deng Xiaoping, appeared reluctant to go beyond expressions of general support for the Kampuchean "people" in their resistance against the Vietnamese, whereas others, notably Hua Guofeng, pointedly associated China with strong support for the Pol Pot administration.

Perhaps the most striking feature of these seemingly contradictory points of leadership emphasis concerned statements of Deng Xiaoping in December and early January. Deng, of course, had been in the forefront of Chinese officials promoting a tough line toward Vietnam in mid-1978. He had pointedly told visitors to China of the alleged threat posed by Vietnam, "the Cuba of Asia," and of the alleged Soviet design to use pro-Soviet developments in places like South Yemen, Afghanistan, and Vietnam for Moscow's design of global expansion and encirclement of China.[51] In late 1978, however, Deng's statements seemed to reflect less concern about the strategic threat to China posed by Vietnam, even though Vietnam was now formally aligned with the USSR and prepared to attack China's ally Kampuchea. And, at that time, he did not echo other Chinese leaders who were warning Vietnam of possible Chinese military countermeasures against it, and was more reserved than other Chinese leaders in his pledges of support for Kampuchea against Vietnam. Deng resumed a tougher line against Vietnam later in January, when he visited the United States. By that time, Beijing had decided to teach Vietnam a military "lesson" in the wake of Hanoi's military invasion of Kampuchea.

One can only speculate about the possible reasons for this temporary change in Deng's approach to Vietnam. The vice-premier almost certainly saw that China's earlier policy of pressure had not worked well and that it might be forced to resort to greater pressure, including the use of armed attack, in order to compel Hanoi to change its policy. Deng doubtless was aware that such an attack would divert resources that were needed for the development of the economy, and would thereby complicate the chances of success in the ambitious modernization program that was the centerpiece of his plan for China's future.

Deng's address to a New Year's Day meeting of the Chinese People's Political Consultative Conference was unusually emphatic in claiming that the threat to China came from the "north": "At present, the threat to peace comes from the north, the source of instability and war in the world lies in the north, and *should there be foreign aggression against our country, it would also come from the north.*"[52]

Deng's argument may have been so strong because it implicitly contradicted the authoritative communiqué issued on 23 December 1978, at the end of the Third Plenum. That communiqué had clearly implied that the threat of aggression to China could come from the south—or any other direction—and had given no special stress to the threat from the north: "The grave danger of war still exists. We must strengthen our national defense, and be prepared to repulse at any moment aggressors *from any direction.*"[53]

Deng's line that China should focus attention on defense of the north received apparent support from an article appearing in the *Guangming Daily* on 19 December 1978. That article offered, without explanation, a detailed defense of the policy of the 19th-century Chinese leader Zuo Zongdang, who had stressed the importance of directing China's defense against the northern threat at the expense of, and in opposition to, others in the Chinese leadership, who urged that China build a stronger defense in eastern and southern regions. The *Guangming Daily* article offered no explanation of why it was recalling this historical issue—the most important strategic debate in 19th-century China—except to claim that Zuo had been misinterpreted by Chinese historians in recent years. In view of the fact that historical allegory has long been used in modern Chinese leadership debates over foreign and domestic policy, it seems fair to conclude that the appearance of this unusual article likely reflected leadership disagreement over foreign policy strategy at this crucial time. The article suggested that the differences may have been strong, inasmuch as it used politically forceful language to defend Zuo against his 19th-century opponents, noting that "the difference [between Zuo and his opponents] was a struggle between patriotism and national betrayal."[54]

People's Daily also seemed to be reflecting differences within the Chinese leadership over the nature of the threat China faced in Asia. A 30 December 1978 *People's Daily* "Commentator" article devoted to Soviet strategy in Asia in general, and in Vietnam in particular, disagreed with unnamed individuals who, it said, had erroneously judged that Vietnam's alliance with the USSR and other recent Soviet moves were of primary concern to China. It disagreed with those "people" who judged that Moscow's primary objective in the region was to threaten and encircle China. The article argued that the danger to China was not so important, and it also implied that general Asian and world resistance would be sufficient to deal with the new Vietnamese-Soviet relationship:

Some people point out that this [Soviet activity in Asia] is intended to encircle China. Of course, the Kremlin has China in mind in pushing expansionism in Asia. But its more important objective is to expand its sphere of influence and rid the continent of the influence of the United States, its chief opponent, thereby threatening peace and security of Japan and other Asian nations in particular. *It is indeed short-sighted and dangerous to overlook this.* The Soviet Union's Asian strategy is an important part of its global counter-revolutionary strategy. It thinks that it has scored a major gain in having Vietnam as its stooge for the pursuit of hegemony in Asia. But, contrary to its wish, this actually serves to show the atrocious features of the Soviet and Vietnamese expansionists and arouse resistance and opposition among the countries and people in Asia. Asia belongs to the Asian people. All efforts in quest of hegemony, worldwide or regional, are destined to fail in the end.[55]

Despite the arguments in pronouncements of Deng Xiaoping, *Guangming Daily*, and *People's Daily*, some high-level Chinese leaders closely associated themselves with the view that Vietnam, backed by the USSR, was indeed a serious threat to China and that China should take more forceful action, including the use of military counterattack. Most notable in this regard was Vice-Premier Li Xiannian, who had more experience than any other top-level Chinese leader in dealing with Vietnam, and who had not been averse to voicing an opinion at odds with the foreign policy views of others in the leadership, notably Deng. He had not been particularly prominent in the more assertive Chinese policy toward Vietnam in 1978 but, beginning in December, he issued a series of unusually strong statements on the question. He implied that Vietnam was directly threatening China and that China might resort to strong measures. As early as 13 December 1978, for instance, Li warned the Vietnamese that "China's forbearance has its limit and the Vietnamese authorities are deluding themselves by thinking that we are weak and can be bullied."[56] On 28 December, Li pointed to the Vietnamese-Soviet alliance as a direct threat, first to China and then to Southeast Asia, and he strongly warned the Vietnamese to stop their "anti-China acts":

> The Soviet social-imperialists have not given up their ambition to subjugate China. And the Vietnamese authorities, backed by the Soviet global hegemonists, are working overtime at their regional hegemonism, opposing China, ostracizing and cruelly persecuting Chinese nationals residing in Vietnam. Not long ago, the Soviet Union and Vietnam concluded a so-called treaty of friendship and cooperation which is in substance a military alliance. *They aim their attack at China* and Southeast Asian countries and have launched a frenzied armed aggression and subversive activities against Kampuchea.
>
> The Vietnamese authorities must stop at once their criminal anti-Chinese and anti-China acts or else they will bear all the consequences.[57]

After the Vietnamese overran Kampuchea, Li was more outspoken than any other Chinese leader in warning against Vietnam's "repeated provocations" against China. He said on 8 January 1979: "We would like to warn Vietnam that the patience of the Chinese people has a limit and no one should turn a deaf ear to what they say. Our principle is this: We will not attack unless we are attacked; and if we are attacked we will certainly counter-attack."[58]

Meanwhile, Deng Xiaoping and other Chinese leaders seemed to disagree over how much support China should provide the Kampuchean administration of Pol Pot in the wake of Vietnam's invasion of late December and early January. He did not go beyond bland expressions of support for the Kampuchean "people" in their struggle to resist the Vietnamese, while other Chinese leaders, notably Hua Guofeng, were much more emphatic in associating themselves with strong support for the Pol Pot regime. For example, when Deng Xiaoping met in Beijing with Kampuchean Deputy Prime Minister Ieng Sary on 13 January, he merely expressed "firm support for the Kampuchean people" in their struggle to resist Vietnamese aggression.[59] On the same day, Hua Guofeng met with Ieng Sary and offered China's strongest statement in support of Kampuchea in several months: "The Kampuchean people's struggle is our struggle. We supported you in the past, we are supporting you now, and we will continue to support you in the future." Hua went on to associate himself closely with Pol Pot; *Xinhua* reported that "Chairman Hua paid high tribute and regards to Comrade Pol Pot and other party and state leaders of Kampuchea and to the Kampuchean armymen and civilians fighting on the frontline."[60]

In short, it appeared that, as the Chinese deliberated over what sort of action to take against Vietnam in the wake of its alliance with the Soviet Union and its attack on Kampuchea, Beijing's policy was at an impasse. For one thing, the assertive policy toward Vietnam, begun in May 1978, had met with at least temporary failure. Vietnam was now aligned with the USSR and was successfully invading China's ally Kampuchea. Other states in Southeast Asia remained suspicious of Chinese intentions. Some observers in the region and elsewhere saw China's failure as stemming from its pressure tactics, which they saw as speeding Vietnam's alignment with the USSR and prompting the Vietnamese to judge that they had little to lose in regard to relations with China if they went ahead and attacked Kampuchea. These observers also began to wonder whether Beijing would follow similar, seemingly misguided policies in other areas.[61]

Not only did China's policy toward Vietnam seem to have failed, but Chinese leaders appeared to be divided over what to do about it. Some comments at this juncture—including those of Deng Xiaoping—seemed to argue for caution, both in assessing the nature of the threat posed to China by Vietnam and in increasing support for Kampuchea. This represented a remarkable—and perhaps politically embarrassing—turnabout for Deng, inasmuch as he was closely associated with the tough policy toward Vietnam through much of 1978. Li Xiannian and Hua Guofeng seemed to have argued for a continuation and increase of the assertive policy toward Vietnam, stressing the threat China faced from the Vietnamese, the need for China to be ready to "counterattack," and stronger support for Kampuchea and Pol Pot.

Thus, as the Chinese decided to launch a military attack on Vietnam—the decision appears to have been made by 21 January 1979, when the media disclosed the transfer of a more experienced military commander to the Vietnam front[62]—they apparently did so with divided counsel and against the background of eight months of repeated setbacks with Vietnam. In view of Deng's comments advocating caution in late December and early January, in contrast with his tough stance earlier, it was fair to conclude that policy toward Vietnam represented the most serious international setback for the vice-premier since his rehabilitation in mid-1977.

U.S. Role

The Chinese policy toward Vietnam had particular implications for the emerging Sino-American relationship. The tougher line coincided with, and was heavily influenced by, progress in Sino-American normalization, culminating in the 15 December 1978 announcement of the establishment of diplomatic relations and Vice-Premier Deng Xiaoping's visit to the United States in late January. Although the United States claimed that it did not publicly side with China in its dispute with Vietnam, the record shows that, beginning at least with Brzezinski's visit to China in May 1978, U.S. leaders took steps that gave an impression to the Vietnamese and others that the United States was siding with China against Vietnam.

At bottom, the compatible policies toward Vietnam strengthened and broadened the common strategic anti-Soviet underpinning of the Sino-American relationship, giving a higher profile to Southeast Asia and giving both sides greater incentive to move toward establishing closer ties and diplomatic relations. China was particularly anxious—in light of its weak position vis-à-vis the USSR in Asia—to convey an impression of American complicity in its policy toward Vietnam. It saw this as helpful in offsetting possible Soviet countermoves against China in defense of Vietnam. Indeed, three major forceful Chinese initiatives toward Soviet-backed Vietnam have been preceded by Chinese efforts to gain

U.S. reassurances and to give an impression that the United States is on China's "side" in the conflict:

- May 1978—Chinese leaders briefed Zbigniew Brzezinski at great length on China's intentions toward Vietnam;[63] at the same time, Brzezinski publicly identified the United States with China's stance against Vietnam. Several days later, Beijing began its tougher pressure campaign against Vietnam.

- January 1979—Deng Xiaoping solidified U.S.-PRC ties and briefed U.S. leaders on China's military intentions toward Vietnam prior to Chinese forces entering Vietnam to teach Hanoi a "lesson."

- January-April 1984—Premier Zhao Ziyang and President Reagan exchanged visits solidifying Sino-American relations after several years of serious tension. Against this background, Chinese military forces upped the ante in the border conflict with Vietnam, leading to the most serious and prolonged fighting there since 1979.

When he traveled to China in May 1978, Brzezinski took along experts on Indochina who held discussions with their Chinese counterparts and spent many hours discussing Vietnam with the Chinese. He also used his remarks at the welcoming banquet in Beijing on 20 May 1978—only four days before the start of China's pressure campaign against Vietnam—to implicitly but clearly identify the United States with Chinese opposition to Soviet-backed Vietnam. He said that the United States "recognizes—and shares—China's resolve to resist the efforts of any nation which seeks to establish global or regional hegemony."[64] The last two words, of course, were code words widely used by China to denote Vietnam.

In late May, as the Chinese began their new tough policy toward Vietnam and unilaterally sent ships to evacuate overseas Chinese, the Soviet Union conducted naval exercises in the South China Sea as an apparent show of force. In what may have been more than a coincidence, U.S. officials ordered one of two active U.S. aircraft carriers of the Seventh Fleet to call at Hong Kong, where the officers on board feted Chinese Communist officials from the British colony. *Xinhua* promptly reported this "friendly" meeting between Chinese leaders and American officers on a U.S. warship docked in what the PRC saw as Chinese territory—the first time that Beijing media were known to have reported such a demonstration of Chinese support for the continued U.S. military presence along their frontier. The carrier soon left Hong Kong for duty in the South China Sea, in what analysts saw as an Amercian show of force for China in the face of the Soviet maneuvers.[65]

In mid-July, Vietnam tried to breathe new life into the dormant U.S.-

Vietnamese negotiations on the normalization of diplomatic relations by telling foreign diplomats and newsmen that Hanoi no longer would require the United States to pay reparations in order to establish diplomatic and trade relations. Beijing was quick to show its disapproval of the new Vietnamese stance;[66] the United States took no significant step forward in trying to normalize diplomatic and economic relations with Vietnam, at least in part to avoid alienating Beijing and upsetting the negotiations on normalizing Sino-American diplomatic relations.[67]

In the latter part of 1978, the United States took several other steps that served to strengthen China's position against Vietnam. The visits of two U.S. cabinet members and the president's adviser on science resulted in unprecedented Sino-American agreements on the transfer of U.S. technology and know-how to China; and in November the United States indicated that, contrary to past practice, it would not oppose the sale of arms to China by West European powers. These moves were warmly welcomed by Chinese leaders, who bluntly portrayed the establishment of closer U.S.-PRC cooperation as the best way to offset the spread of Soviet influence through alleged surrogates in Vietnam and elsewhere.[68] U.S. leaders did not dissociate themselves from this view.

Several weeks before the Vietnamese invasion of Kampuchea began on 25 December 1978, the United States altered its previously noncommittal position on the Vietnamese-Kampuchean dispute and came down on the side of Pol Pot's Kampuchea—a paradigm of human rights abuse but China's ally and Soviet-backed Vietnam's enemy. For example, the State Department announced on 3 December that the United States supported the territorial integrity of Kampuchea, and it warned that Hanoi's actions in the Vietnamese-Kampuchean dispute would affect the pace of U.S.-Vietnamese normalization of relations.[69]

The 15 December communiqué on the establishment of U.S.-PRC diplomatic relations duly reaffirmed both sides' opposition to international "hegemony," but Hua Guofeng publicly stated that the normalization would be useful against "regional" as well as global hegemonism[70]—a statement that clearly associated the United States with China's stance against Vietnam and was not countered by any public U.S. statement. Subsequently, the United States served, in late January, as an international sounding board for Deng Xiaoping to express the now agreed-upon Chinese case against Vietnam and to advise the world that reports of a Chinese military buildup along the Vietnamese border meant that China intended to attack Vietnam if the latter did not change its policies. The United States waited until well after Deng had returned to China, and had held discussions in Japan on the way home, before advising that it did not share the Chinese view regarding the advisability of a military attack against Vietnam. In the meantime, the United States allowed Kampuchean Prince Norodom Sihanouk (an official representative of a government not officially recognized by the United States) to meet with Deng in the official residence in Washington provided to the Chinese visitor. After the meeting, Sihanouk confirmed reports that China was supplying Pol Pot forces with military and other goods via Thailand. Less than a week later, President Carter issued his strongest statement of support for Thailand against possible attack from Vietnam, warning that the United States remained "intensely interested and deeply committed" to the inviolability of Thailand's borders.[71]

NOTES

1. By contrast, Li Xiannian led Chinese delegations to more important countries—the Philippines and Bangladesh—at this time. Compare Chinese media treatment of the travels of the two leaders in *DR China*, January–March 1978.

2. A very useful assessment of Chinese perceptions of the international balance of power at this time is in Banning Garrett and Bonnie Glaser, *War and Peace: The Views from Moscow and Beijing* (Berkeley: University of California Press, 1984), pp. 57–100.

3. See, for example, Allen Whiting, "Assertive Nationalism in Chinese Foreign Policy," *Asian Survey*, August 1983; and Carol Hamrin, "Emergence of an 'Independent' Chinese Foreign Policy and Shifts in Sino-U.S. Relations," in James Hsiung, ed., *U.S.-Asian Relations* (New York: Praeger, 1983).

4. Garrett and Glaser, *War and Peace*, documents this point well.

5. An insightful analysis of this period is in [H. Lyman Miller], *Chinese Political Debate Since the December Third Plenum*, FBIS special report (1979).

6. *FBIS Trends* supplement, "Peking Leadership Dispute over Purge of 'Gang' Followers," 24 February 1978.

7. Hua's remarks appeared in *DR China*, 7 March 1978.

8. FBIS, *The Fifth Chinese National People's Congress*, special report on Communist media (1978), p. 4.

9. Hua's speech is in *DR China*, 27 March 1978. Deng's speech is in *DR China*, 21 March 1978.

10. FBIS, *Chinese Army Political Conference: Persistent Leadership Differences amid Mounting Pressure for a Wider Purge*, FBIS special report (1978).

11. FBIS, *Chinese Leadership Conference and CCP Plenum. November–December 1978. Ratification of the Modernization Program*, FBIS analysis report. (1979).

12. See, for instance, Central Intelligence Agency, *China: The Continuing Search for a Modernization Strategy*, ER80–10248 (1980), p. 5.

13. Coverage of Hua Guofeng's visit to Iran is in *DR China*, 30 August 1978.

14. See Chinese press coverage in *DR China*, 14 August 1978.

15. See Chinese press coverage in *DR China*, 18 December 1978.

16. See in particular Li Xiannian's remarks in the Philippines during March 1978, which are analyzed in *FBIS Trends*, 22 March 1978, pp. 12–13.

17. See analysis in Harry Harding, "China and the Third World," in Richard Solomon, ed., *The China Factor* (Englewood Cliffs, N.J.: Prentice-Hall, 1981).

18. See U.S. Congress, Joint Economic Committee, *Allocation of Resources in the Soviet Union and China* (Washington, D.C.: U.S. Government Printing Office, 1984), pp. 159–60.

19. Huang's remarks appear in *DR China*, 22 May 1978.

20. See analysis in *FBIS Trends*, 25 October 1978, pp. 2–4.

21. The editorial appeared in *DR China*, 18 December 1978. For background on the communiqué, see U.S. Library of Congress, Congressional Research Service. *China-U.S. Relations*, issue brief 76053 (periodically updated).

22. Reports of Li's remarks appear in *DR China*, 13 November 1978.

23. Deng's press conference was noted in *DR China*, 26 October 1978.

24. See Chinese press coverage of Deng's visit in *DR China*, 23 and 24 October 1978.

25. Ibid.

26. *DR China*, 6 November 1978.

27. Huang's trip is covered in *DR China*, 7 June 1978.

28. See authoritative Chinese comment on the Nonaligned Movement in *DR China*, 13 and 25 July 1978.

29. Ibid

30. See coverage in *DR China*, 17, 19, and 21 July 1978.

31. Li's visit is covered in *DR China*, December–January 1978–79.

32. This section relies heavily on an article by Robert Sutter in David W. P. Elliott, ed., *The Third Indochina Conflict* (Boulder, Colo.: Westview Press, 1981).

33. See *FBIS Trends*, 22 June 1977.

34. Ibid., 8 September 1977.

35. Ibid., 23 November 1977.

36. Ibid., 20 July 1977.

37. Ibid., 5 October 1977.

38. Ibid., 25 January 1978.

39. Ibid., 11 January 1978.

40. Ibid., 5 January 1978.

41. For background, see U.S. Senate, Committee on Foreign Relations, *Vietnam's Future Policies and Role in Southeast Asia* (Washington, D.C.: U.S. Government Printing Office, 1982), pp. 42–43.

42. Note in particular U.S. Congress, House Committee on Foreign Affairs, Subcommittee on Asian and Pacific Affairs, *A New Realism: Factfinding Mission to the PRC, July 3–13, 1978* (Washington, D.C.: U.S. Government Printing Office, 1978).

43. Note, for instance, Huang Hua's trip to Zaire in June 1978 and the visit of a Chinese military delegation to the Congo in late June 1978. Both reported in *DR China*.

44. See speeches of Huang Hua and others before the U.N. disarmament sessions in late May and June.

45. For further analysis, see *FBIS Trends*, 1 June 1978.

46. Ibid., 14 June 1978.

47. Ibid., 28 June 1978.

48. For further analysis, see ibid., 6 July 1978.

49. Ibid., 26 July 1978.

50. See *Far Eastern Economic Review* analysis of this period.

51. See U.S. Congress, House Committee on Foreign Affairs, *A New Realism*.

52. *Xinhua*, 1 January 1979 (emphasis added).

53. *Xinhua*, 23 December 1978 (emphasis added).

54. *Guangming Daily*, 19 December 1978.

55. *People's Daily*, 30 December 1978 (emphasis added).

56. *Xinhua*, 13 December 1978.

57. *Xinhua*, 28 December 1978 (emphasis added).

58. *Xinhua*, 8 January 1979.

59. *Xinhua*, 13 January 1979.

60. Ibid.

61. Personal, informal survey of several China specialists, 1979.

62. See *FBIS Trends*, 24 January 1979.
63. I am indebted to Nayan Chanda for this point.
64. *Xinhua*, 20 May 1978.
65. *Christian Science Monitor*, 15 June 1978.
66. *Xinhua*, 25 July 1978.
67. A *Washington Post* editorial supported this argument.
68. See U.S. Congress, House Committee on Foreign Affairs, *A New Realism*.
69. *Washington Post*, 4 December 1978.
70. *Xinhua*, 16 December 1978.
71. *New York Times*, 7 February 1979.

6

TACTICAL ADJUSTMENTS IN THE FACE OF SOVIET PRESSURE, 1979-80

The results of China's military "lesson" to Vietnam were mixed. Chinese armies seriously damaged Vietnamese border areas, diverted Vietnamese forces from Kampuchea to northern Vietnam, further complicated Vietnam's economic planning, and demonstrated China's willingness to use force if necessary to halt Soviet-backed Vietnamese expansion in Southeast Asia. But Vietnam managed to return tit for tat and received ample support from its Soviet ally. Most notably, the Chinese assault resulted in a reported 20,000 Chinese casualties and a large increase in Chinese defense spending at a time when PRC leaders were trying to curb defense spending increases in order to assist the development of China's civilian economy. The Vietnamese also managed to all but end the previously substantial official Chinese influence in Laos, and to contain the Chinese-supported Pol Pot guerrillas in Kampuchea. Meanwhile, the exodus of over 250,000 refugees from Vietnam to China severely strained the PRC's resources and further exacerbated its economic difficulties.[1]

These setbacks added to growing international and domestic pressures on Deng Xiaoping and his reform-minded associates, brought on particularly by increased Soviet military and political pressure around China's periphery and setbacks in economic modernization and political reform at home. In response, Chinese leaders discussed and debated foreign policy options, and decided to initiate several tactical adjustments in China's approach to foreign affairs. These included the start of Sino-Soviet negotiations at least ostensibly designed to improve bilateral relations, the decline in China's heretofore outspoken interest in identifying closely with the United States on a strategic plane against the USSR, and greater Chinese willingness to broaden political ties and other contacts with a variety of third world governments, international political movements, and foreign Communist parties heretofore shunned as unhelpful or antagonistic to China's anti-Soviet objectives. Despite such alterations, however, Chinese actions and policy pronouncements made it amply clear that Beijing's tactical adjustments were still focused on the basic Chinese need to stabilize the Asian environment in the face of Soviet pressure by means of effective, pragmatic diplomacy, reliance on continued strong international opposition (especially U.S. opposition) to the USSR, and the maintenance of Sino-American understanding against suspected Soviet designs in Asia.

SOVIET AND U.S. POLICIES

The Soviet support and assistance for Vietnam was only a part of what Chinese leaders clearly saw as a newly enhanced Soviet effort to encircle and intimidate China. That effort was not undertaken in response specifically to China's action against Vietnam, but was part of a broader, across-the-board step-up in Soviet military activity that included the following:[2]

- President Brezhnev and Defense Minister Ustinov toured the Soviet Far East and viewed a major Soviet military exercise not far from the Chinese border in March 1978.

- Around the time of the Chinese incursion into Vietnam, it became clearer that the Soviet Union had established a new Far East command.

- During China's action against Vietnam, Soviet forces along the Chinese border were more active in a perceived effort to intimidate China. Before launching its strike at Vietnam, China reportedly took the precaution of evacuating civilian population centers along the frontier with the USSR that might be vulnerable to possible Soviet retaliation.

- Shortly after the Chinese forces returned from Vietnam in mid-March 1979, Moscow conducted "ahead of schedule" the largest military exercise it had ever held near the Chinese border, according to Chinese media comment.

More broadly, the Soviet Union was in the process of improving the size, equipment, organization, deployment patterns, and rapid mobilization capabilities of its forces in Asia. This effort included the new Far East Command but also involved the following:

- A major modernization of military equipment in the Far East, in parallel with similar modernization efforts elsewhere in the Soviet armed forces

- Activating additional, low-priority divisions facing China

- Augmenting the deployment of Soviet forces in Mongolia (Soviet forces in southeastern Mongolia were seen as a particular threat to Beijing and as capable of cutting off Manchuria from the rest of the country)

- Beginning to deploy new forces in the disputed southern Kurile Islands— forces intended mainly to intimidate Japan

- Acceleration of the deployment of more modern air and naval forces in the Far East

- Making more visible to China, Japan, and other Asian states the Soviet threat of mass destruction by deploying better strategic weapons, eventually including the SS-20 missiles and the Backfire bombers, to the Far East. (The increased accuracy of the former was seen as a significantly increased threat to China's small nuclear deterrent, which in many cases reportedly relied on reinforced bunkers for protection against a Soviet first strike.[3] The SS-20 gave the Soviets the accuracy to annihilate the limited number of such Chinese sites.)

This impressive Soviet military buildup—which continued unabated into the 1980s—underlined Soviet objectives that went beyond past concern with inhibiting China from challenging the border with the USSR. It gave the Soviets a major offensive military advantage over China and steadily widened the gap between the military capabilities of Chinese forces and those of the USSR. Basic Soviet objectives in the buildup now included the following:[4]

- The Soviets sought to ensure that their military capabilities in East Asia remained adequate against not only China but also any combination of adversaries, particularly what was now seen as an emerging American-Japanese-Chinese alignment.

- The Soviets also sought to ensure, through the threat constantly posed on China's northern border, that China would be persuaded not to take any strong actions against Soviet friends and clients along its periphery; Vietnam and India were cases in point.

- The Soviets also sought to create a base of operations to assist in the future exploitation of opportunities for further advance in Southeast and Southwest Asia. For example, the Soviet ability to establish an important military base at Cam Ranh Bay in the 1980s was dependent on its stepped-up military deployment throughout the Far East, especially along China's northern frontier.

U.S. policy, meanwhile, appeared to undergo a temporary change after China invaded Vietnamese border provinces and the Soviet Union issued strong warnings of possible countermeasures involving its augmented forces in the region. The United States provided political backing for a Chinese-supported proposition calling for withdrawal of Vietnamese forces from Kampuchea in tandem with a Chinese withdrawal from Vietnam, and Washington indirectly warned the USSR that "steps which extend the conflict [in Indochina] would have serious consequences" on world peace.[5] The United States also announced that it would not allow the Chinese incursion to upset forward movement in Sino-American relations.

But the United States avoided reaffirming strategic support for China as Beijing faced increased Soviet military pressure in the wake of its incursion into Vietnam; and U.S. Secretary of the Treasury Michael Blumenthal reportedly criticized the incursion when he visited China in February 1979.[6] U.S. naval forces were not reported deployed—as had occurred in 1978—to counter the Soviet naval presence near China during the Sino-Vietnamese confrontation. U.S. officials also avoided comment in support of China as it faced the unprecedented Soviet military exercises along the Sino-Soviet border in March 1979.[7] Some U.S. news reports even noted that U.S. officials were preparing to pull back further from involvement in Asia and to adopt a new "quarantine doctrine" that would isolate the United States from intra-Communist conflicts that were expected to dominate the East Asian mainland over the next several years.[8]

This kind of U.S. behavior, for a time at least, raised some questions regarding U.S. policy in Asia and future Sino-American relations. For one thing, on the U.S. side it could have been argued that during 1978 the United States was unwise in allowing its interest in better relations with China to influence its policy in Indochina so strongly, resulting in what appeared to many to be a decided American "tilt" against Vietnam and in favor of China. And it could have been viewed as misguided for U.S. leaders to have identified the United States so closely with the tough Chinese policy toward Vietnam—especially since that policy quickly proved to be far from successful in securing Chinese interests in the region and was subject to less than uniform Chinese leadership support.

From the Chinese perspective, the apparent reduction in U.S. support in the wake of Beijing's incursion could have been seen as poorly timed, inasmuch as it came when Beijing was facing greater Soviet military pressure on its northern border. As the Chinese withdrew from Vietnam without a clear military victory, their leaders may have been inclined to look abroad for an explanation of their lack of success. From one perspective, the United States could be made to take the blame—after all, U.S. leaders first encouraged China's tough stance against Vietnam, then appeared to pull back support when the Soviet Union began to apply strong pressure on China.

This type of U.S. behavior could also have been interpreted as "weakness" vis-à-vis the Soviet Union—a development that might have had some impact on China's interest in closer relations with the United States. In particular, Beijing was strongly interested in better relations with the United States as a means to offset Soviet pressure on China. If U.S. support was seen as weak, then Chinese interest in better Sino-American ties could flag. Indeed, apparently vacillating U.S. actions during the China-Vietnam crisis and subsequent developments caused Beijing to be at least somewhat disillusioned with U.S. willingness to stand by China against Soviet "hegemony" in Asia, and helped to prompt the Chinese to formulate new tactics designed to ease Soviet pressure by seeking modest accomodation with the USSR.[9]

INTERNAL CHINESE COMPLICATIONS

Domestic developments were taking a turn for the worse as far as Deng Xiaoping and his reform-minded associates were concerned. In order to deal with domestic problems without the distraction of leadership discussion and debate over foreign policy issues, Deng may have chosen to adjust China's foreign tactics so as to reach a broader PRC leadership accord in this area, in preparation for focusing on further domestic reform. In any event, at this time China faced serious economic and social dislocations prompted by the cutback in central control of economic development, rapid importation of foreign goods and services, a construction boom and resulting inflation, and large-scale efforts by petitioners to seek redress of past grievances. Unemployed urban youth began experimenting with Western ideas and life-styles—to the delight of the Western media but the horror of Communist Party conservatives.[10]

Following the close of the Third Plenum, moreover, there were renewed efforts to achieve political reforms and leadership changes that had been compromised upon at the plenum. The efforts included attempts to redefine the political line of the Gang of Four as "leftist" rather than "rightist," and to reopen an assessment of controversial developments in the party's history, notably the Cultural Revolution. The aim was to promote a more thoroughgoing purge of cadres recruited and promoted during and since the Cultural Revolution who still remained committed or beholden to that period's Maoist ideology and policies. Press comment at the time portrayed the purge as an essential prerequisite to effective modernization and equated it with Mao's elimination of opposition to his policies during the Yanan rectification movement of the 1940s.[11]

The calls for reform fairly soon ran up against resistance from strongly pro-Maoist opponents. And the reforms were blocked by more moderate leaders, including Chairman Hua and Vice-Chairman Ye Jianying, who argued that the purge of pro-Maoist leaders remaining in the administration would harm the party's stability and unity, and consequently would hinder progress in modernization efforts.[12]

Events in March and April 1979 caused the vigorous challenge mounted by the reformers to drop off sharply. Instead, more moderate views upholding compromises made at the Third Plenum were reaffirmed in renewed calls to maintain leadership "stability and unity." And Beijing emphasized a new line stressing the importance of upholding the ideological orthodoxy seen in the "four principles"—allegiance to the socialist road, to CCP rule, to the dictatorship of the proletariat and to Marxism-Leninism-Mao Zedong thought. Commentary during this period indicated that a variety of practical difficulties facing China—including a strained international environment following its punitive attack on Vietnam, the outbreak of social unrest and political dissidence in several cities, and a growing realization of serious imbalances in the economy—together with a resurgence of leftist criticism of reform policies, provided the impetus for the strong reaffirmation of the more orthodox views that reformers had been challenging.

In this more fluid political situation, some Chinese leaders began indirectly to question publicly some of the implications of the strongly anti-Soviet, pro-Western approach in Chinese foreign policy of the previous year.[13] They employed a series of press articles using allegories from Chinese history and from early Soviet history. Some of the articles suggested that China could afford neither to "import" modernization from the West nor to pursue a confrontational foreign policy against the USSR and its associates. Rather, they advocated that China should adopt the approach of Lenin during the days of the New Economic Policy in the early Soviet Union—it should relax restrictions on capitalistic practices at home while making amends with enemies abroad. This would gain China a "breathing space" from foreign threat and allow it to ensure that social stability was maintained, and economic development and military strengthening were carried out at a steady pace. Leadership support for some change in foreign policy was also seen in the rehabilitation of officials who had been criticized for favoring a "pro-peace" foreign policy involving improvement of relations with both the USSR and the United States, and relaxation of tensions with China's neighbors.

Leaders under Deng met these oblique criticisms, and growing international and domestic strains, with tactical adjustments in China's foreign policy. Chinese policy became somewhat less forceful in pushing opposition to Soviet hegemonism and criticism of Soviet "proxies" in the third world. Beijing came to see its past unsophisticated, anti-Soviet, pro-Western approach as excessive, potentially dangerous, and possibly counterproductive to its basic concern in establishing an effective modernization strategy within a secure international environment. Nevertheless, the core of Chinese policy continued to rely on close ties with the West, the United States in particular, to offset the growing Soviet power in Asia and to help Chinese economic development.

The significant adjustments in Chinese foreign policy included the following:

- Concerned with what it now saw as China's possibly greater vulnerability to growing Soviet pressure, Beijing put aside its past uncompromising stance and called for talks with the USSR on improving Sino-Soviet relations.

- China revived talks with Vietnam, although it showed no sign of compromise so long as Vietnamese troops remained in Kampuchea. Beijing worked feverishly to ensure strong international support for Kampuchean resistance to Vietnam's occupation, and tried to unite more closely with ASEAN on this issue and to improve China's image in Southeast Asia by cutting back on its relations with pro-Chinese Communist insurgencies in Southeast Asia.

- China continued to value highly the development of closer ties with the United States—a stance that led to notable moderation in its policy regarding sensitive issues in Sino-American relations, such as Taiwan and Korea. But Beijing soft-pedaled its past emphasis on common Sino-American strategic interest in confronting Soviet expansion.

- China reduced its past identification with unpopular anti-Soviet regimes in the third world. It attempted to spread its influence through a more sophisticated political approach that used a greater variety of channels of political, diplomatic, and economic interchange, and avoided the past self-righteous opposition to developing nations that retained close ties with the USSR or its allies.

- Moderation in China's past strident anti-Sovietism and more flexible standards on Communist ideology after the Third Plenum opened the way to its greater interest in developing relations with Communist parties previously shunned as revisionist or pro-Soviet.

SINO-SOVIET RELATIONS

Beijing's offer to open negotiations with Moscow to improve relations between the two countries came in the immediate aftermath of China's attack on Vietnam. In one sense, it signaled a significant departure from Beijing's firm approach to relations with the USSR over the previous ten years as China dropped its long-standing preconditions to talks on improving relations. The 3 April 1979 *Xinhua* dispatch that revealed the offer for talks—in the course of reporting the Chinese decision that day to end the 1950 Sino-Soviet treaty of alliance—stated that Beijing had proposed negotiations with the Soviet Union to resolve "outstanding differences and improve relations."[14] Subsequently, the Chinese made it clear that they had dropped their demand that Soviet troops be withdrawn from disputed border territory before there could be progress in Sino-Soviet relations.

Moscow reacted cautiously. In contrast with its efforts during the previous years to use propaganda restraint and other gestures to signal Soviet interest in eliciting Chinese agreement for establishing greater channels of communication, Moscow did little positive to respond to the Chinese initiative. The Soviets apparently suspected, among other things, a Chinese attempt to divide Moscow from its Vietnamese ally, which was then beginning talks with China. On 17 April 1979, Soviet Foreign Minister Andrei Gromyko presented a note to the Chinese ambassador in Moscow suggesting that the two sides draft "a document on principles in relations," and asking for China's views on the subject and aims of the talks.[15] Beijing responded with a communication that called for a continuation of the periodic Sino-Soviet border talks and proposed that the negotiations deal with defining guiding principles for relations between the two countries, eliminating "obstacles" to the normalization of their relations, and developing trade, scientific, technical, and cultural exchanges. Beijing proposed that the two sides sign appropriate documents in accordance with the results of the talks.[16]

Although the second agenda item suggested that China might have intended to introduce old preconditions once the Soviets agreed to the talks, the first and third items mirrored Soviet overtures to China made repeatedly since the revival of Sino-Soviet exchanges in late 1969. On 4 June, Gromyko handed a memorandum to the Chinese ambassador setting forth the general Soviet position on the talks and stressing the need for an agreement on principles governing their relations.[17] But Gromyko added a controversial agenda item—attempting to use it to turn Beijing's long-standing charge that Soviet foreign policy was "hegemonist" against the Chinese. He said that the new agreement on principles governing Sino-Soviet relations should declare that the "two sides...agree not to recognize anyone's special rights or hegemony" in world affairs.

The Chinese initiative for talks did not prompt a significant reduction in polemics by either side. Moscow's failure to reduce media attacks was particularly noteworthy, given Soviet efforts to use a cutback in propaganda to improve the atmosphere in Sino-Soviet relations at the start of the border talks in 1969 and after Mao's death in 1976. However, Gromyko's proposal on "hegemony" touched off a flurry of acrimonious Sino-Soviet comment about which side practiced "hegemonism" in foreign affairs. The debate, along with such negative events as a serious Sino-Soviet border clash in July 1979,[18] the highly successful visit of U.S. Vice-President Walter Mondale to China in August, and repeated Chinese leadership statements to the Western press downplaying the importance of the upcoming talks with Moscow, strongly suggested that little progress could be expected in the sessions.

China set a particularly negative tone for the revived talks with Moscow in a 15 October *People's Daily* article by Ren Gubing.[19] This marked the first such signed article since 1977 by the commentator known for his caustic anti-Soviet stance and advocacy of uncompromising international opposition to Soviet "expansionism." Ren focused his scathing attack on Moscow's proposal to discuss hegemonism at the United Nations that fall. The resurfacing of the distinctly anti-Soviet commentator closely followed Soviet and Chinese agreement to begin the formal negotiations in Moscow later in the fall, despite continued disagreement over the agenda for the sessions. The timing of the article thus suggested that its arguments were related not only to the Soviet U.N. proposal but also to the dispute over the inclusion of the anti-hegemony issue in the bilateral negotiations. The resurrection of Ren, an action that must have been viewed in Moscow as provocative, also tended to confirm China's basic pessimism about the outcome of the Moscow negotiations.

As a result, when the talks finally got under way, Chinese and Soviet media gave them only brief, factual coverage. The five preliminary and six plenary meetings of the delegations were capped by the session on 30 November between Chinese Vice-Foreign Minister Wang Youping and Soviet Foreign Minister Gromyko. Subsequent reporting made it clear that in private the Chinese took an unyielding position early in the talks. Beijing reportedly demanded that the Soviets remove "obstacles" to improved relations before China would agree to a statement on principles governing Sino-Soviet relations.[20] The Chinese specifically insisted that Moscow reduce Soviet forces along the Chinese border to the level of the early 1960s, withdraw Soviet troops from Mongolia, cease support for Vietnam's occupation of Kampuchea, and work to resolve the Sino-Soviet border dispute.

Moscow in turn emphasized its unwillingness to agree to the Chinese conditions. Soviet officials repeatedly stressed that progress in the talks would depend on the attitude of the Chinese, and that improvement in Sino-Soviet relations would not occur at the expense of other countries. At the talks, the Soviets also proposed a statement of opposition to "hegemony," an end to Sino-Soviet polemics, regular Sino-Soviet diplomatic meetings (including summit meetings), and expanded trade, technical, and cultural exchanges. Apart from the proposal on hegemony, which was recent, the other offers echoed Soviet proposals made to China over the past decade as a means to reduce acrimony and restore an atmosphere more like normal relations between China and the USSR.

BROADER ANTI-SOVIET EFFORTS

The thrust of Chinese comment and policy behavior on other foreign issues in 1979 made it clear that Beijing was interested only in a relatively limited tactical adjustment in its approach to the Soviet Union and opposition to Moscow's hegemonism. For example, Chinese comment on Western Europe included full coverage of the Conservative Party's return to power in Great Britain in May 1979 that highlighted favorably Margaret Thatcher's advocacy of larger defense procurements and increased cooperation between the United States and Western Europe against the USSR.[21] And Premier Hua Guofeng, during his October-November 1979 visit to Western Europe, moderated his anti-Soviet rhetoric according to his hosts' diplomatic sensitivities when speaking at official functions; nonetheless, he made it clear that Beijing was still pressing the view that China and Western Europe share fundamental strategic interests in confronting Soviet hegemony.

Typically, in addressing a welcoming banquet in France hosted by President Giscard on 15 October 1979, Hua outlined increasingly "unscrupulous acts of aggression and expansion" by Moscow as a source of common concern to Beijing and Western Europe; but he referred to the Soviet Union and its allies only indirectly as the "hegemonists and their proxies." In London, where Prime Minister Thatcher's views permitted stronger rhetoric, Hua in a banquet speech on 30 October implicitly compared Soviet ambitions for world domination with those of Nazi Germany, and he saluted the British prime minister for "unequivocally identifying the source of war danger and calling for effective countermeasures." He also referred to the Soviets indirectly as "hegemonists." In his farewell banquet in London on 1 November, Hua reiterated his earlier parallel between the current world situation under threat of Soviet expansionism and the situation of the 1930s, recalling Europe's dismissal of Winston Churchill's "farsighted warning" against a policy of appeasing aggression as a "tragic lesson which ought to be remembered."[22]

VICE-PRESIDENT MONDALE'S VISIT TO CHINA

Chinese coverage of U.S. Vice-President Walter Mondale's August 1979 visit to China underlined the tactical adjustment in Beijing's approach to the two superpowers. Most notably, while the vice-president appeared to go out of his way to offer the strongest American statement of support for China's security, during a speech at Beijing University, the Chinese side soft-pedaled the strategic connection to Washington—a contrast with comment at the time of Deng Xiaoping's January 1979 visit to the United States.[23]

Beijing gave extensive play to Vice-President Mondale's visit as having given new momentum to Sino-American relations. But it focused primarily on the effects of the visit on bilateral relations, welcoming U.S. pledges to grant most-favored-nation tariff treatment to Chinese imports and other commercial gestures made by Mondale. Strategic aspects of Sino-American relations were given due acknowledgment but were not stressed in comment during the visit. In welcoming the vice-president at a banquet on 28 August, for example, Deng Xiaoping reaffirmed the conviction that a coincidence of strategic interests underlies Sino-American ties, stating, as he had during his Washington visit, that both sides should approach their relations "from a global perspective and with a view to the longterm political and strategic interests involved." Attacks on Moscow were muted during the visit, and Deng's pronouncement that Beijing and Washington share an "inescapable responsibility" to "oppose hegemonism and foreign domination in all its forms" was the only Chinese reference—and an indirect one at that—to the Soviet Union.

During Deng's visit to Washington in January, his statements and other Chinese comment had focused much more sharply on the coincidence of Sino-American strategic interests as the core of the two countries' relations. While Deng had made a clear effort to tone down his attacks on Moscow when speaking at formal affairs hosted by administration officials, he had bluntly denounced the Soviet Union by name when addressing less official forums during his visit.[24]

SOUTHEAST ASIA

Chinese negotiations with Vietnam, begun in April 1979, made even less progress than Beijing's later talks with Moscow, and were accompanied by transparent PRC efforts to tighten military and political pressure on Hanoi and to shore up international opposition—especially in ASEAN—to the Soviet-backed Vietnamese occupation of Kampuchea. Significant benchmarks in the Chinese effort included the following:

- Kampuchea—In May 1979, Beijing sent special envoys to intercede with Prince Sihanouk, then in North Korea, to remain firm in opposition to the Vietnamese occupation and to avoid an international settlement that would legitimize the Vietnamese takeover.[25] Over the course of the year, Beijing comment backed away from close identification with Pol Pot's bloody leadership. By year's end, it was actively hailing the united front of all "patriotic" Kampucheans within the newly reorganized Democratic Kampuchean Government, now under the titular leadership of Khieu Samphan.[26]

- Vietnam—Beijing in July 1979 used the defection of Vietnamese leader Hoang Van Hoan to China to mount an unprecedented direct attack on the legitimacy of the Vietnamese regime.[27] Within a few months, China was calling directly for the overthrow of the "Le Duan clique," and its media began giving some air time to reports of the activities of armed resistance forces in Vietnam.[28]

- ASEAN—During the year Beijing had the Chinese-based clandestine radios that beamed to Southeast Asia in the name of anti-government Communist insurgents curb their attacks on indigenous governments in favor of attacks against the Vietnamese and their Soviet backers.[29] To reassure Thailand, Beijing in June had the Chinese-based clandestine radio beamed to Thailand cease operations. By year's end, Beijing media were no longer carrying Chinese anniversary messages to the Southeast Asian Communist parties, and representatives of the Communist parties resident in China were no longer referred to by the Chinese press.

TAIWAN AND KOREA

Chinese policy toward Taiwan and Korea was not affected significantly by the tactical adjustments made after the Chinese incursion into Vietnam. Beijing's policy in both areas remained governed heavily by the continued improvement in its bilateral relationship with the United States. As a result, the Chinese continued to deepen their moderate approach to Taiwan while softening their anti-American stance in Korea. The latter approach led to a certain degree of cooling in North Korean-Chinese relations.

Chinese policy toward Taiwan remained governed by the 1 January 1979 New Year's greetings to Taiwan, from the Chinese NPC standing committee, which had dramatically elaborated past Chinese calls for the island's unification with the mainland.[30] Going well beyond previous authoritative government proposals for reconciliation with Taipei, the NPC greetings combined offers for a cessation of military hostilities and for a variety of contacts between the two sides with assurances that Beijing would take Taiwan's different social and economic conditions into account when incorporating the island into the PRC.[31]

The NPC message came against the background of the announcement of the establishment of American-Chinese diplomatic relations, which also took effect officially on 1 January 1979. The greetings conveyed Beijing's most elaborate authoritative appeal to Taipei for reconciliation since the founding of the PRC in 1949, and offered unprecedented assurance for the future of the island. At a 1 January meeting of the Chinese People's Political Consultative Conference (CPPCC), Deng Xiaoping stated that the NPC's proposals constituted Beijing's "major policy, basic position and attitude toward the return of Taiwan and the motherland's reunification."[32]

The message pledged that Beijing would take Taiwan's "present realities" into account in incorporating the island into the PRC, and would "respect the status quo" on the island and "adopt reasonable policies and measures" that would "not cause the people of Taiwan any losses." Both these promises, and the scope of the blueprint offered for uniting Taiwan with the PRC, went well beyond previous Beijing appeals for reconciliation with the Taipei regime, most notably during 1955-58 and again in 1973. In both the former period, coinciding with Sino-American talks in Geneva, and in the latter, following the beginnings of Sino-American détente, Beijing offered no more than negotiations leading to the island's "peaceful liberation" and opportunities for people on the island to visit friends and relatives on the mainland.

Outlining steps that could lead to reconciliation with Taiwan, the NPC message proposed that the two sides first negotiate an end to the "state of military confrontation" existing along the Taiwan Strait. Apparently as a token of sincerity, Defense Minister Xu Xiangqian announced on 1 January that the People's Liberation Army forces in Fujian would cease their ritual shelling of Taiwan-held offshore islands.[33]

The NPC message urged that both sides subsequently establish postal and communications links to facilitate cultural, academic, and technological ties, and remove barriers to visits between the island and the mainland. It also suggested that both sides would benefit from economic ties, stating that through trade each could "make up for what the other lacks and create economic interflow." All of these steps, the message noted, would help overcome the "lack of mutual understanding" caused by the "prolonged separation."

The NPC greetings played strongly on the nationalism and feelings of common cultural heritage of Chinese living on Taiwan. It pointed out that Taipei had "always taken a firm stand of one China and opposed an independent Taiwan," a common position that formed the "basis of our cooperation." All Chinese, in Taiwan or on the mainland, "share a compelling responsibility for the survival, growth, and prosperity of the Chinese nation," the message stated. Making an appeal to sentiments of common cultural traditions, it declared that no "descendant of the Yellow Emperor" wished to disappoint the expectations of both "our ancestors and our descendants" by prolonged national disunity.

In its new approach, Beijing consistently avoided references to "liberation" of Taiwan and dropped derogatory references to the Taipei leadership in favor of the term "Taiwan authorities." It nonetheless continued to steer clear of any formal renunciation of the use of force against Taiwan.

This moderate approach to Taipei was complicated at the end of 1979 by the Kaohsiung incident, which resulted in the arrest of scores of leaders of the political opposition following a riot at a political rally in the southern Taiwan city of Kaohsiung. On the one hand, Beijing tried to exploit the incident as an example of the "oppressive" Nationalist administration cracking down on "patriotic" opposition. On the other hand, Beijing was clearly concerned about the inclination of many of the oppositon leaders to favor self-determination for Taiwan.[34]

The result was a Chinese effort to walk a fine line that would avoid alienating Taipei, encouraging Taiwan's independence, or alarming the United States over PRC policy. It was seen in Chinese comment in early 1980 that maintained a relatively moderate approach on the question of the island's reunification with the mainland, but gave heightened attention to what it portrayed as popular opposition on Taiwan to the Taipei regime. That year Beijing ignored the 28 February anniversary of the 1947 Taiwan uprising, an occasion regularly used in the past to voice PRC policy toward Taiwan; but China pressed its views on the Taiwan issue at a usually authoritative level in connection with the annual Spring Festival. This set a pattern that would be followed in later years.

By ignoring the Taiwan uprising anniversary, Beijing avoided marking an event with implicitly hostile connotations for Taipei and supportive connotations for those opposition leaders in Taiwan favoring self-determination or independence for the island. The Spring Festival, focused on Chinese kinship and community solidarity, was apparently viewed as a more congenial framework for the current conciliatory PRC approach to Taiwan. Such considerations had not stopped Beijing from marking the uprising anniversary in past years, however, regardless of the focus of its position. For example, it made a pitch to Taipei for accommodation when the anniversary was celebrated in 1973 for the first time in several years. Similarly, Beijing comment on the occasion in 1979 strongly underscored the main themes of the PRC's appeal for "peaceful reunification" made a few weeks earlier in the NPC New Year greetings to Taiwan.[35]

Beijing's upgraded Spring Festival activities directed at Taiwan in 1980 included a letter to the Taiwan people on 15 February from the CPPCC National Committee and on 16 February from the Taiwan Democratic Self-Government League, a political organization formed in reaction to the 1947 Taiwan uprising and thereafter co-opted by the PRC as a coexisting "democratic party."[36] The latter organization also hosted a Spring Festival party on 18 February that was addressed by CCP Polit-buro member and United Front Work Department Director Ulanhu.[37]

Comment on Taiwan in the 1980 Spring Festival activities did not deviate from the main themes stressed in Beijing's conciliatory and gradualist approach to the Taiwan question set down in the 1979 NPC message. Speaking at the party on 18 February, Ulanhu reiterated Bei-jing's pledge to "respect the realities on Taiwan" in incorporating the island into the PRC, and its policy of preferring Taiwan's "peaceful" re-unification with the PRC. The CPPCC letter of 15 February recalled that the NPC's 1979 New Year greetings had "put forward the basic princi-ples and policies for solving the Taiwan problem," and urged Taiwan, as commentary had done in the past year, to open communications and shipping links with the mainland as a first step.

The Spring Festival comment followed a declaration first made by Deng Xiaoping in a 16 January speech that Taiwan's reunification with the PRC represented one of the three "major tasks" for China in the 1980s.[38] Deng's statement did not appear to signal a more aggressive ap-proach to Taiwan reunification, since he noted further in his speech that modernization was the principal task and that its completion would pro-vide better prospects for reunification with Taiwan.[39]

While reaffirming Beijing's standing policy on the Taiwan issue, comment during the 1980 Spring Festival also voiced authoritative sup-port for active political resistance to the Kuomintang by denouncing Tai-pei's "suppression" of the opposition movement in the wake of the Kaoh-siung incident. Beijing comment portrayed the opposition movement as a potentially significant factor in weakening Kuomintang control of the government on Taiwan, but also seemed to reflect concern that the movement's growth might lend impetus to Taiwan independence rather than to reunification with the mainland.[40]

The 15 February 1980 CPPCC letter denounced Taipei's use of the Kaohsiung incident as a pretext to suppress "patriotic" opposition to the Kuomintang, and demanded the release of those arrested in the wake of the incident. At the same time, it praised the Taiwan "compatriots'" traditions of "opposing 'two Chinas' and 'Taiwan independence,' oppos-ing schism, and fighting for reunification." More authoritatively, at the meeting on 18 February, Ulanhu declared that Beijing supported Tai-wan's "patriotic and democratic movement" but opposed " 'two Chinas' concept and 'Taiwan Independence.' "[41]

Meanwhile, Beijing began to signal in more detail, how it wished to incorporate Taiwan through the process of "peaceful reunification." In June 1980, it suggested that the island could enjoy the "special" status of Hong Kong and Macao. A Beijing radio broadcast to Taiwan on 16 June reported statements by Guangdong Province Party Chief and Governor

Xi Zhongxun during a visit to Macao in which he said that Hong Kong and Macao are "actually special zones" whose "historical status should be maintained to promote stability and prosperity." Taiwan, Xi said, could also "enjoy the status of a special zone" following its reunification with the mainland. The issue of territorial sovereignty aside, Xi stated, "pertinent measures applicable to such cases should be flexible." Beijing had not in recent years drawn any parallel between the political status of Hong Kong and Macao and the potential status of Taiwan, although Xi's suggestion was in keeping with Beijing's flexible approach to the Taiwan question as elaborated in Chinese media since the normalization of Sino-American relations in December 1978. While avoiding precise indications of how Taiwan might be incorporated into the PRC, Beijing consistently expressed a general preference for Taiwan's "peaceful reunification," and pledged to "respect" the economic and social "realities on Taiwan." In December 1978, a Beijing radio broadcast to Taiwan had suggested a parallel between Tibet's "peaceful liberation" under the 1951 agreement and Taiwan's potential unification with the mainland. More recently, the Hong Kong Communist press had suggested in June 1980 that Beijing's new policy of enhanced autonomy for Tibet might be applied to Taiwan.[42]

SIGNS OF SINO-KOREAN DISAGREEMENT

A distinct coolness in Sino-Korean relations began to emerge in 1978, coincident with the rapid forward movement in China's relations with the United States and Japan, and resulting moderation in China's anti-American stance on Korea. The strain began to be seen in public meetings between the two sides and continued until China shifted to a more independent posture in the third world, that gave pride of place to North Korea, in late 1981. Problems between the Communist neighbors were in evidence in Beijing's subdued treatment of the 25 April 1979 North Korean army anniversary, with Chinese comment cooler and its leadership turnout lower in rank than in the recent past.[43] A 25 April *People's Daily* article on the Korean army anniversary illustrated Beijing's reserved treatment. It failed to employ the standard descriptions of the Koreans and Chinese as "comrades in arms," and referred to relations between the two "peoples" rather than, as had been usual, between the two countries' "peoples and armies." Similarly, a *Xinhua* account of an anniversary meeting held by a Chinese People's Liberation Army (PLA) unit failed to offer the usual characterization of the atmosphere at the gathering. The account also reported on the Chinese speaker's greetings to the Korean army, omitting his remarks on Sino-Korean relations and support for Korean reunification.

The Chinese leadership's limited participation in the anniversary celebrations appeared to reflect a decision to tone down the normal show of support on an occasion having sensitive implications for U.S. and Japanese interests on the Korean peninsula. At the PLA meeting, for instance, there was no representative from the Chinese Defense Ministry's Foreign Affairs Bureau, for the first time since 1974. Chinese representation at the Korean military attaché's film reception at the Korean embassy on 25 April was also at a lower level than in the past; the usual additional embassy reception was not reported to have been held. This time the film reception was attended by a PLA deputy chief of staff, whereas in 1974, the last time only a film reception was held, the PRC was represented by a vice-minister of defense. Beijing itself drew attention to the absence of any party representatives at the reception when it reported that the Chinese turnout included officials of "other government departments involved." A CCP representative had attended all the main North Korean embassy Army Day receptions since 1973 and several of the film shows.

The visit of North Korean Premier Yi Chong-ok to Beijing in January 1981 underscored the cooling in relations that had taken place over the previous three years.[44] Yi's arrival on 10 January 1981 failed to trigger the customary welcoming *People's Daily* editorial, and his departure on 14 January was not marked with the usual concluding statement in the press. These omissions served to cloud the assertion by both sides that a unanimity of views was reached during the talks.

Beijing was the first to call attention to its reduced ardor in relations with Pyongyang by failing to issue a routine welcoming editorial in the party paper, and both sides registered a degree of estrangement by failing to publicize the usual characterization of the atmosphere at the welcoming ceremony. Similarly, Korean media's atypical failure to report on the second and concluding rounds of talks on 11 January may have signaled that differences had been aired the previous day. *Xinhua's* version of the talks on the 11th indicated that Chinese Premier Zhao Ziyang had offered routine Chinese support for Pyongyang's latest reunification proposal, terming Kim Il-song's call for a Korean confederation at the Korean Communist Party Congress in October 1980 "reasonable and correct."

Both sides used the banquet speeches to reiterate their standard positions on questions such as Korean reunification and U.S. troop withdrawal from the South, but Pyongyang and Beijing diverged in their treatment of the occasions. Korean media characterized the first banquet on the 10th as "friendly," while *Xinhua* failed to do so. Korean and Chinese reporting on the departure of the North Korean delegation for Burma on 14 January continued to reflect discrepancies. Korean media did not report any remarks by either premier on the occasion, but *Xin-*

hua cited Chinese Premier Zhao Ziyang as saying the trip had been "highly successful," and asserted that Yi was "very much satisfied with the fruitful results" of the talks. The lack of a formal joint statement at the end of the visit accorded with recent Chinese practice, but when CCP Chairman Hua Guofeng had visited Pyongyang in 1978, both the Korean Commuist Party Daily, *Nodong Sinmun*, and the *People's Daily* had published concluding statements that closely followed the form of communiqués. Similarly, in November 1980 the visit by the Yugoslav premier was marked with a Chinese press statement.

RELATIONS WITH OTHER THIRD WORLD COUNTRIES

In the years following Mao Zedong's death, and especially in the year after Deng Xiaoping's return to power in 1978, China had followed a strongly anti-Soviet orientation in its policy among the developing countries of Asia, Africa, and Latin America. Coincident with the tactical shift seen in its posture toward the superpowers in the wake of its military incursion into Vietnam in February-March 1979, Beijing came increasingly to see its past strident anti-Soviet stress in the Third World as counterproductive, and it began to readjust that policy. The result was a slow but steady reemphasis over the next few years on greater Chinese interest in fostering better relations with the developing countries as a key element in Beijing's portrayal of a more independent image in foreign affairs.

Beijing was nonetheless careful to ensure that this kind of image building and search for tactical advantage did not jeopardize the concern to achieve stability around its frontiers. Thus, China appeared to use its "independence" from the United States and the West in areas more peripheral to its basic security and development concerns, such as Latin America, Africa, and the Middle East, as a means to offset and balance the continued anti-Soviet and implicitly pro-Western thrust of its policy in much more important third world areas, such as Southeast Asia.

Of course, Beijing had long held that China is a member of the Third World and that the developing countries are a vital force in the international struggle against the "hegemony" of the superpowers. It had been quite strident in the initial period following Deng's return to power in fostering political opposition to expansion of Soviet influence among the developing countries. Following a strategy of working with established Third World governments, Beijing had continued previous efforts to put aside its earlier ties with more radical and divisive "revolutionary" groups there. In the Chinese lexicon, Beijing now followed a strategy of "united front from above" against the forces of imperialism and domination, as opposed to the past policy of "united front from below."[45]

In their strong efforts to build a common front against the USSR, Chinese officials and propaganda had often been hamhanded and, as a result, had alienated China from the main currents of thinking among many third world leaders. Thus, a number of leaders in developing countries grew increasingly suspicious of Chinese intentions as the PRC put aside past differences with the United States and the West for the sake of strategic and economic advantage. These officials became more susceptible to Soviet charges that China had "sold out" to imperialist and reactionary forces in its eager search for leverage against the USSR. Indeed, the Chinese showed they were willing to cooperate with some of the most reactionary third world governments—such as Chile's Pinochet regime—so long as they were suitably anti-Soviet. And Beijing not only sharply attacked Vietnam and Cuba as proxies of the USSR, but also privately criticized or shunned other states that were considered to be too beholden to the Soviet Union for economic aid or political support.

Coincidentally, China was keeping its new aid commitments to the developing countries to a minimum, and began to show interest in competing with other developing countries for aid from international organizations and for access to Western markets.[46] Of course, there were good reasons for reducing its past, often generous, aid commitments to certain developing countries:

- China needed resources at home for the ambitious modernization program.

- Past Chinese aid commitments to third world countries had often been poorly utilized—the showpiece of Chinese aid in Africa, the Tan-Zam Railway, for example, did not run properly after being completed by China.

- Aid often fostered governments that turned against China. Vietnam and Albania were the most important examples of this trend; but other instances included the regimes in South Yemen and Mozambique, which had received considerable support from China in the past, only to turn to more pro-Soviet policies later on.

- Large amounts of Chinese aid to particular developing countries sometimes tended to prompt the USSR to offer even greater aid in order to compete directly with China and overwhelm its influence. As a result, China lost influence despite its past investment.

The combination of China's controversial pro-Western, anti-Soviet political orientation and its more niggardly aid effort had diminished its influence in many developing countries by 1979. In response, Chinese leaders, especially those in the Foreign Ministry and the International Liaison Department of the CCP, began a series of low-keyed visits to third world states. Although China's renewed emphasis on policy independence and closeness to the developing world would not emerge full blown for two more years, by 1979 several signs of tactical change were already in evidence:

- Beijing began to moderate its strident anti-Soviet rhetoric and to pull back from close public identification with some conservative third world regimes merely because they were anti-Soviet. A small example was in China's less frequent use of media reports from such unprogressive anti-Soviet bastions as Chile. A more substantive instance was Beijing's altered support for Egypt's efforts to reach a peace agreement with Israel. China initially saw the efforts as a useful means to check Soviet penetration into the Middle East. But once Arab opposition to Cairo became apparent, Beijing pulled back to a more reserved approach that attempted to balance continued support for the Arabs and for Egypt.

- Unless basic Chinese security interests were directly affected, as they were in the opposition to Vietnam, Beijing increasingly tried to avoid the limelight on controversial third world issues. Questions such as the conflict over ownership of the western Sahara, the civil war in Chad, the Ethiopian-Somalian conflict over contested border lands, and, later, the Iran-Iraq war found China increasingly taking a publicly neutral position. At the same time, Beijing continued to voice strong support for positions that enjoyed a broad consensus in the third world, such as opposition to Israel and South Africa, support for liberation groups directed against them, and support for a more equitable international economic order.

- China used its scaled-down aid effort to build as much political goodwill as possible. It tended to focus on high-profile projects that were finished cheaply and quickly, with ample opportunities for favorable publicity. Typical examples were Chinese-constructed sports stadiums and auditoriums, and small Chinese health teams throughout Africa.

- Beijing began more pragmatic exploitation of third world markets for its economic advantage. The growing trade with Africa and the Middle East, for example, remained heavily in China's favor, providing a major source of foreign exchange.[47] Moreover, the Chinese began efforts to use the lucrative Middle East arms market as a source of foreign exchange and for political advantage.[48] The first substantial opening came with Egypt. Although China had supplied Cairo with some $10 million worth of spare parts after Egypt broke with Moscow in 1976, the real breakthrough was not seen until Egyptian President Anwar Sadat disclosed in mid-1979 that China was selling Egypt 50 aircraft as part of a new arms deal. It was judged by some experts that the deal involved 90 planes, 40 of which were a gift and 50 were sold. By January 1980, China had signed a new military protocol with Egypt. This package was estimated to have included six newly built Romeo-type diesel submarines, military aircraft including F-6s and F-7s, Chinese surface-to-air missiles, spare parts, ammunition, and maintenance services. With this arrangement, China was now selling Egypt—presumably backed by Arab oil money—hundreds of millions of dollars worth of weaponry.

• Beijing attempted to shore up its influence in the third world through more extensive political and technical contacts. This involved not only the traditional lavish entertainment for visiting third world leaders, but also increased Chinese exchanges with representatives of political parties, labor groups, women's organizations, military officials, and other interest groups.[49] These exchanges cost little in monetary terms, but were useful in building a broader base of political influence. They had the added benefit of deepening Chinese understanding of opinions in particular developing countries, so that Beijing could avoid alienating leaders or offending particular sensibilities as the Chinese pursued their broader foreign policy objectives. A highlight of Beijing's more ecumenical approach to contacts with political parties in developing countries was International Liaison Department Deputy Director Wu Xueqian's visit to ten African countries in late 1979. This was followed in mid-1980 by a visit to several African and Middle Eastern countries by the director of that department, Ji Pengfei.[50]

RELATIONS WITH COMMUNIST PARTIES

During their visits to Africa and the Middle East, Ji Pengfei and Wu Xueqian demonstrated China's new willingness to have contacts and establish relations with third world political parties that in the past had been shunned as "revisionist" or "pro-Soviet." This approach was seen also in China's increased flexibility throughout the international Communist movement. Beijing's more ecumenical approach, its greater tolerance of international groups previously seen as pro-Soviet, and its more liberal interpretation of revisionism led it to begin, in particular, exploratory contacts with the Italian, Spanish, and French Communist parties.

• On 4 April 1979, a *Xinhua* report broke with past Chinese treatment of the Italian Communist Party (PCI) by providing an uncritical, straightforward account of the five-day PCI Congress and of the reelection of Enrico Berlinguer as the Central Committee's secretary-general. Although Beijing had stopped portraying the PCI as completely subservient to Moscow in June 1976—viewing the party as having moderated its past stern opposition to NATO and to the European Economic Community in order to win electoral support—it continued to treat the PCI as a revisionist party in regular Chinese media reportage. Beijing also continued to support the rival Italian Marxist-Leninist Party. The new trend in Chinese reportage was quickly followed by contacts that led to a reconciliation between China and the PCI at the time of Berlinguer's visit to China in April 1980.[51]

- In August 1979, Chinese media began to refer neutrally to the Spanish Communist Party and to its leaders. In December 1979, party leader Ji Pengfei received Spanish Communist journalists in Beijing, leading to a full reconciliation between the two parties in the early 1980s.[52]

- Contacts between the more Soviet-oriented French Communist Party (PCF) and China began more cautiously. The PCF listed two Chinese journalists as observers at its 23rd Congress in May 1979, but there was no Chinese reporting on that congress. That summer, Beijing allowed a PCF representative to visit China as part of an official French parliamentary delegation, after having refused such representatives under similar circumstances in the past.[53]

These contacts with the West European parties—as well as Beijing's reestablishment of party ties with the Yugoslavs in 1977—clearly showed an intention to put aside the ideological and anti-Soviet considerations that had dominated and narrowed Chinese party relations in the past. For a time, Beijing attempted to rationalize its more flexible stance with an ideological gloss to explain how China now saw the distinction between revisionism and orthodoxy. In a word, China saw the distinction as resting on the principle of opposition to "hegemonism."

CCP Secretary-General Hu Yaobang explicitly enunciated this new basis of the CCP's foreign relationships for the first time in his remarks to Italian journalists on 15 April 1980.[54] The CCP, he stated, was "willing to establish, restore and develop relations with all working class parties that uphold independence and a correct position." The CCP would oppose all self-proclaimed Communist parties, he went on to say, that "bully other parties, interfere with other countries' internal affairs, and even invade and occupy other countries' territories by force." Hu's formulation of the basis for CCP ties with foreign parties appeared to build on the new definition of revisionism put forward in a highly authoritative speech by Party Vice-Chairman Ye Jianying on Chinese National Day in 1979, in which "revisionism" was characterized as "oppression of the people as home and pursuit of hegemony abroad."[55]

On that basis, Hu specifically ruled out the possibility of a resumption of CCP ties with the Communist Party of the Soviet Union (CPSU). A bitter Beijing radio commentary on 22 April 1980—the 110th anniversary of Lenin's birth—appeared to apply the new definition of revisionism specifically to the Soviet Union without actually branding the CPSU "revisionist." Outlining at length Lenin's enunciation of the Soviet Union's foreign policy on the basis of peace and mutual international respect, the commentary cited the "Brezhnev clique's . . . nibbling at Chinese territory and provocation of border disputes," and its "annexation" of Afghanistan as a ruthless betrayal of Lenin's foreign policy principles.[56]

NOTES

1. For background, see U.S. Senate, Committee on Foreign Relations, *Vietnam's Future Policies and Role in Southeast Asia* (Washington, D.C.: U.S. Government Printing Office, 1982).

2. This section draws heavily on the excellent review of such Soviet moves and their implications for China in Harry Gelman, *The Soviet Far East Buildup and Soviet Risk-Taking Against China* (Santa Monica, Calif.: Rand Corp., 1982).

3. See, for instance, Harlan Jencks, *From Muskets to Missiles* (Boulder, Colo.: Westview Press, 1982), p. 159.

4. See Gelman, *Soviet Far East Buildup.*

5. For background, see David W. P. Elliott, ed., *The Third Indochina Conflict* (Boulder, Colo: Westview Press, 1981), pp. 188–89. For this specific quote, see *Washington Post*, 18 February 1979.

6. Chinese coverage of Blumenthal's trip appears in *DR China*, 1–5 March 1979.

7. *New York Times*, 21 February 1979.

8. See article by Richard Burt in *New York Times*, 15 March 1979.

9. See H. Lyman Miller, "From the Third Plenum to the April Adverse Current: The Domestic Politics of Sino-Soviet Detente," paper presented at the annual meeting of the New England Regional Conference of the Association for Asian Studies, 20 October 1979. See also Daniel Tretiak, "China's Vietnam War and Its Consequences," *China Quarterly* no. 80 (1979).

10. FBIS, *Chinese Political Debate Since the December Third Plenum*, analysis report, (Washington, D.C. 1979).

11. Ibid.

12. Ibid.

13. An insightful assessment of this debate is in Carol Hamrin, "Emergence of an 'Independent' Foreign Policy and Shifts in Sino-U.S. Relations," in James Hsiung, ed., *U.S.-Asian Relations* (New York: Praeger, 1983).

14. See *DR China*, 3 April 1979.

15. *DR USSR*, 17 April 1979.

16. For background, see M. S. Ukraintsev, "Soviet-Chinese Relations: Problems and Prospects," *Far Eastern Affairs* (Moscow) no. 3 (1982): 15–24.

17. *DR USSR*, 4 June 1979.

18. See *FBIS Trends*, 25 July 1979.

19. Appears in *DR China*, 16 October 1979.

20. For background, see William E. Griffith, "Sino-Soviet Rapprochement?," *Problems in Communism*, March–April 1983.

21. *FBIS Trends*, 9 May 1979.

22. Chinese media coverage of Hua's trip is reviewed fully in *FBIS Trends*, 15 November 1979. In all four countries he visited, Hua asserted that the key to European security lies in greater West European strength and unity. *Xinhua* reported that, in his speech in Paris on 15 October, Hua praised French efforts to strengthen national defense and cited the Chinese premier's assessment that "a united and strong Europe is an important factor" in world peace and stability. In his welcoming banquet speech in London on 30 October, Hua observed more strongly that "a united and strong Europe serves to stay the hand of any warmonger and caution him against rash adventures."

Hua's stress on the need for increasing West European reliance on its own efforts for its defense had been a staple of Chinese comment since before the mid-1970s, when Beijing began to portray the Soviet Union as gaining the edge in world competition with a declining United States. While Hua did not refer directly to the dangers of excessive reliance on the United States for its defense during his tour, that aspect of the Chinese view of West Europe's strategic situation was supplied in a long *Shijie Zhishi* (World Knowledge) commentary carried by Beijing Radio on 7 November, which did not specifically mention the Hua trip but seemed timed to follow it up. Underscoring the same need for West Europe to "develop its own strength" and to follow a "balance-of-power strategy" in the current "multipolar world," the commentary warned that declining U.S. power cannot in the long run be relied on, since Washington will pursue its own "vested interests" in the end.

In that context, Hua repeatedly underscored the need for increased Chinese and West European cooperation out of common strategic interests. Chinese comment throughout the trip repeatedly emphasized the same themes, as did Beijing's authoritative assessment of the Hua tour as a whole in an 11 November *People's Daily* editorial: "It is imperative that both the people of China and the people of West Europe exert their joint efforts to defend world peace and security" in Asia and Europe.

Even in assessing Beijing's bilateral relations with each of the countries he visited, Hua repeatedly noted the importance of such ties for overall common strategic concerns. The *People's Daily* editorial on the trip summarized such statements by Hua, noting that "the strengthening of ties of friendly cooperation" between China and Western Europe "constitutes an important development which will stem aggression and expansion and promote world peace." The most concrete expression of such Sino-European strategic cooperation was Hua's tour of the Rolls Royce aircraft engine manufacturing facilities in Derby, England, with which Beijing had been cooperating for production of Spey jet engines in China since 1975. *Xinhua*'s reporting on Hua's visit to the Rolls Royce plant noted statements by plant officials expressing pleasure at Chinese trial production of the engines and the declaration by the Rolls Royce chairman that the company was "willing and ready to transfer appropriate technology" to China, despite whatever "irritation" might be felt by "some people."

While urging extensive Sino-West European cooperation, Chinese leaders' statements during the trip and Beijing commentary on it took pains to insist that such cooperation remain informal and consultative. Beijing's position seemed intended to blunt anticipated Soviet criticism of the tour, and it implicitly acknowledged differences in strategic views between Beijing and the European hosts. Paralleling concurrent Beijing denials of an interest in forming an "axis" with the United States and Japan against the Soviet Union, *Xinhua* reported Foreign Minister Huang Hua's 2 November London press conference statement that his tour was not intended to "forge an alliance of any kind."

Chinese commentary had suggested early in the tour that Beijing did not anticipate a complete identity of views on strategic issues to result from Hua's talks, and a 7 November *Xinhua* commentary at the end of the visit acknowledged that none had been reached, while suggesting an overarching consensus of general views. The *Xinhua* commentary observed that because of the "different circumstances" of each of the countries involved, different views on issues would "surely" result and, even in cases where views coincided, differences over "means and tactics" needed to solve various issues would inevitably emerge. Such differences, the commentary noted, "should not constitute an obstacle" to joint solution of questions of common concern or to efforts to "defend world peace from different angles and by different means."

Clearly demonstrating Chinese sensitivity to Soviet reaction to the Hua tour, a 5 November *Xinhua* correspondent's commentary ridiculed Soviet press attacks on Hua's anti-Soviet statements and on his talks with the European leaders as an "unsolicited confession" of hegemonism. The commentary asserted that in statements during his tour, Hua had not named the source of aggression and expansionism when he referred to the threats posed to the world by the "hegemonists," and it questioned "who on earth, except the enemy of peace" would be uneasy about China working "in concert with" West Europe in the defense of peace. It observed that tension had existed in Europe for years before the Hua tour because the Soviet Union had deployed its massive military strength against West European targets, adding that the establishment of self-defense measures against this threat was a "sacred duty" of the European countries.

23. See the analysis in *FBIS Trends*, 6 September 1979.

24. While Chinese leaders often moderated their traditional anti-Soviet invective when visiting foreign captials where such rhetoric might embarrass their hosts, they showed less reserve about denouncing Moscow more explicitly when leaders of those countries visited Beijing.

25. See *DR China*, 5 June 1979.

26. See *DR China*, 28 December 1979 and 2 January 1980.

27. See *DR China*, 7 July and 3 September 1979.

28. For background, see *FBIS Trends*, 4 September and 14 November 1980.

29. See, for instance, *FBIS Trends*, 25 June 1980.

30. The Chinese pronouncement appears in *DR China*, 2 January 1979.

31. A useful analysis of China's posture at this time appears in *FBIS Trends*, 4 January 1979.

32. Deng's remarks are in *DR China*, 2 January 1979.

33. Noted in *FBIS Trends*, 4 January 1979.

34. See the detailed analysis in *FBIS Trends*, 5 March 1980.

35. During 1973–79, the anniversary always prompted a meeting hosted by the Chinese People's Political Consultative Conference and addressed by Beijing's Taiwan affairs specialist, Liao Chengzhi.

36. See *DR China*, 19 and 26 February 1980.

37. The previous year, the Taiwan Democratic Self-Government League hosted a film reception, but no high-level CCP leader was named as being in attendance. In addition, in 1979 the PRC-controlled Kuomintang organs in Beijing, as well as CPPCC and overseas Chinese affairs offices in several provinces, held parties to appeal to Taiwan to consider seriously Beijing's new approach to the island as enunciated in the NCP's New Year's greetings.

38. Noted in *FBIS Trends*, 5 March 1980.

39. In the same vein, at a CPPCC New Year gathering in 1979 to discuss the NPC's landmark message to Taiwan, Deng had declared that Taiwan's reunification with the PRC was "placed on our concrete agenda" as one of the three significant aspects of China's current situation.

40. Since the beginning of Beijing's conciliatory approach toward Taiwan, PRC media had reported and offered low-level commentary on instances of political opposition to the Nationalists in Taiwan, but had previously withheld authoritative comment.

41. Cited in *PBIS Trends*, 5 March 1980. Beijing's concern over the fate of the opposition movement in Taiwan became evident in the period immediately following the incident. A 16 December 1979 commentary on the incident, broadcast to Taiwan, suggested that the riot had been in reaction to "a series of actions to suppress democracy" taken by Taipei since the normalization of relations between Beijing and Washington. A *Xinhua* commentary on 30 December stated that the Kaohsiung affair was the "natural outcome of intensified conflicts" sparked by the Taiwan people's "long discontent" with the Kuomintang's "autocratic rule," and rebutted charges, attributed to Taipei, that the incident had been organized by the Taiwan independence movement in collusion with Beijing. A 27 January 1980 *Xinhua* dispatch claimed that "mass arrests and persecution" of non-Kuomintang public figures since the Kaohsiung incident were aimed at suppressing "the patriotic and democratic movement" that had been developing vigorously on the island in recent years and at silencing the ever louder calls for reunification with the PRC.

42. A good review of this media coverage is in *FBIS Trends*, 2 July 1980.

43. Media coverage of the anniversary is reviewed in *FBIS Trends*, 9 May 1979.

44. The visit is assessed in detail in *FBIS Trends*, 22 January 1981.

45. For an excellent review of China's policy toward the third world up to 1980, see Harry Harding, "China and the Third World," in Richard Solomon, ed., *The China Factor* (Englewood Cliffs, N.J.: Prentice-Hall, 1981).

46. For an assessment of Chinese foreign aid efforts, see U.S. Congress, Joint Economic Committee, *Allocation of Resources in the Soviet Union and China—1982* (Washington, D.C.: U.S. Government Printing Office, 1983); and *Allocation of Resources in the Soviet Union and China—1983*. (Washington, D.C.: U.S. Government Printing Office, 1984).

47. For Chinese foreign trade figures, see Central Intelligence Agency, *China: International Trade* (updated quarterly).

48. The best available assessment of China's arms sales to the Middle East is in Yitzhak Shichor, "The Middle East in Chinese Defense Policy," in Gerald Segal and William Tow, eds., *Chinese Defence Policy* (London: Macmillan, 1984). See also Joint Economic Committee, *Allocation of Resources—1983*.

49. The frequency and diversity of such contacts rose markedly during this period. See *China Quarterly*, "Chronology," for March, June, September, and December 1979, and March, June 1980.

50. See *DR China* and *China Quarterly*, "Chronology," March 1980, September 1980 for coverage of these visits.

51. See the review in *FBIS Trends*, 11 April 1979.

52. See assessment in *FBIS Trends*, 16 July 1980.

53. Useful background and data are in *FBIS Trends*, 24 February 1982.

54. *DR China*, 15 April 1980.

55. *DR China*, October 1979.

56. For background, see *FBIS Trends*, 30 April 1980.

7

REACTION TO THE SOVIET INVASION OF AFGHANISTAN

The adjustments made in foreign policy after April 1979 represented a clear precursor of the more numerous tactical shifts seen in China's "independent" approach to foreign affairs that would emerge more fully in 1981-83: China's tactical flexibility seen in negotiations, rather than all-out confrontation with the USSR and Vietnam; its pulling back from its past unsophisticated search for anti-Soviet leverage in the third world, in international organizations, and within the international Communist movement; and its reduced public identification with the United States for strategic support.

A considerable body of circumstantial evidence indicates that Deng Xiaoping personally felt more comfortable with a strong anti-Soviet, pro-Western slant in China's foreign policy and would not—on his own—have advocated even such tactical compromise in this approach. But internal and international events pressured Chinese foreign policy decision makers, sometimes pushing Deng and the leadership consensus toward a less strident and more nuanced approach to foreign affairs.[1] That kind of approach seems to have been favored by such longtime foreign policy professionals as Ji Pengfei and Wu Xueqian, who probably had the backing of higher-level leaders, possibly including Li Xiannian or Chen Yun.[2]

It is important to note, however, that these distinct preferences actually did not make a great deal of difference in the underlying structure and basic framework of Chinese foreign policy. So long as China remained relatively weak in the face of growing Soviet military and political pressure, it was compelled to choose either to accommodate or to resist with the help of outside support, mainly from the United States. And, as economic modernization continued to get first priority, Chinese military capabilities vis-à-vis the Soviets remained inadequate, thereby requiring some sort of tacit or explicit Sino-American strategic understanding against the USSR. The goal of economic modernization also made the West more important as a source of technical and financial support, and as a major trading partner. These realities established basic parameters for Chinese foreign policy—limits that could not be breached without a wholesale reorientation of domestic and foreign policies of the previous decade.

The Soviet invasion of Afghanistan in December 1979 reinforced Chinese awareness of the limits of Beijing's independence and freedom of action in foreign affairs. Faced with a new Soviet advance along its southern periphery—only one year after the Soviet-backed Vietnamese invasion of Kampuchea—Beijing reacted with extreme concern. The PRC leadership under Deng Xiaoping reverted to a policy stressing China's common interest with the United States and other Western powers in opposing such Soviet expansion. At the same time, the Chinese—well aware of their exposed position vis-à-vis Soviet power—avoided actions that could have provoked Soviet military response. The careful effort to build an international strategic counterforce against Soviet power was to dominate Chinese foreign policy for the next year.

The seriousness with which Beijing viewed Moscow's intervention in Afghanistan was apparent in both the authority and the substance of its public comment. A PRC government statement was issued on 30 December 1979; on the following day Vice-Foreign Minister Zhang Haifeng called in the Soviet ambassador for an "interview," and People's Daily published an editorial on the Soviet action.[3]

The government statement was particularly important because such statements traditionally had been reserved for events that Beijing perceived as critically and directly affecting Chinese interests. The last such statements, in January 1979, concerned the Vietnamese invasion of Kampuchea; they had previously been issued at major junctures in the Vietnam war, in 1971 on the Indo-Pakistani war, and in 1975 on the Indian annexation of Sikkim. Beijing's concern was also underlined in the decision to publish editorial comment. Previous instances of Soviet interference in third world countries—in Angola in 1975, in the Shaba disputes involving Zaire of 1976 and 1977, and in the 1978 Somali-Ethiopian war—had been denounced in lower-level People's Daily "Commentator" articles.[4]

The toughly worded government statement "vigorously condemned" Moscow's "wanton violation" of all norms of international behavior and warned that its "hegemonistic action" posed a "grave threat to peace and security in Asia and the whole world." The statement called the Soviet intervention a "grave step for a southward thrust to the Indian Ocean," and it warned that Moscow's extension of the Brezhnev Doctrine of "limited sovereignty" to nonaligned and Islamic countries with which it had signed treaties of friendship and cooperation was an ominous portent. The statement "firmly demanded" the cessation of the Soviet intervention and aggression in Afghanistan, and the immediate withdrawal of Soviet forces.

Zhang Haifeng's lecture to the Soviet ambassador went further than the government statement in underscoring direct Chinese security concerns. According to the *Xinhua* account of the "interview" on 31 December, Zhang stated flatly that, because Afghanistan is China's "neighbor," the Soviet intervention "poses a threat to China's security" that "cannot but arouse the grave concern of the Chinese people."

The *People's Daily* editorial elaborated Beijing's charges as set down in the government statement. It called the Soviet action "the most serious act of aggression" by Moscow since the 1968 invasion of Czechoslovakia, compared Moscow's justifications to those of Hitler on the eve of World War II, and suggested that Moscow's direct use of its own military forces outside the bloc marked a "new stage" in its "aggression and expansion."

Despite the evident gravity with which Beijing viewed the Soviet intervention in Afghanistan, its public statements gave no indication that it was contemplating any unilateral response. None of the Chinese comment offered even a perfunctory commitment of the Chinese government and people to support the Afghan resistance to Soviet occupation as, for example, Beijing had pledged to the Czech people in 1968. Beijing's comment instead called for a strong international response, particularly from the United States.

The PRC government statement, exemplifying Beijing's effort to muster world reaction, pledged that "the Chinese Government and people will work tirelessly with all countries and people who love peace and uphold justice to frustrate Soviet acts of aggression and expansion." Similarly, the *People's Daily* editorial warned that world peace could be maintained only if the world's people "exert pressure on those hegemonists who stop at nothing to engage in aggression and expansion," in order to "stop them from committing aggression" and "force them to observe the most rudimentary principles" of international behavior.

That Beijing was looking to Washington for a strong response to the Soviet actions was pointedly underscored in *Xinhua's* 3 January account of PRC Ambassador to Washington Chai Zemin's banquet for Secretary of State Cyrus Vance on the first anniversary of the normalization of Sino-American relations.[5] In the context of reporting on Chai's routine observation that strengthened Sino-American relations are in the interests of "peace, security, and stability in the Asia-Pacific region and the world at large," *Xinhua* quoted Chai's statement that "we should by no means underestimate the gravity" of the Afghan invasion, as well as his call for "all peace-loving and justice-upholding countries" to consider how to take "forceful joint countermeasures to the Soviet acts of aggression."

Chai's call was echoed by Foreign Minister Huang Hua at a 3 January banquet in Beijing hosted by U.S. Ambassador Leonard Woodcock to mark the same occasion.[6] According to *Xinhua*, Huang stated in his speech that Moscow's "hegemonistic action" gave rise to "strong repercussions throughout the world and put people on alert." He maintained that "we should deal with [the situation] seriously" and "take all effective measures to frustrate the Soviet adventure in Afghanistan," and he stressed that "only when all the Asian and Pacific countries, as well as other countries opposed to hegemonism, strengthen their friendly cooperation can world peace be effectively maintained and security and stability in the Asian and Pacific region be safeguarded."

Chinese comment on the Soviet invasion also suggested that Western—and implicitly U.S.—indecisiveness in meeting Soviet challenges had created the opportunity for Moscow's actions in Afghanistan.[7] Linking the Soviet action to failure to deal firmly with the Soviet-backed Vietnamese invasion of Kampuchea a year earlier, the *People's Daily* editorial recalled that "certain friends in the world have indulged in the illusion of making certain concessions to the aggressors" in hopes of obtaining a "political settlement" of the Kampuchean question. "This kind of attitude," the editorial warned, "has not only encouraged Hanoi but has also boosted the courage of Moscow in laying its hands on Kabul." Noting Afghanistan's strategic position in South Asia, the editorial predicted that "subsequent developments" in the Afghan crisis would "exert an important impact" on the "pattern" of Soviet-U.S. rivalry and the world situation in the 1980s.

RENEWED INTEREST IN U.S.-CHINESE STRATEGIC TIES

Against this backdrop of increased concern, Beijing took satisfaction in the visit U.S. Secretary of Defense Harold Brown, portraying consultations between the two sides as having special significance in the context of Moscow's intervention in Afghanistan. Comment preceding the visit had signaled Beijing's support for firm U.S. steps in response to the Soviet actions in Afghanistan, and Beijing clearly welcomed Secretary Brown's forthright denunciations of Moscow's actions and his calls for parallel Sino-American responses to them.[8]

China's satisfaction with Secretary Brown's readiness to criticize

Moscow openly and to call for parallel Sino-American action in response to Soviet moves was clearly reflected in Chinese reporting as his visit progressed.[9] Initial comment on the visit's purpose stayed within limits established during previous high-level U.S. visits since the normalization of relations, and did not link the secretary's trip to the world situation in the wake of the Soviet invasion of Afghanistan. Such linkage became the underlying theme of Chinese reporting as the visit proceeded, however.

Beijing's initial expectations for Secretary Brown's visit were reflected in *Xinhua*'s report on his arrival, which observed only that the visit was intended to allow both sides to "exchange views on the present international situation and bilateral relations."[10] The measured Chinese approach was maintained in *Xinhua*'s 6 January report of the speech at the welcoming banquet by Secretary Brown's host, Chinese Defense Minister Xu Xiangqian. Xu bitterly denounced Soviet actions in Afghanistan and called for all countries to "unite and take effective measures and fight relentlessly" against Soviet hegemonism. He did not, however, call specifically for joint Sino-American responses to the Soviet intervention in Afghanistan, instead repeating the usual statement that Beijing and Washington view their relations from "long-term political and strategic considerations."

Chinese readiness to place the visit within the larger context of Moscow's intervention in Afghanistan increased visibly following Secretary Brown's forthright stance against the Soviet actions at the 6 January banquet, and particularly after the first session of working-level talks the next day with Vice-Premier Geng Biao. *Xinhua*'s report on the Geng-Brown talks on the 7th, for example, noted that after a "lengthy" discussion on the Afghan situation, both sides agreed to hold "follow-on discussions" on the impact of Moscow's actions on the region and to "consult further on appropriate responses." Xu Xiangqian's comments at a banquet on 9 January were similarly optimistic on prospects for Sino-American collaboration, declaring that talks during Secretary Brown's visit were "especially significant in light of the current situation," and that the developing relations between Washington and Beijing "will exert an influence which is not to be ignored for the maintenance of peace in Asia and the world." The *Xinhua* correspondent's commentary summarizing the results of the visit borrowed Secretary Brown's observation in his 6 January banquet speech that the defense talks had taken place "at a critical moment" and noted, again using Brown's words, that both sides agreed to "take parallel actions" in opposing Soviet hegemonism. With respect to Afghanistan, the *Xinhua* correspondent stated that both sides planned to "make respective responses that they consider appropriate" and to hold further consultations in the future.

As *Xinhua* reported his remarks on 8 January, Deng Xiaoping appeared particularly eager to press Sino-American collaboration against the Soviet Union in his talks with Secretary Brown that day. *Xinhua*, which at that time rarely quoted the substance of Chinese leaders' comments when receiving foreign guests in Beijing, reported Deng's remarks at unusual length. It thus highlighted the vice-premier's conviction that Moscow's policies of "hegemonism and global expansionism" will never change and that nations and peoples should "unite and deal seriously" with Soviet aggression. Washington and Beijing, *Xinhua* quoted Deng as stating, should "do something in a down-to-earth way" to respond to Moscow.

Xinhua's handling of Secretary Brown's talks with Deng Xiaoping was also remarkable for its treatment of Deng's call for the world's peoples to "unite" against Moscow. *Xinhua*'s English-language report on 8 January translated Deng's remark as a call for all nations to "enter into an alliance" against Moscow. It emended its rendering on 10 January, first by transmitting a service message noting that Deng had called on all nations to "unite" against Moscow, and shortly thereafter by retransmitting the entire item on the Deng-Brown meeting with a notation that the original had contained "several mistranslations."[11]

China complemented its efforts to encourage U.S.-led opposition to Soviet expansion around its periphery with generally upbeat comment about what was portrayed as a new sense of resolve in U.S. policy toward the USSR. Thus, Beijing registered strong approval of what it perceived to be a major about-face in the Carter administration's strategic policies toward the Soviet Union in the wake of Moscow's invasion of Afghanistan. Chinese media hailed the president's State of the Union address in January 1980 as encapsulating the major shift in U.S. foreign policy toward a more resolute defense of U.S. interests against Soviet challenges, and portrayed a growing consensus behind the president. Beijing at the same time welcomed new advances in Sino-American bilateral relations as having heightened strategic significance in the current international context.[12]

Beijing's highly favorable evaluation of President Carter's State of the Union address came in a 30 January *People's Daily* article attributed to commentator Fang Min.[13] Observing that the president's address marked a "new and uncompromising stand" in U.S. relations with the Soviet Union, Fang noted in particular that the president predicted that the 1980s would be a decade of international turmoil, that he avoided referring to détente with the USSR, and that he pledged to increase defense spending and meet the challenges to U.S. vital interests by all necessary means, including military force. Fang contrasted at length the current administration stand on relations with the Soviet Union and its conduct of such relations since 1977, noting that during the past three years Washington had "said much and done little," had been "irresolute and indecisive," and had been "relatively weak and helpless" in the face of repeated Soviet challenges.

Fang called the Soviet intervention in Afghanistan "sobering medicine for people in power in the United States," and he concluded from President Carter's address that the president recognized "the dangers of undue restraint and concession" under the "former U.S. policy of appeasement and accomodation" of Moscow. The president's current effort to move the United States from its state of "inertia" internationally to defend U.S. interests and "play a leading role in the world," Fang suggested, "accurately reflects the popular sentiments" in the United States. While acknowledging that "it remains to be seen" how the administration adjusted its policies to meet its rhetoric, Fang concluded that "after the outbreak of the Afghan situation, the United States has obviously felt it necessary to 'mend the fold.'"[14]

The positive treatment of the president's address capped a sharply favorable swing in Chinese media treatment of the Carter administration's conduct of Sino-American strategic relations following the Soviet intervention in Afghanistan. Chinese media welcomed various actions taken by the administration to modify U.S. relations with Moscow as a result of the Soviet action and praised its steps to increase defense spending. Chinese media treatment of the administration also reversed Beijing's long-standing characterization of Washington as uncertain of U.S. interests internationally, susceptible to Soviet pressure, and helpless in the face of Soviet intransigence; these unfavorable judgments had been evidenced most recently in treatment of the U.S. response in 1979 to reports of a Soviet combat brigade being stationed in Cuba.[15]

Accompanying an increasingly favorable evaluation of the U.S. president's policies toward Moscow, Chinese media began to portray broad congressional and public support for a firm stance against the Soviets. The 25 January People's Daily commentary on the president's State of the Union address, for instance, observed that Congress' applause for the speech "showed that a tremendous change has taken place in the political atmosphere" in Washington since the Soviet intervention in Afghanistan, and noted that "even Senator McGovern expressed his support" for the president.[16] Previous Chinese commentary critical of what it characterized as U.S. weakness and indecision in meeting Soviet challenges in recent years had attributed such behavior in part to the lack of a public consensus behind U.S. foreign policy in the wake of Vietnam, and in particular to division between the president and the Congress over the U.S. role abroad.

Concurrent with its positive appraisal of the administration's stance against the Soviet Union, Beijing sought to draw out the wider international significance of several recent advances in Sino-American bilateral ties. While Beijing repeatedly had urged in the past that China and the United States should view their bilateral relations from the "long-term political and strategic" perspective, Chinese media had played down such "strategic" ties during 1979 but now appeared to go to somewhat greater lengths to stress such linkage in the present international setting. This greater emphasis was consistent with Chinese calls, following the Afghan events, for closer international "unity" and cooperation against the Soviet Union, and it seemed to have gained particular impetus from the 5-13 January visit to China of Secretary of Defense Brown. Chinese media during the visit had noted with favor the remarks by Carter administration officials that Washington had dropped its evenhanded approach to its relations with Beijing and Moscow in the wake of the Afghanistan incident. Instances of a stronger linkage between Sino-American bilateral and strategic relationships included the following:

- *Xinhua*'s 24 January report on Vice-Premier Deng Xiaoping's comments to U.S. delegates to the first session of the Sino-American joint commission on scientific and technological cooperation cited Deng's denunciation of the Soviet intervention in Afghanistan. According to the *Xinhua* report, Deng stressed the need, under such tense international circumstances to "unite and deal seriously with Soviet hegemonism," and added that "such unity should be concrete in content" and based on "solid work." In that respect, Deng observed, the six scientific and technical cooperation agreements signed during the joint commission's sessions were "a very good thing."[17]

- *Xinhua*'s 24 January report on final congressional approval of most-favored-nation trading status for the PRC noted that many members of Congress supported the measure as a "significant movement forward" in the interests not only of both countries but also of "stability and peace in the world." Beijing in the past had stressed the urgency of such preferential trading status to the development of Sino-American bilateral relations, but PRC media had not previously suggested that the issue was of strategic importance. Beijing seemed to be drawing tacit satisfaction from Washington's shift away from evenhanded treatment of China and the Soviet Union when the 24 January *Xinhua* report on the congressional passage noted that Senator Henry Jackson and Congressman Charles Vanik—leading opponents of granting most-favored-nation tariff status to the USSR—had favored giving such status to China.[18]

In the area of Sino-American military cooperation—a topic with extremely sensitive strategic connotations for the Chinese and their defensive posture against the expanding force of the USSR—Beijing media avoided comment on the Pentagon's announced readiness to sell defensive military equipment to China. *Xinhua* reported the Pentagon's announcement neutrally in a brief dispatch on 25 January.[19]

SINO-SOVIET RELATIONS

Consistent with Deng Xiaoping's claim to U.S. Secretary of Defense Harold Brown that the USSR would never change its policy of hegemonism,[20] Beijing reverted to a tough anti-Soviet public posture and suspended vice-ministerial talks with the USSR on 20 January. Its effort to dismiss any notion of the possibility of a Sino-Soviet rapprochement under existing circumstances was taken to the highest level, with unusual publicity being given to anti-Soviet statements made by top PRC leaders:

- On 17 April 1980, *Xinhua* reported CCP Vice-Chairman Deng Xiaoping's press conference statement, after receiving Italian Communist Party delegates led by Secretary-General Berlinguer, to the effect that Moscow's stationing of "one million troops" along China's borders and its "troublemaking" in Indochina constituted a "serious threat" to China.[21]

- On 21 April, *Xinhua* reported CCP Chairman and Premier Hua Guofeng reiterating Deng's statements to the Japanese press corps in Beijing, and he added that "so long as Soviet hegemonist policy remains unchanged, Sino-Soviet relations will not improve."[22]

- On 30 April, *Xinhua* reported Hua's comments to a Japanese visitor that Beijing would "not change its position of opposing hegemonism" as long as Moscow did not change its policies.[23]

Regarding Chinese ideological differences with Moscow, *Xinhua* similarly cited leadership statements to make it clear that Beijing saw no potential at present for a restoration of party ties with the CPSU:

- On 15 April, *Xinhua* cited General Secretary Hu Yaobang's statement to the Italian press corps accompanying Berlinguer that a resumption of CCP-CPSU ties was out of the question.[24]

- On 22 April, the PRC Foreign Friendship Association leader, Wang Bingnan, according to *Xinhua*, stated at a reception marking the 110th anniversary of Lenin's birth that China would "intensify the struggle" against the "Brezhnev clique," which "completely betrayed Leninism."[25]

- On 5 May, *Xinhua* cited Deng Xiaoping's comment to a visiting African leader that the USSR was "not a socialist country but a social-imperialist country."[26]

In addition to going out of its way to publicize anti-Soviet statements by authoritative leaders, *Xinhua* reported a rally on 30 April in Xinjiang protesting an incident that had occurred along the border with the Soviet Union there the previous year and had been protested by Beijing at that time.[27] The characterization of the incident and its consequences in *Xinhua*'s report of the new "accusation rally" were identical to those in its report of a PRC Foreign Ministry note and of a protest rally in Xinjiang over the incident the previous summer. *Xinhua* gave no reason for the new publicity for the incident, except to note that a veterinarian captured during the clash in 1979 had been returned by the Soviet Union in February 1980, "only after repeated negotiations and struggle by our government."

Indeed, the return of the veterinarian had been part of Soviet attempts to probe for a opening in China's tough stance:

- On 14 February 1980—the 30th anniversary of the signing of the Sino-Soviet alliance—the Soviets had released the Chinese veterinarian captured during the border incident the previous summer.

- On 20-28 March, the Soviet Foreign Ministry's chief China specialist, Mikhail Kapitsa, made the first of three annual visits to China as the guest of the Soviet embassy.

- On 7 April, an authoritative *Pravda* article called on China to reopen talks on Sino-Soviet border issues or on improving Sino-Soviet relations.[28]

Beijing strongly rebuffed the Soviet overtures for improved relations, citing Sino-Soviet differences over Vietnam, Afghanistan, Mongolia, and the Sino-Soviet border. In addition to strongly worded anti-Soviet statements by Chinese leaders, PRC intentions were made clear by incidents later in the year:

- On 21 July, three people accused of spying for the USSR were publicly sentenced in China.[29]

- On 25 August, Beijing protested the alleged Soviet harassment of Chinese diplomats in the USSR.[30]

- In October, an incident was noted along the Soviet border with Inner Mongolia.[31]

BROADER ANTI-SOVIET EFFORTS

China's broader international posture also focused on the need to foster resistance to Soviet expansion—in Europe, Japan, and the third world.

The Chinese nonetheless remained carefully circumscribed in committing themselves to direct support for the Afghan resistance or even for their close ally, Pakistani, presumably out of concern over prompting adverse Soviet military reaction. At the same time, Beijing increased its interest in improving its influence in the third world states important in the Afghan context, notably India.

Beijing cautiously attempted to adjust its bilateral ties with South Asian states during a trip to Pakistan by Foreign Minister Huang Hua on 18-23 January 1980.[32] Chinese media coverage of the visit was unusually muted, and statements of unilateral Chinese support for Pakistan and for Afghan resistance to Soviet occupation were cautiously subordinated to a call for wider international assistance. Beijing also went to unusual lengths to induce improved relations with India's newly installed government under Indira Gandhi, a leader whom China in the past had criticized for tilting India toward the Soviet Union.

Huang's reticence was in part designed to avoid offending Pakistani sensitivities in the current situation. Thus, although he pointedly remarked upon his arrival that his long-planned visit to Pakistan had taken on "new significance" because of "recent developments in Afghanistan," his public statements of support for Pakistan were relatively guarded and *Xinhua* coverage of the visit was unusually terse. *Xinhua* departed from normal practice, for example, by reporting none of the banquet toasts during the visit; and its report on the foreign minister's talks with Pakistan's President Zia stated only that the two leaders had discussed "the development of the regional situation" and had "exchanged views on further strengthening cooperation" between the two countries. In a press conference on 22 January, Huang, according to *Xinhua*, added that both sides had agreed to "continue their consultations" and would take "some follow-up actions" to "increase their cooperation."

The only substantive declaration of Chinese support for Pakistan came in *Xinhua*'s account of Huang's press conference at the end of his visit, which noted that the foreign minister had "reaffirmed" that "the Chinese Government and people firmly stand by the Pakistani people in standing up to the external threat." Even here, however, *Xinhua* seemed to play down the PRC commitment by quoting Huang's statement that the West European countries, Japan, and the United States "should offer genuine assistance to Pakistan and all other countries that are faced with threat and aggression," assistance that "should be commensurate with the present developments" and "should not be symbolic or temporary out of expedient considerations."[33]

On 20 January 1980, Huang Hua visited an Afghan refugee camp, where he declared that "the Afghan people are not isolated in their struggle" and that "the Chinese people will do what they can to help relieve your suffering."[34] However, the *Xinhua* accounts of his remarks implied that Chinese assistance to the Afghan cause was limited to humanitarian relief supplies sent directly to the refugee camps within Pakistan. Huang's suggestion at his 22 January press conference that "timely, adequate, and effective assistance should be given to the Afghan people and their resistance movement," moreover, appeared to be tied to the kind of assistance that he thought the West European countries, Japan, and the United States should provide.

While thus voicing support for the Afghan resistance effort and regularly reporting Soviet difficulties in suppressing the rebellion, Beijing showed sensitivity to Soviet charges of direct Chinese military support to the rebels. In a rebuttal of such "fabrications," a 25 January *Xinhua* correspondent's commentary claimed that Moscow was attempting to divert world opinion from its worsening predicament and to provide new excuses for perpetuating its occupation of Afghanistan.[35]

In an apparently related effort to stem what it saw as growing Soviet influence in South Asia, Beijing went to unusual lengths to cultivate good relations with the new government in India and took favorable note of India's belated criticism of the Soviet intervention in Afghanistan. In sharp contrast with its comment on Gandhi's election defeat in March 1977, which protrayed her regime as unpopular, dictatorial, corrupt, and pro-Soviet, Chinese media reported her return to power in January 1980 without criticism; and on 14 January, *Xinhua* carried a political profile of her that failed to mention any of the excesses that Beijing had attributed to her previous administration. Significantly, Premier Hua Guofeng's 15 January 1980 message to Gandhi on her election expressed the hope that the trend in improved Sino-Indian relations "will continue to develop in the interest of peace and stability in Asia," and was notably more enthusiastic than Hua's comparable March 1977 message to Morarji Desai, who had gained the prime minister post upon Gandhi's ouster.[36]

Beijing's conciliatory approach was also demonstrated by Huang Hua's attendance at the Indian embassy's 26 January banquet marking Indian's 30th National Day and the extensive coverage the *Xinhua* account gave to remarks by Huang and the Indian ambassador on their mutual commitment to improving Sino-Indian ties.[37] Huang was the highest-ranking Chinese leader to have attended the embassy's National Day celebrations since Vice-Premier and Foreign Minister Chen Yi attended such a banquet in 1961, prior to the deterioration in relations accompanying China's 1962 military strike into India. A Chinese vice-foreign minister had headed the Chinese delegation in 1979; and although an improvement in Sino-Indian relations was signaled with the long-delayed visit of Indian Foreign Minister Vajpayee to Beijing in

February 1979, relations were immediately soured by China's incursion into Vietnam while Vajpayee was still in China.

Beijing showed concern when the Gandhi government initially wavered on opposition to the Soviet invasion of Afghanistan at the U.N. General Assembly's special session on the issue earlier in January 1980. But Chinese media repeatedly presented subsequent official Indian criticism of the Soviet action, beginning with *Xinhua*'s 17 January report of Gandhi's denial that India supported the Soviet move. *Xinhua* had earlier called the Indian representative's remarks at the 11 January U.N. General Assembly session defending the Soviet action an "odd approach" to the invasion, and promptly and favorably reported the U.S. State Department's 12 January criticism of India's position. On 14 January, *Xinhua* noted reports of criticism of the stance by Indian opposition leaders.[38]

China was also prompt in rebutting what it claimed were Soviet efforts to foment Indian fears of renewed Chinese attacks against India. *People's Daily* in a 22 January commentary responded to an 18 January *Tass* claim that China was massing military forces on India's northern border to "mount an attack at any time," calling the report "clumsy rumor mongering" designed to divert attention from Afghanistan.

Despite all these efforts, however, Beijing's initial overtures to Prime Minister Gandhi were rebuffed, and a temporary downturn in relations was seen in a 1 March *People's Daily* commentary that denounced as "slander" statements made by Gandhi on 21 February that the PRC had occupied portions of Indian, Bhutanese, Nepalese, and Burmese territory, and "poses a danger" to the Indian border.[39] Her comments, the paper charged, were intended to "hinder a reasonable solution" to the Sino-Indian border issue and to "sow discord" between China and its South Asian neighbors. After flatly blaming India for precipitating the Sino-Indian border dispute in the 1950s and 1960s, the commentary recalled that the newly elected Indian government had expressed a desire to raise "all questions," including the border issue, in seeking improved Sino-Indian relations, a "gesture" that China "welcomes." Such an effort, the commentary suggested, was impaired by "unfriendly statements and actions."

The steady, heavy drumbeat of China's anti-Soviet exhortations—focused on the Afghanistan issue—was seen throughout the rest of the year during high-level Chinese exchanges with the United States, Japan, and Western Europe. Chinese commentary on international consideration of the Kampuchean issue also underlined stern anti-Soviet, anti-Vietnamese themes. Chinese Vice-Premier Geng Biao made an unusually strong call during a welcoming banquet for him in Washington on 27 May for a more effective U.S. response to Soviet aggression and expansion. He stressed that the Soviets and Soviet-backed Vietnamese had taken aggressive action in Southwest and Southeast Asia that were not problems of regional defense but "issues that concern the entire situation of global struggle and actions of a long-premeditated strategic offensive." Geng maintained that Moscow and Hanoi presented a "strategic challenge" that required "a strategic response." He concluded emphatically:

> Now is the time for us to make a decision—a correct choice between two alternatives: to persist in and step up our struggle or to weaken and give up our struggle. Failure to make the decision now would leave no time for future choice. It would mean either surrender or war.[40]

PRC Premier Hua Guofeng used a May-June 1980 visit to Japan to focus on the importance of close Sino-Japanese collaboration in foreign affairs and economic development, particularly in the wake of the Soviet intervention in Afghanistan. While Beijing had traditionally maintained that the growth of Sino-Japanese friendship played an important role in world affairs, Chinese comment on Hua's visit went to unusual lengths to emphasize the increasing congruence of long-term Chinese and Japanese international and economic needs in the context of a rapidly changing Asian situation, particularly following the Soviet intervention in Afghanistan.

A *Xinhua* correspondent's report on 3 June, summarizing the results of the visit, concluded that "the tension in the world exacerbated by the Soviet invasion of Afghanistan" had made closer Sino-Japanese cooperation "the need of the times." The correspondent went on to observe that Moscow's actions and Vietnam's "expansion in Southeast Asia" threatened Japan "not only militarily but also economically by the possible disruption of oil supplies and its traditional markets in Southeast Asia." Recalling that Hua had raised the possibility during Prime Minister Ohira's visit to China in 1979 that the USSR might threaten Japanese interests by seeking control of oil routes in the Middle East, the *Xinhua* correspondent noted that "this time"—in the wake of the Soviet Afghan intervention—Hua and Ohira "reached basic agreement on the current international situation." In such a context, *Xinhua* added, China could do much to alleviate Japan's energy concerns, with Japanese financial and technical help to tap Chinese coal resources.[41]

Chinese comment on Western Europe reflected concerns about the need for continued unity, both among the European governments themselves, and with the United States in NATO, against Soviet expansion. It focused on France's independent foreign policy and its ambivalent treatment of the Soviet invasion of Afghanistan. Chinese reporting on

French President Giscard's meeting with Soviet President Brezhnev in May 1980 reflected Beijing's dismay over what China perceived to be a major rift in the unanimity of the West European reaction to the Soviet intervention in Afghanistan. Subsequently, Chinese commentary praised Giscard's and West German Chancellor Helmut Schmidt's call, following their meeting at Bonn in July, for a "powerful and independent Europe" in the face of relentless Soviet pressure. At the same time, however, it betrayed Chinese anxieties that the call might harm West European strategic cooperation with the United States.[42]

Meanwhile, in Southeast Asia, the Chinese directly linked the Kampuchean issue with the Afghan question as crucial to a successful international resistance to the USSR. They issued strident warnings against any weakening or compromise in the face of Soviet intimidation and placed thinly disguised pressure on those, including some in ASEAN, that appeared willing to seek a middle ground over Indochina.[43]

Beijing's concern that the issue of Vietnamese troop withdrawal remain foremost was made clear in its reaction to the ASEAN proposal, tabled at the United Nations, for an international meeting on Kampuchea in 1981. Beijing's first comment on the proposal came in a 15 September *Xinhua* account of talks between Premier Zhao Ziyang and Kenyan President Daniel Arap Moi.[44] *Xinhua* reported Zhao as saying, in a statement consistent with PRC views on similar past proposals, that China was not opposed to convening such a meeting but that its purpose must be to carry out the 34th General Assembly resolution on Vietnamese troop withdrawal. He said that a meeting would be meaningless if Vietnam had no intention of withdrawing its troops, and he insisted that, as a token of sincerity, Vietnam must begin removing troops before any meeting began. Moreover, he said, the meeting should first set a time limit for the withdrawal of all troops, provide for supervision of the withdrawal, and adopt "feasible measures" to ensure Kampuchea's self-determination without foreign interference.

While attempting to maintain close solidarity against Vietnam, Beijing subsequently appeared to be throwing cold water on efforts by ASEAN to promote a political solution to the Kampuchean question. Beijing tactfully but firmly deflected suggestions made during the China visit of Thai Prime Minister Prem Tinsulanon in October 1980 and Singapore Prime Minister Lee Kwan Yew in November 1980 that the Democratic Kampuchean regime be discarded as the focus of anti-Vietnamese resistance in favor of a more palatable alternative.[45] Chinese statements during the visits reflected Beijing's continuing ambivalence toward the convening of an international conference on Kampuchea, as called for in the U.N. resolution on the Kampuchean problem.

NOTES

1. See, for example, Kenneth Lieberthal's article in Harry Harding, ed., *China's Foreign Relations in the 1980s* (New Haven: Yale University Press, 1984).

2. See Carol Hamrin's article in U.S. Congress, Joint Economic Committee, *The Chinese Economy in the 1980s* (Washington: USGPO, 1985).

3. See *DR China*, 31 December 1979 and 2 January 1980.

4. For useful background, see *FBIS Trends*, 4 January 1980.

5. See *DR China*, 3 January 1980.

6. Ibid.

7. See analysis in *FBIS Trends*, 4 January 1980.

8. For an insightful assessment of the visit and later U.S.-Chinese consultation on security matters, see Jonathan Pollack, *The Lessons of Coalition Politics* (Santa Monica, Calif.: Rand Corp., 1984).

9. See analysis in *FBIS Trends*, 16 January 1980.

10. For Chinese media coverage of the visit, see *DR China*, 7–11 January 1980.

11. Despite *Xinhua's* efforts to correct its translation of the passage, it was possible that the insertion of the term "alliance" in the original English-language report was deliberate. That it was simply an error seemed unlikely, in view of the care Beijing always took in discussing strategic relationships with other countries, and the fact that Deng's formula was well known and unambiguous. Beijing was not known ever to have proposed an "alliance" against hegemonism, although until 1979 it regularly called for the formation of an "international antihegemony united front" directed against the Soviet Union. Beijing had, in fact, taken particular care to indicate that its strategic relationships with other countries were not alliances. In his press conference on the normalization of U.S.–Chinese relations in December 1978, for example, Hua Guofeng insisted that China's newly normalized relations with Tokyo and Washington did not constitute the formation of an alliance. See *FBIS Trends*, 16 January 1980.

12. For useful background, see *FBIS Trends*, 30 January 1980.

13. See *DR China*, 31 January 1980.

14. Earlier comment on the president's address had been favorable. An initial 23 January *Xinhua* report on the address had highlighted his commitment to defend the Persian Gulf area against threat of foreign control, and a brief *People's Daily* commentary on the 25th observed that the president had departed from the normal precedence of domestic affairs over foreign affairs to concentrate heavily on "how the United States will deal with the grave Soviet challenges in the 1980s." Noted in *FBIS Trends*, 30 January 1980.

15. See *DR China*, 5 and 12 October 1979.

16. See *FBIS Trends*, 30 January 1980.

17. *DR China*, 24 January 1980.

18. *DR China*, 25 January 1980.

19. *DR China*, 28 January 1980.

20. *DR China*, 8 January 1980.

21. *DR China*, 17 April 1980.

22. *DR China*, 22 April 1980.

23. *DR China*, 1 May 1980.

24. *DR China*, 15 April 1980.

25. Cited in *FBIS Trends*, 7 May 1980.

26. *DR China*, 6 May 1980.

27. See *DR China*, 24 July 1979 and 2 May 1980.

28. For background on the Soviet moves, see William E. Griffith, "Sino-Soviet Rapprochement," *Problems Of Communism*, March–April 1983, especially the article by Mikhail

Kapitsa and Oleg Rakmanin noted there. See also the articles by "Professor Yurkov" in *DR USSR*, 3, 4, and 10 March 1982; Donald Zagoria, "Moscow-Beijing Detente," *Foreign Affairs*, Spring 1983; and Jonathan Pollack, *The Sino-Soviet Rivalry and Chinese Security Debate* (Santa Monica, Calif.: Rand Corp., 1982).

29. *DR China*, 21 July 1980.

30. *DR China*, 29 August 1980.

31. *DR China*, 6 October 1980.

32. See, in particular, *DR China*, 21 and 23 January 1980.

33. In contrast, when Pakistan was facing Indian-abetted dismemberment in late 1971, Beijing was markedly less restrained in its pledge of unilateral support. At an early November banquet in Beijing for a visiting Pakistani delegation led by People's Party Chairman Zulfiqar Ali Bhutto, acting PRC Foreign Minister Ji Pengfei voiced the Chinese government's and people's "resolute support" for Pakistan's "just struggle," and highlighted joint Sino-Pakistani cooperation without focusing on the need to mobilize international support. This direct support was reiterated by other Chinese leaders when Indian troops moved into East Pakistan later in November, and was given substance in a December government statement that declared that China was providing "material assistance" as well as political support to the Pakistanis. See *FBIS Trends*, 30 January 1980.

34. *DR China*, 21 January 1980.

35. Noted in *FBIS Trends*, 30 January 1980.

36. Ibid.

37. See *DR China*, 28 January 1980.

38. See assessment in *FBIS Trends*, 30 January 1980.

39. *DR China*, 3 March 1980.

40. *DR China*, 28 May 1980.

41. *DR China*, 4 June 1980.

42. Beijing concerns over the implications of France's independent defense policies were raised pointedly in a *Xinhua* article on 14 October 1980, the day before Giscard arrived in China for an official visit. The report praised at length several French steps to improve its national defense in the context of the "menace of Soviet expansionism," but also cited Paris' conclusion that French security is directly related to its neighbors' and that therefore France must pursue its "independent defense" together with efforts to strengthen cooperation with its allies in NATO. See *FBIS Trends*, 29 October 1980.

43. Chinese concerns were seen in a series of *People's Daily* articles prior to the U.N. General Assembly debate on Kampuchea in September 1980. The articles denounced USSR-Vietnam efforts to legitimize the Vietnamese occupation of Kampuchea and stressed that U.N. actions, particularly the credentials fight over the seating of a Kampuchean representative, must be viewed as strategic efforts to contain Soviet and Vietnamese aggression.

Three articles by the *People's Daily* "Commentator" stressed the larger strategic significance of the Kampuchean issue by portraying recent Soviet and Vietnamese military and diplomatic moves in the area as "naked coercion" of Thailand and other ASEAN countries to accept as a "fait accompli" the Vietnamese occupation of Kampuchea through the "puppet" Heng Samrin regime. In Commentator's domino theory, this would have completed the first step in Hanoi's efforts to create an "empire" throughout Southeast Asia, using the Kampuchean "model"—a model also useful to the USSR in South Asia. Specifically, Commentator argued, Vietnam was increasing its military forces along the Thai border—backed by Soviet advisers and equipment—and was threatening an invasion while making duplicitous offers to negotiate for peace in order to secure ASEAN agreement to talks with the Heng Samrin regime and to deflect attention from the real issue—the withdrawal of Vietnamese forces from Kampuchea. The 13 September Commentator article claimed that 7–12 September talks between Soviet and Vietnamese foreign ministers had launched a new "double barreled" military and diplomatic offensive against ASEAN, and that the USSR and Vietnam were determined to create "still greater chaos and instability in this area."

Commentator charged on 24 September that the Vietnamese offer to renew talks with the PRC was a similar ploy to mask its military operations in the Thai-Kampuchean border areas and distract attention from its occupation of Kampuchea. The previous day's PRC Foreign Ministry note rejecting the Vietnamese request, Commentator said, constituted a "merciless exposure" of the Vietnamese "propaganda stunt in anticipation of what will happen at the current session of the U.N. General Assembly session." The 13 and 24 September Commentator articles both stressed that the only solution to the Kampuchean problem would come through the withdrawal of Vietnamese forces from Kampuchea in accordance with the 1979 U.N. General Assembly resolution. See review in *FBIS Trends*, 24 September 1980.

44. *DR China*, 16 September 1980.

45. See *DR China*, 27 and 28 October 1980, 12 November 1980.

8

DEVELOPING AN INDEPENDENT FOREIGN POLICY, 1981-83

Chinese leaders continued to work hard to foster a strong international front against the USSR through early 1981. For instance, during the height of the crisis in Poland in early 1981, Chinese leaders and media commentary took a firm stance against armed Soviet intervention in Poland and underscored the importance of the Beijing-Washington relationship in that context. PRC leaders used the Polish developments to reemphasize that oppositon to Soviet hegemonism must be global, not isolated by region, and that the United States, Western Europe, and Asian countries must unite to contain the USSR.

While endorsing a strong Western stance against Soviet interference in Poland, Beijing revealed some concern that the spotlight on Poland might blind the West to examples of Soviet and Soviet-backed interference in areas closer to China. *Xinhua* reports on Chinese discussions with Western leaders indicated that the Chinese officials emphasized that Poland must be viewed as only one part of a worldwide Soviet drive to achieve hegemony, which must be opposed on all fronts through increased strategic cooperation. In a meeting with British Foreign Minister Lord Carrington on 3 April 1981, Deng Xiaoping cautioned that the Afghan and Kampuchean problems "should not be overshadowed by the problems of Poland, the Middle East and the Iran-Iraq war."[1] Zhao Ziyang continued this line of reasoning during his talks with Swedish Prime Minister Thorbjoern Faelldin. According to *Xinhua*, Zhao said on 7 April that "the Soviet strategic cockpit remains in Europe, but it mainly employs out-flanking tactics"—some involving third world areas around China. In talks the following day, Zhao maintained that "regional peace is inseparable from global peace" and that the Kampuchean issue was "not a regional question."[2] He stressed in these conversations and in an interview with Japanese newsmen at this time that the Soviet Union was intensifying its aggression and expansion on a global scale, and that Asian and Pacific countries, the United States, and Western Europe must unite in a "joint effort" to contain the USSR.[3]

Nevertheless, as the year wore on, China's public anti-Soviet effort flagged. Altered international and domestic circumstances complicated Deng Xiaoping's preferred anti-Soviet, pro-Western orientation. The changed circumstances included the challenge that the new Reagan Administration, with its strong commitment to Taiwan, posed to China's understanding of the normalization agreement with the United States; domestic economic and political problems that slowed reform efforts in these areas, reduced Deng Xiaoping's prestige, and curbed for a time Chinese interest in closer ties with the West; and renewed Soviet efforts to initiate a dialogue and possible improvement of relations with China.

These shifts came against a backdrop of growing Chinese assurance concerning the international balance of forces that had developed in the wake of the Soviet invasion of Afghanistan. For the first time in almost a decade, Beijing saw an international balance evolving that was likely at least temporarily to hold the threat of Soviet expansion at bay. Moscow's ability to use military power to extend its influence was also seen as sapped by growing economic, political, and military problems the Soviet leaders faced both at home and abroad.[4]

China adjusted its foreign approach tactically to accord better with these altered circumstances. It moved to an international posture more independent of the United States, closer to the developing countries of the third world, and less hostile to the USSR. In many respects, China's new tactics represented a logical follow-on to the policy initiatives undertaken in 1979 but put aside in favor of a stronger anti-Soviet, pro-Western approach in the immediate aftermath of the Soviet invasion of Afghanistan.

While the underpinning of China's foreign policy remained the search for a stable environment in Asia, it was uncertain, as PRC policy evolved in 1981-83, whether Beijing judged it could achieve such stability with a foreign posture truly independent of the United States and the West, and substantially less hostile to the USSR, or whether Beijing at some point would have to halt and reverse its pullback from the United States for fear of jeopardizing this link so important for maintaining China's security and development interests in the face of persistent Soviet pressure in Asia. China chose the latter course by early 1983. It began retreating from some of the tactical adjustments seen in the previous two years, notably seeking to patch up Chinese relations with the Reagan administration.

DOMESTIC DIFFICULTIES

The economic and political problems that appeared to provide new incentives for tactical adjustment in Chinese foreign policy by 1981 came against a background of domestic developments throughout most of 1980 that showed increasing momentum for reformers led by Deng Xiaoping. A new milestone was reached at the Fifth Plenum of the 11th CCP Central Committee, held at Beijing in February 1980.[5] The meeting focused on reforming party leadership to facilitate modernization and substantially changing central leadership institutions in order to ensure longer-term continuity and implementation of practical modernization policies. The plenum removed several high-level critics of reform policies; elevated to high positions younger leaders, many of whom were closely associated with Deng Xiaoping; and restored the party Secretariat to high status in the implementation of policy.

The plenum's decisions on the central leadership and organization appeared to be intended to inspire similar organizational streamlining at lower levels of the party. Other plenum actions—including its long-awaited rehabilitation of the Cultural Revolution's primary target, former chief of state Liu Shaoqi—similarly lent impetus to partywide reform and rectification. The plenum's militant communiqué amounted to a call to political battle against persisting resistance to leadership reform and modernization policies.

Later that year, Hua Guofeng was reduced in status when he gave up the premiership to the governor of Sichuan, Zhao Ziyang, a protegé of Deng and a prime advocate of economic and political reforms. Administrative and economic changes in line with Zhao's experience in Sichuan were promoted throughout China. The long-awaited trials of the Gang of Four began at Beijing in November and tended to further discredit Hua Guofeng and leaders like him who had supported Maoist policies in the Cultural Revolution and were resisting sweeping political changes and practical economic reforms.[6]

At the turn of 1980-81, however, developments started working against the reformers. Signs of apparent growing political dissidence—such as direct challenges to the leadership of the CCP, the outbreak of disturbances in several cities, anti-party politicking, bombings, strikes, and school boycotts—combined with major economic dislocations, requiring new decisions to scale down Chinese economic reform and to reassert administrative control over the economic readjustment begun in early 1979. Together, these developments stalled those in the Chinese leadership who were pressing for more political change, raised additional problems for reform-minded officials led by Deng Xiaoping, and reduced for a brief time China's economic incentive for closer involvement with the West. When combined with Beijing's more sanguine view of the Asian balance, strong opposition to Reagan administration pronouncements on Taiwan, and keen interest in exploring options with a Soviet leadership in the midst of political succession, these domestic difficulties acted to undermine support for the strongly pro-U.S., anti-Soviet posture preferred by Deng Xiaoping. At least because he wished to avoid a possibly serious confrontation over Chinese foreign policy at a time when he already faced problems on economic and political issues, Deng gave ground and the center of the Chinese leadership consensus moved toward a more balanced public posture between the superpowers.[7]

The economic problems stemmed in many respects from the increased use of innovative economic reforms—many employed on an experimental basis—throughout 1979 and 1980. Collectively, they involved a package of sweeping economic changes that could have been called China's version of Lenin's New Economic Program, adopted in the 1920s in the USSR. Problems with the economy, however, continued to plague the PRC leadership:

- Import demand generated by the original ten-year plan grew, pushing the foreign trade deficit to slightly more than $1 billion in 1979 and to almost $2 billion in 1980. (These were small by most international standards but were seen as extraordinarily and dangerously large by autarky-minded Chinese leaders.)

- Relaxation of restrictions on personal travel led many youth previously sent to the countryside to rejoin their families in the cities, pushing the number of urban unemployed to more than 20 million.

- A budget deficit of over $10 billion in 1979 led to a substantial increase in the money supply and serious inflationary pressure.[8]

By late 1980, Chinese leaders acknowledged that the new economic policies—while successful in many ways—had led to such negative consequences as budget deficits, inflation, foreign trade deficits, declining growth rates, persisting large pockets of poverty in rural areas, and more urban unemployment. It was also said that the goal of putting the economy back on the track of self-sustained growth in three years would require an additional two years.

During 1981 it was learned that there was an absolute decline in some critically needed commodities, notably energy. The planned budget deficit for 1980 was exceeded by 50 percent, leading to further overdrafts from the central bank, an increase in currency in circulation, and persistent inflation.

Beijing did not publicize any of the speeches made by top party leaders at a December 1980 work conference, but on 1 February 1981 the usually reliable left-wing Hong Kong journal *Cheng Ming* summarized the main points of speeches reportedly delivered by Deng Xiaoping, Zhao Ziyang, and CCP Vice-Chairmen Chen Yun and Li Xiannian. The views *Cheng Ming* attributed to Chen Yun, relating almost entirely to economic matters, were reflected in authoritative Beijing press comment on economic readjustment since early December 1980. The political views the journal ascribed to Deng set a pattern for authoritative Chinese comment on the political situation in China at the turn of that year.[9]

Deng's speech underscored evident concern over political disorders and other challenges to party leadership seen in editorials published on 17 January and 8 February in the *People's Daily*. The January editorial, "Political Stability Is the Guarantee of Economic Readjustment," carried forward a line introduced in a 5 December 1980 editorial on political work. It cautioned that there are "many factors of instability" that, if not dealt with, could prevent successful economic readjustment, hamper the "four modernizations," and slow political reforms. The editorial identified factors making for instability at both ends of the political spectrum. On the one hand, it hinted that right-wing elements had pressed for drastic curtailment of the party's leading role; *People's Daily* stated that leadership of the party was stipulated in the constitution, and "whoever wants to change it is on a very dangerous road." On the other hand, the editorial denounced remnant leftist elements, calling it "imperative" to strike firmly at unrepentant "rebels" who "still uphold the misdeeds of Lin Biao and the 'gang of four' and . . . indulge themselves in the 'four bigs' [criticizing party leaders] and beating and smashing and looting."[10]

The 8 February *People's Daily* editorial was entitled "Democratic Reform of the State Must Be Realized Step by Step Under Conditions of Stability and Unity." In the vein of the January editorial, it expressed concern over political instability and threats to party leadership, and suggested that political reform, like economic readjustment, must be delayed while those problems persist. After reviewing in detail the reforms begun since the Third Plenum of late 1978, the editorial stated that democratization must "go through a process and cannot possibly be accomplished in one move"—reform is "a complex question" that calls for preparation, planning, and experimentation. It cautioned those pressing for rapid reform that stability and unity are "indispensable" prerequisities to "pushing forward democratization" of the state. "Turmoil," it said, "cannot promote democracy and is detrimental to the democratic reform of the state."[11]

Subsequent comment specifically addressed the issue of leadership reform. In late February, Beijing media publicized a report made a few months earlier by the permanent secretary of the party's Discipline Inspection Commission.[12] The report showed that problems of indecisiveness and vacillation, caused by leadership differences, continued to complicate decision making at all levels of the Chinese administrative structure. For example, the secretary mentioned efforts by Deng Xiaoping to "streamline" the Chinese bureaucracy. He said that even though Deng's initiatives had been widely discussed for years, they "still cannot be implemented in many places" because of cadre foot-dragging or outright opposition. He added that decisions on such sensitive issues as the rehabilitation of officials discredited during the Cultural Revolution frequently still remained in abeyance because "no one will solve problems" and "no one will assume responsibility." He called such "irresponsibility" the root cause of the "bureaucratism" that had undermined the power and prestige of China's administration in recent years.

A *People's Daily* editorial on 10 March made it clear that Deng and other reformers still did not have the power to conduct a sweeping purge of remaining leftists and other opponents in the leadership.[13] It pointedly criticized cadres who had resisted reform policies pursued since the Third Plenum, and characterized such resistance as a fundamental impediment to the "four modernizations":

> Since the third plenary session of the 11th party Central Committee, some comrades have failed to understand, even resented, the party's line, and this is the crux of the problem. Very obviously, if this problem is not solved, or not properly solved, it is impossible to correctly appraise the current situation or thoroughly understand the necessity of further economic readjustments and political stability and impossible to really uphold the four basic principles. As far as leading cadres are concerned, if they fail to thoroughly overhaul their thinking, set things right and rid themselves of the "left" things, once the climate is right, they will experience a relapse and again make the same mistakes.

The editorial went on to recall the Yanan rectification campaign of the 1940s as a model for ridding the current leadership of the "pernicious" influence of "leftist" deviation: "It was only after overcoming the 'left' mistakes that the Chinese revolution became victorious. And only after we have seriously cleared up and corrected the 'left' mistakes will our four modernizations program embark on a path of sound development."

However, instead of calling for demotions or dismissals of negligent or unsympathetic leaders, as advocated by reformers in the past, the editorial restricted itself to calling for a "study campaign" that would allow all comrades to clear up their thinking and to make self-criticisms in a "gentle" atmosphere of "sincere heart-to-heart" talks. It called on party members to unite even with officials who had made "serious mistakes" in the past. It added an implicit acknowledgment that the prevailing consensus among leaders in China would not allow the kind of major leadership changes favored by some reformers, noting that such changes would make it "very difficult to maintain and develop stability and unity" in China.

This slow, compromise approach to leadership reform was clearly in evidence after the convening of the long-delayed sixth plenary session of the 11th Central Committee, which was held in Beijing on 27-29 June 1981.[14] While Hua Guofeng was removed as party chairman, he remained a party-vice chairman. Reform-minded officials Hu Yaobang and Zhao Ziyang were appointed party chairman and vice-chairman, respectively—a major victory for Deng Xiaoping, who replaced Hua as chairman of the CCP's Military Affairs Commission. However, officials who had been thought to resist Deng's efforts to purge party ranks and to condemn Maoist excesses of the past—notably CCP Vice-Chairman Ye Jianying—retained their high party posts. They were presumably influential in determining the plenum's balanced assessment of Mao Zedong and CCP history since 1949, in contrast with the harsher censure favored by other leaders, including Deng and Hu.

On the economic front, meanwhile, the regime moved to deal with persistent problems by means of stern countermeasurers announced in 1981 to reduce the projected budget revenues and expenditures by 9 and 13 percent, respectively, and to provide a balanced budget. A large cutback in spending was to be achieved by a 45 percent reduction in the planned capital contruction target for 1981. This resulted in a sharp reduction in plans to purchase foreign industrial equipment. Additional restrictions were made in planned expenditures for national defense and government administration. It was also decided that further experimentation with economic reform should not be extended beyond those enterprises where it had already been introduced, and that a "consolidation" of experiments with these reforms was necessary.[15]

In a major government report on 1 December 1981, Premier Zhao Ziyang disclosed the following facts:

- China would need at least until the mid-1980s to complete the economic readjustments originally scheduled to end in 1982.

- The economy would not grow very fast in the current 1981-85 five-year plan period. (No specific plan for the period had been announced.)

- A 4 percent growth rate in industrial and agricultural output was targeted for 1982; this was slightly higher than the 3 percent announced for 1981.

- Heavy industrial production would fall 5 percent and light industry production would rise 12 percent in 1981.[16]

As Chinese leaders conferred repeatedly on these difficult political and economic problems—that had a major bearing on their own political standing and future leadership roles—they appear to have discussed as well important foreign policy issues. Circumstantial evidence—mainly in the form of a spate of press and journal articles on historical incidents having obvious relevance to contemporary Chinese foreign policy— suggested that tactics in relations with the United States and the Soviet Union in particular, and foreign policy in general, were also under review. As in leadership discussions that accompanied the changes in Chinese foreign policy approaches in the spring of 1979, at least some in the Beijing leadership appeared to want to pull back from the hard line against the USSR, and from close ties with the United States, that were favored by Deng Xiaoping.[17]

Some argued that China's weak domestic situation and the uncertainty of international circumstances around China dictated a more moderate foreign policy—one that would seek a degree of détente with the Soviet Union while avoiding tying China so closely to the United States as to risk greater hostility from Moscow and jeopardize Beijing's future ability to exercise sovereignty over Taiwan. Others increasingly saw an opportunity for China—posed by the USSR becoming bogged down in foreign adventures and domestic difficulties—that would allow China to distance itself from what it saw as the pro-Taiwan, heavy-handed Reagan administration policies in the third world, in favor of a policy of national independence that served to enhance Chinese interests in the third world and the international Communist movement, and appealed to Chinese nationalistic sensibilities at home. Of course, a more aloof and critical posture toward the United States could have been seen as a way of indirectly increasing Chinese leverage to press the Reagan Administration for policies more compatible with Beijing's interests regarding Taiwan and other questions. Meanwhile, the economic retrenchment meant that Chinese interest in close ties with the United States and the West flagged, at least for a time, leading to a slowdown in the growth of economic contacts that were often accompanied by Western social ideas and political institutions seen as incompatible with Chinese socialism.

Western scholars have attempted to determine who at the upper levels of the leadership would advocate changes in China's approach in foreign affairs—toward the United States and the Soviet Union in particular. Carol Hamrin and Kenneth Lieberthal have done some very useful work in this area, arguing in favor of a view that postulates strong linkages between changes in Chinese domestic reforms and foreign policy—seeing the two sides as closely related in domestic-foreign "policy packages" favored by competing leadership groups in China.[18] Put simply, the argument holds that Deng's domestic economic and political reforms and his pro-Western, anti-Soviet posture were mutually reinforcing parts of one policy package that was opposed by more conservative leaders who favored different approaches in both domestic and foreign affairs.

Despite its utility, however, this line of analysis has a few difficulties in helping us understand the basic determinants of Chinese foreign policy. For one thing, the evidence for serious debate over foreign policy in the Chinese leadership remains thin—mainly confined to circumstantial evidence, often ambiguous remarks by Chinese officials, and the allegorical articles. For another, the sharp distinctions postulated in competing "policy packages" have not been able to be played out fully. In particular, the strategic reality of China's relatively weak and vulnerable position in Asia has not allowed those conservative leaders—if they exist— to carry out a foreign policy that does not focus on dealing primarily with Soviet pressure through reliance on an international balance of power heavily influenced by the United States. Moreover, China's recent development strategy has made it very difficult for Beijing to turn away from the West in favor of reliance on a development model of autarky or on interchange with the socialist community and the third world. As a result, the distinctions seen in the Chinse leadership over possible desirable changes in foreign policies have amounted to little more than tactical shifts in China's ongoing effort to secure its unsteady environment and to get on with the main task of development, by means of a foreign policy focused on fostering international opposition to the USSR and cooperation with the United States and the West.

SINO-AMERICAN RELATIONS

Comment by candidate and later President Ronald Reagan on China and Taiwan clearly provided a major impetus to Chinese leaders as they considered and reevaluated their approach to foreign affairs. Even though Beijing continued its strong efforts to shore up U.S. and other international support in order to resist and check Soviet power, China reacted strongly to what it saw as Reagan's "two Chinas" policy. Beijing's response also demonstrated a new sensitivity to actions by the Carter administration regarding Taiwan in late 1980:[19]

- A 14 June 1980 *People's Daily* "Commentator" article bristled at candidate Reagan's call for a resumption of official ties with Taiwan. This marked the first time Beijing had used an authoritative press commentary to express dissatisfaction with any aspect of U.S.-Chinese relations in over ten years.[20]

- A week later, Beijing registered new sensitivity to U.S. arms transfers to Taiwan in a 20 June *Xinhua* "Commentator" article that called on Washington to "stop forthwith" its arms sales to Taiwan. This represented a sharp contrast with Beijing's virtual public silence on this issue in the year and a half since the normalization of U.S.-Chinese relations.[21]

- A 28 August *People's Daily* "Commentator" article, issued in the wake of vice-presidential candidate George Bush's visit to China and the release of candidate Reagan's formal statement on China policy earlier in the month, warned of "grave retrogression" in U.S.-Chinese relations if such a policy—based on the U.S. Taiwan Relations Act—were implemented. The article suggested that a pro-Taiwan policy would make impossible Sino-American cooperation in the "struggle against hegemonism," and would reduce candidate Reagan's pledge to cooperate with all countries against Soviet aggression to nothing but "empty talk."[22]

- On 15 October, China officially protested an agreement on diplomatic immunity between organizations coordinating U.S.-Taiwan relations, accusing the Carter administration for the first time of breaking commitments made in normalizing U.S.-China relations. The fact that the administration cited the Taiwan Relations Act to justify the agreement apparently was a major factor in Beijing's judgment that the administration's adherence to the normalization agreement was in doubt and that a formal representation over this comparatively small matter was needed.[23]

Both the Reagan administration and China attempted to ease differences as they prepared for Secretary of State Alexander Haig's visit to China in June 1981—the first high-level contact between China and the newly installed American administration. China remained wary of U.S. intentions, however. Overall, Chinese media coverage suggested that the secretary was received correctly but with less warmth than the last such U.S. visitor, Secretary of Defense Brown of the previous administration, who had visited China in January 1980.[24]

At the welcoming banquet for Secretary Haig on 14 June, Foreign Minister Huang Hua offered a toast remarkable for its list of areas of disagreement between the two countries. Alluding unmistakably to the Taiwan issue, Huang pointedly included in the list the principles of sovereignty and noninterference that were due "mutual respect," given the past "twist and turns" in Sino-American relations. Only passing reference had been made to the principles during Secretary Brown's visit. In a remark unprecedented on such occasions in recent years, Huang referred to "quite a few differences" in policy and views, and went on to allude to specific areas in which American and Chinese policies diverged. He cited China's support for the "Arab and Palestinian peoples in their struggle against Israel's policy of aggression," for "the people of Southern Africa in their struggle for national independence," and for the "reasonable demand" of developing countries for a new international economic order.[25]

According to Xinhua, Huang Hua omitted any assessment of progress in Sino-American relations—customarily a feature of toasts welcoming high-level U.S. officials, including Secretary Brown in 1980.[26] The omission was underscored this time in Xinhua's failure to report any remarks by Vice-Chairman Deng Xiaoping to Secretary Haig regarding the significance of the Beijing-Washington relationship.[27]

Chinese media nonetheless signaled that they were reassured of U.S. intentions by Secretary Haig. A turning point appeared to have been reached on the second day of the talks. On 16 June, Xinhua reported that at the outset of Deng Xiaoping's meeting with Secretary Haig—in the presence of journalists—Deng pointedly told his guest that he was "pleased" that the talks had "proceeded very well."[28] Beijing later indicated its satisfaction with the talks when Premier Zhao accepted an invitation to visit the United States and invited President Reagan to visit China.[29]

The same day, Xinhua also approvingly cited Haig's appraisal of the visit as "unus ally productive, unusually significant, unusually successful." Huang Hua, in his closing toast that evening, emphasized a convergence of Chinese and U.S. strategic interests, and credited Secretary Haig's visit with having yielded "positive results." According to Xinhua, Huang "warmly congratulated Mr. Haig on his successful visit."[30]

But on the same day President Reagan, at a press conference in Washington, reiterated his firm support for the Taiwan Relations Act and U.S. arms sales to Taiwan, causing Beijing in a 17 June Xinhua dispatch at the end of the Haig visit to admonish "Americans in the U.S. Government" who "just after" Secretary Haig's visit to China "still advocate clinging to" the Taiwan Relations Act and continued U.S. arms sales to Taiwan. The Xinhua commentary, which was normally used to assess the results of an important visit such as that by Secretary Haig, focused almost entirely on the Taiwan question. In contrast, Xinhua's summaries of the visit of Vice-President Mondale in September 1979 and of Secretary Brown in January 1980 discussed bilateral agreements and other accomplishments of the visits, and the prospects for anti-Soviet strategic cooperation between China and the United States.[31]

After repeating Beijing's well-known views on the Taiwan Relations Act, the commentary stated that the provision in the act for sales of defensive arms to Taiwan is "tantamount to a de facto revitalization" of the " 'Mutual Defense Treaty'...which places...Taiwan under the military protection of the United States," thus "severely infringing upon China's sovereignty" and demonstrating that some "Americans in the U.S. Government...are bent on giving Taiwan international status as an independent political entity."

The commentary warned that anyone who thinks China will have to "swallow the 'bitter pill' " because it needs "American support on the question of combatting Soviet hegemonism" should remember the Sino-Soviet split. Evoking an analogy between the state of Sino-Soviet relations on the eve of the break and the current state of Sino-American relations, *Xinhua* recalled that in the late 1950s, China "waged a resolute struggle against...bullying...in order to defend the principles of independence, sovereignty, and equality, not hesitating to bear the consequences of a break," thus showing "the daring spirit of the Chinese people."

The *Xinhua* dispatch summed up by saying that the results of Secretary Haig's visit "indicate that the two countries have identical or similar views" on global strategy, and that "some progress has been achieved in their bilateral relations." It "remains our hope," the commentary concluded, "that this identity of views and the progress made in Beijing will stand the test of future actions. But in view of the incessant out-of-tune voices from Americans in the U.S. Government...we cannot but make the necessary reply."

This kind of tough language, unprecedented since the opening to the United States began in the 1970s, signaled the start of an unusually strident Chinese effort to press for changes in U.S. foreign policy, especially toward Taiwan. Over the next year and a half, Chinese leaders pushed hard for U.S. concessions on Taiwan in order to bring U.S. policy into accord with Chinese interests. They were especially insistent on the need to reduce and ultimately end U.S. arms sales to Taiwan, asserting, among other things, that Beijing would not move ahead with purchases of U.S. arms until the United States clarified its position on arms transfers to Taiwan. Chinese leaders pressed for U.S. concessions on providing better access to American markets and technology; they also made major issues out of other bilateral disputes, including alleged Chinese liability to U.S. investors for railway bonds issued by the Chinese government 75 years earlier, the propriety of American air carriers serving both Taiwan and the mainland, China's desire to join the Asian Development Bank, and the petition for political asylum in the United States by a Chinese tennis player, Hu Na.[32]

The Reagan administration took several steps that appeared to be designed to meet Chinese complaints:

- It decided in January 1982 that it would not sell Taiwan a more advanced aircraft, the F-X fighter, but would continue selling the kind it had been providing in the past.

- It sent Vice-President Bush to China in May 1982 with letters from President Reagan to Chinese leaders that formally disavowed American interest in a "one China, one Taiwan" policy.

- It entered into negotiations with the Chinese to ease differences over U.S. arms sales to Taiwan. The result was a 17 August 1982 Sino-American communiqué that placed qualitative and quantitative limits on U.S. arms sales to Taiwan.

- It took steps to liberalize U.S. technology transfers to China.[33]

From a U.S. perspective, each of these steps represented a greater U.S. concession to Chinese concerns than any previous American administration had been willing to make. The positive impact of the moves, however, was offset in Chinese eyes by continued actions and remarks by U.S. leaders, especially President Reagan, that Beijing saw as offending Chinese sensibilities, especially over Taiwan. China complained repeatedly that the United States was trying to treat China as a "card" in the American confrontation with the Soviet Union, and that the American side had relegated China to the role of "junior partner" that had no alternative but to accept American policy regarding Taiwan. At the same time, Beijing took sharper issue with U.S. foreign policy in general, especially in the third world, and with the American position on many international economic and disarmament questions.

The reasoning behind China's altered approach was far more complex than a mere reflection of its anger over the Reagan administration's policy. Even its long-standing fear of being tricked or taken advantage of by outside powers does not adequately explain the new approach.[34] The policy was clearly reinforced by China's generally more sanguine view of the international balance of power affecting its interests at this time. Viewing the immediate Soviet threat as diminished, and Soviet leaders as bogged down with a host of domestic and international problems, the Chinese saw that they now had more room for maneuver in the great power triangle, and therefore attempted to press their advantage with the United States.

By mid-1981, Chinese comment came to view Soviet expansion as at least temporarily checked by a series of international and domestic blocks. Perhaps of most importance, the United States was seen by China—for the first time in over a decade—as having a strongly anti-Soviet stance. Eventually, by mid-1982, the Chinese would see the Soviet

Union as passive in the face of U.S. initiatives in such key areas as the Middle East;[35] Beijing would then begin to revise its view of the international balance prevalent since the 1970s, when it had portrayed the USSR as the "rising" and "expanding" superpower, and the United States as the "declining" and "passive" one. The Chinese now would come to the view that a protracted stalemate was in the offing between a powerful but hobbled Soviet Union and a resurgent West led by the United States.[36]

A key implication for China in this gradually altered view of the East-West balance was that Beijing—for the first time in a decade—no longer had to be in the fore in fostering an international front with the United States against Soviet expansion. China could rest reasonably assured that the United States would play this leading role, with or without active Chinese encouragement. In contrast with its view of previous U.S. administrations, Beijing claimed to see no advocates of "appeasement" in the Reagan administration. Rather, it highlighted the rapid buildup of U.S. strength seen in such events as the unusually smooth passage—unprecedented since the 1960s—of U.S. defense budget increases larger than any before in peacetime.

As a result, Beijing—if it chose—could afford to distance itself somewhat from the United States. The incentive for such a change was provided in some measure by the Reagan administration's policies and rhetoric, especially regarding Taiwan. Other factors also came into play, however:

- Chinese leaders were aware that at least some strategists in the Reagan administration—in their strenuous efforts to build anti-Soviet support worldwide—placed special strategic importance on good U.S. relations with China against the USSR. This was a key theme in the public statements on China by Secretary of State Haig and Assistant Secretary of State John Holdridge during 1981 and 1982.[37] As a result, China almost certainly calculated that this perceived American "need" for China gave the PRC considerable leverage as it pressed for concessions on Taiwan and other issues. Thus, Beijing could use harsh criticism of the United States, along with China's new public avowals of an interest in improved relations with the USSR, to alarm these American strategists into making more concessions designed to keep China on the U.S. "side" in the American confrontation with the USSR.

- Beijing also attempted to play on political sensibilities on the China issue within the United States. Knowing that candidate Reagan had followed a long American tradition of raising the sensitive issue of China policy in the U.S. presidential campaign of 1980, Beijing realized that his opponents in the future would probably be only too glad to take political advantage of any "mishandling" by President Reagan of the U.S.-Chinese relationship. Thus, according to these calculations, the desire by the administration to avoid a public downturn in U.S.-China ties could be expected to prompt politically sensitive leaders in the administration to be more accommodating to Chinese demands and pressure for concessions.[38]

- Beijing's new, independent foreign approach, with its increased criticism of the United States, allowed China to rebuild its credentials as an independent actor in foreign affairs with important third world states, such as North Korea, and with progressive groups and parties, including the international Communist movement. It served to counter Soviet exploitation of China's previous avowed desire for a close strategic relationship with the United States to charge that Beijing had "sold out" third world and other interests for the sake of collaboration with the "imperialist" West.

- China's new stance also provided evidence to the USSR of possible Chinese interest in striking out in a more independent foreign policy direction that would allow for an easing of tensions with the USSR. This presumably would encourage the Soviet Union to moderate its stance vis-à-vis China in the interest of fostering Sino-Soviet détente.

In addition, the new Chinese foreign approach fit in with domestic priorities. China's more sober development programs by 1981 reduced, at least for a time, the role that Western technology and investment were expected to play in the nation's growth. While U.S. and other Western businesses remained important in developing selected areas of China's economy, such as energy, constraints caused by poverty and technological incompatibility reduced the importance of economic ties to the West for the time being. Moreover, Chinese leaders expressed disillusionment with U.S. willingness to open its markets to Chinese goods enough to lower the PRC trade deficit with the United States, or to allow a freer flow of U.S. advanced technology to China. Accordingly, China was less concerned that its more independent posture would alienate U.S. or other Western economic support for its modernization.

The slowdown in Chinese economic growth meant that military modernization was delayed further; the leaders continued to wait until the economy developed to a point where Beijing could afford to invest in a major upgrading of military capabilities. In the interim, military planners were compelled to rely on increasingly inadequate equipment to defend against growing Soviet power. Chinese leaders probably were reluctant to move into a closer relationship with the United States that might seriously antagonize the USSR, unless there were major offsetting benefits; and they would be open to opportunities for a political dialogue and possible accomodation with the USSR that would serve to keep Sino-Soviet friction under careful control, and perhaps even allow the Chinese to reduce defense spending and concentrate scarce resources on economic modernization.[39]

Beijing leaders also had political differences over the close alignment

with the United States and strong hostility to the USSR, with some arguing that Beijing had more to gain from a more evenhanded policy toward both superpowers that would allow China to play one against the
other. Chinese compromises on nationalistic principles in dealings with
Americans over Taiwan and other issues also were sensitive domestic
political issues.[40] The Chinese also appear to have had expectations
about U.S. policy toward Taiwan and U.S. assistance to China's modernization that were less than realistic, and repeatedly bumped up against
the reality of Reagan administation policy actions and pronouncements.
Deng Xiaoping was strongly identified with the previous close ties with
the United States, including the sensitive compromise over Taiwan in the
1978 normalization communiqué. He presumably came under criticism
for this policy at this time when his domestic economic and political programs were running into difficulty.

Since evidence strongly suggests that Deng preferred a more pro-
U.S., anti-Soviet orientation in Chinese foreign policy, one can conclude
that he was compelled to give way and join the chorus in support of
China's more independent line vis-a-vis the United States in 1981. At a
minimum, Deng adjusted his stance in order to remove this foreign
policy question as a possible focus of leadership division at a time of
strenuous efforts to alter Chinese economic and political systems prior
to the Chinese 12th Party Congress in September 1982.

CONFRONTING REAGAN ADMINISTRATION POLICIES

The major benchmarks in China's more independent and critical approach to the United States came in quick succession. Speaking at a 1 July
1981 rally celebrating the 60th anniversary of the Chinese Communist
Party, Hu Yaobang provided the highest-level public evidence that Beijing was likely to react strongly to U.S. actions judged to be inimical to
its interests regarding Taiwan. In a lengthy passage defending the CCP's
patriotic record, Hu assured the assembled top leaders that under his
leadership the party would not tolerate "any servility in thought and
deed" in the face of "hegemonist threats of force" and in relations
"with all stronger and richer countries." He immediately followed this
pledge with a reiteration of China's vow to reunify Taiwan with the
mainland.[41]

Beijing's particular concerns about U.S. policy toward Taiwan were
spelled out by *People's Daily* on 4 July, when it published excerpts from
a journal article entitled "On the 'Taiwan Relations Act.'" The article
provided the most detailed examination of the Taiwan Relations Act yet
published in the party paper. The article generally repeated positions

that had been voiced in less authoritative media earlier in the year, but it added a new tone of urgency in discussing the implications of U.S. policy decisions for both Sino-American relations and Taiwan's future. That the article was meant to be a serious reminder to Washington is suggested by the fact that excerpts from it were released on the U.S. Independence Day.[42]

The *People's Daily* editor's note that prefaced the excerpts said they were being published as a rejoinder to "some people" in the United States who wanted to carry out the Taiwan Relations Act "in an all-around way"—a proposal that, according to the editor, "clearly violates" the 1979 joint Sino-American communiqué. The excerpted article began by criticizing "U.S. Government leaders" who declared that there was "no contradiction" between developing relations with China in accordance with the communiqué and acting along the lines of the act. It concluded with the warning that Sino-American relations "are now at another crucial moment" of either advancing in the direction charted in the joint communiqué or "retrogressing" because of the interference of the Taiwan Relations Act.

The article, for the first time since normalization, explicitly raised in public a hypothetical scenario in which China eventually might choose to use force against Taiwan.[43] That Beijing took the risk of sounding bellicose—a risk it had taken pains to avoid—suggested that it felt compelled to address more convincingly the concerns of "some people" in the United States who sought to ensure a "peaceful settlement of the Taiwan problem" by enhancing Taiwan's security. The article argued that such an approach had the opposite result, since it encouraged Taipei to reject contacts and talks with Beijing. As a result, according to the article, China eventually might be forced to consider, "against its wish," the use of "nonpeaceful methods" to attain its immutable goal of a unified China. Prior to the article, Beijing had carefully stopped short of raising this possibility for over a decade.

In a speech in October 1981, marking the 70th anniversary of the 1911 revolution, Hu Yaobang claimed, in an obvious effort to distance China from the United States, that the days were gone "when China was dependent on imperialism in diplomatic affairs. We formulate and carry out our foreign policy independently . . . we firmly oppose imperialism and hegemonism."[44]

While Chinese public characterizations of Premier Zhao Ziyang's and Foreign Minister Huang Hua's respective meetings with President Reagan in October and November 1981 remained cool and correct, Western press reports said that a Chinese ultimatum was delivered demanding a cutoff of U.S. arms supplies to Taiwan over a four-year period. Chinese officials subsequently linked this demand with their 30 September 1981 overture from National People's Congress Chairman Ye Jianying to the Nationalist leaders on Taiwan, calling for talks on peaceful reunification of Taiwan with the mainland. Repeatedly claiming that U.S. arms supplies made Taipei less willing to talk with the mainland, Beijing demanded a cutoff in the arms supplies in the interest of peacefully settling the Taiwan issue.[45]

Concurrently, in late 1981, Beijing began tagging the United States as well as the USSR with the hegemonist label reserved in the recent past for the Soviet Union alone. With concern over U.S. intentions toward Taiwan showing through, Chinese statements argued that U.S. policy on various third world issues failed to take due account of strategic objectives and allowed Moscow opportunities for gain. This line of criticism was given authoritative expression by Foreign Minister Huang Hua during his visit to Japan in mid-December. Speaking at the Sino-Japanese ministerial conference on 15 December, he cited Taiwan as an "outstanding" example of Washington's failure to consider the "overall strategic situation" in formulating policy toward the third world. In addition to Taiwan, Huang recited a list of regions—the Middle East, southern Africa, and Central America—where U.S. policy allegedly provided Moscow with opportunities for expanding its influence.[46]

Charges of U.S. "hegemonism" in Central America were a particular contrast with Chinese comment earlier in the year. Beijing media at that time went on record in support of U.S. efforts to back the government of El Salvador against Soviet-supported intervention. That the new double hegemony line enjoyed full leadership support was underlined by Deng Xiaoping. In talks with Yugoslav journalists on 15 December 1981, Deng told them that he considered both the United States and the Soviet Union to be hegemonists in foreign affairs—the first time he had so labeled the United States in many years.[47]

On 31 December 1981, a *People's Daily* "Commentator" article put on the public record the most explicit statement to date of China's demand that an understanding be reached with the United States on the phasing out of arms supply to Taiwan. The essence of the article's message was that the time had come, three years after U.S.-PRC normalization, for U.S. unilateral action to cease and for the United States and China to work out ways of resolving the arms issue.[48]

Li Xiannian used a late January 1982 leadership meeting on the occasion of the Spring Festival to convey the indirect but clear message that China would not pursue its interest in cooperating with the United States at the expense of its claim to sovereignty over Taiwan. Thus, after reaffirming Beijing's willingness to develop diplomatic relations and economic and cultural contacts with all countries on the basis of the principles of peaceful coexistence, Li delivered a stern message: "We will never barter away principle, let alone depend on alms. It is absolutely intolerable that anyone should try to encroach upon China's national sovereignty, interfere in our internal affairs, and obstruct the reunification of our country. We can never tolerate that."[49]

Beijing's more independent approach to the United States and its unrelenting pressure on the Taiwan issue were graphically underlined during Vice-President Bush's visit to China in May 1982. Its treatment of the 5-9 May official visit was carefully designed to drive home to the Reagan administration the need to resolve the festering problem of U.S. arms sales to Taiwan. The vice-president held talks with top-level Chinese leaders—Foreign Minister Huang Hua, Premier Zhao Ziyang, and Deng Xiaoping. Coverage of the talks and speeches was dominated by the Taiwan arms issue, with strategic and other forms of cooperation, as well as international issues, all but ignored. *Xinhua* reported only passing references by Zhao at the welcoming banquet to past bilateral progress and the importance of the relationship to China, and it omitted most of the vice-president's lengthier remarks in this vein while highlighting his statements of U.S. commitment to the one-China principle.[50]

While the vice-president was welcomed as an "old friend" of China, his talks were characterized in somber terms, with little indication of progress toward breaking the deadlock on the Taiwan issue. Thus, Beijing used formulas—such as "frank and sincere"—highlighting persistent divergence of views. *Xinhua* quoted Deng as expressing the "hope" that the vice-president's visit would help to "dispel the shadows and dark clouds overhanging our relations."[51] Such treatment contrasted with that given previous high-level U.S.-China talks—including those during Vice-President Mondale's official visit in August 1979—which had typically been characterized as "cordial" or "friendly" as well as "frank."[52]

Conspicuously absent from Beijing's coverage of the Bush visit was any discussion of strategic cooperation. In this respect, media treatment was similar to that given Mr. Bush's August 1980 visit during the election campaign, and markedly different from that accorded other high-level U.S.-China exchanges, including the Mondale and Haig visits. Thus, formerly typical Chinese comments regarding the importance of anti-Soviet cooperation and the potential for overcoming difficulties as long as both sides handled them in that perspective were absent this time, and the vice-president's references to the importance of the strategic relationship in toasts and in his press conference were not reported in the Chinese media. Similarly, his remarks about the improved understanding on global issues achieved during his talks, and his critique of Soviet "hegemonist expansionism," were not published by *Xinhua*, whereas similar comments by Secretary Haig the previous June and by other high-level U.S. visitors before then had been highlighted.

The 17 August 1982 Sino-American communiqué provided only a

brief respite in Chinese pressure on the United States. In the communiqué, the Reagan administration said that U.S. arms sales to Taiwan would not exceed "either in qualitative or in quantitative terms" the level of supplies during the past four years, and that the United States intended gradually to reduce its sale of arms to Taiwan, leading to what the communiqué called a "final resolution." The United States also disavowed a policy of "two Chinas" or "one China, one Taiwan," and said that the U.S. government "understands and appreciates" the PRC policy of seeking a peaceful resolution of the Taiwan question, as seen in recent PRC proposals for reunification talks with Taiwan. The U.S. side strongly implied that its agreement to curb arms supplies to Taiwan was contingent on a continuation of Beijing's peaceful approach to the island.

For its part, Beijing strongly affirmed its "fundamental" peaceful policy toward Taiwan. It also allowed the communiqué to go forward without reference to a fixed date for a U.S. arms cutoff, as the Chinese had demanded in the past. At the same time, Beijing did not downgrade relations when the Reagan administration formally notified Congress on 19 August that the United States would extend its current coproduction arrangement in Taiwan for F-5E/F fighters for two more years.

Both sides averred in the joint communiqué that they would take unspecified future measures to achieve "final settlement" of the issue of U.S. arms sales to Taiwan "over a period of time."

A Chinese Foreign Ministry spokesman's statement and a *People's Daily* editorial on 17 August hailed the communiqué on the Taiwan arms question as meeting China's minimum requirements, but treated the agreement as only a significant first step in a process that must lead to a final settlement of the issue.[53] Both in authoritative commentary on the communiqué and in reacting to American statements, the Chinese were concerned to limit Washington's latitude in applying the terms of the agreement in ways that departed from their own interpretations.

Both the Foreign Ministry spokesman's statement and the editorial hailed the joint communiqué as incorporating Beijing's "fundamental requirements" for ultimately resolving the Taiwan arms question. These demands, as enumerated in the editorial and as implicit in Chinese comment on the issue during previous months, included a U.S. commitment not to increase the quality and quantity of arms supplied to Taiwan, to reduce arms supplies over time, and ultimately to reach a "final resolution" of the issue. The Foreign Ministry statement explicitly interpreted the last point as "certainly" implying that arms sales must be "completely terminated" over a period of time.

Beijing treated the communiqué as having "eased" the "crisis" threatening Sino-American relations, but at the same time it stressed that the agreement "only marks a beginning" of a process that the Chinese would monitor carefully. As *People's Daily* put it, the communiqué had "broken the deadlock" on the Taiwan arms issue, but "the dark cloud that has blurred the prospects of Sino-American relations has not been completely swept away." Washington had given "promises," the editorial observed, "but we shall have to wait and see whether or not it will prove its sincerity by its actions."

China's satisfaction with the conclusion of the communiqué on Taiwan arms supply was so hedged with wary reservations that the accompanying commentary had little to say about the prospects for Sino-American relations overall. The communiqué pledged both sides to strengthen their ties bilaterally in various fields and to hold "appropriate consultations" on both bilateral and international issues, but neither the Foreign Ministry statement nor the editorial repeated these points.

The commentary was virtually devoid of any reaffirmation of the strategic basis of the relationship, a theme that until 1981 was prominent in Beijing's statements. The communiqué made only the weak claim that healthy Sino-American ties were conducive to "peace and stability" in the world, and served the cause of "opposing aggression and expansion." Neither the Foreign Ministry spokesman nor *People's Daily* went further. By contrast, the 1979 communiqué had renewed both countries' opposition to hegemony, a reaffirmation that the accompanying *People's Daily* editorial observed would "help opposition to major hegemonism as well as minor hegemonism, to global hegemonism as well as regional hegemonism"—terms that signified Moscow and Hanoi, respectively.

Foreign Minister Huang Hua's 6 October 1982 speech to the Council on Foreign Relations in New York—during his attendance at the U.N. General Assembly session—represented the most comprehensive and authoritative discussion of Sino-American relations since the 17 August communiqué, and underscored Beijing's continued determination to press for U.S. concessions. Stressing that the communiqué marked only the beginning of efforts to resolve the arms questions, Huang strongly underscored Beijing's insistence that Washington meticulously observe the document's provisions. He warned that "some people" in the United States still sought to undermine the political basis of Sino-American relations and that if their efforts "swayed U.S. policy," relations between the two countries would "go down the drain."[54]

Following the joint communiqué, Beijing had regularly criticized public statements by administration officials and selected public figures and press commentary in the United States for "distorting" the communiqué. This was extended to President Reagan himself in a 10 October 1982 *People's Daily* commentary rebutting his comments on 6 October linking reduction in U.S. arms sales to Taiwan to Beijing's use of peaceful means for reunification. Such linkage, the party paper warned, "completely violates" the spirit to the communiqué and sets "preconditions" that called into question the administration's sincerity in implementing it.[55]

Huang went on to open the realm of Sino-American economic relations to high-level Chinese complaint. He deplored current "discriminatory restrictions" on the export of high technology and sophisticated equipment to the PRC, and "intensified" U.S. restrictions on imports from China. Implying that these restrictions raised doubts about Washington's enduring commitment to its relationship with Beijing, he wondered aloud whether the administration regarded China as "a friend or an adversary."

Huang's unusually direct discussion of difficulties in technology transfer went so far as to ridicule U.S. pledges to ease restrictions on it as little more than "loud thunder" that produces "little rain." Beijing had normally refrained from public comment on this issue. Chinese media had given more extensive coverage to problems in negotiating a new textile agreement—the second round of which was then under way in Washington—and in structuring the U.S. importation of canned Chinese mushrooms. In both cases, Beijing had criticized what it viewed as attempts by U.S. manufacturers and government officials to restrict the level of imports without regard for the realities of Sino-American trade. Typically in that regard, Huang pointed out that China, by virtue of its repeated trade deficits since trade relations with the United States had been resumed in the early 1970s, was being "unfairly treated."

Persistent Chinese complaints during ensuing months over Taiwan, textiles, and technology transfer were joined by issues including the Hu Kwang Railway bonds and the seeking of asylum in the United States by tennis player Hu Na.[56] President Reagan's interpretation of the 17 August 1982 communiqué, during an interview with the conservative publication *Human Events* in February 1983, prompted a formal Chinese protest—the first formal representation by China in response to remarks by the president on the Taiwan issue.[57]

Subsequently, Chinese leaders endeavored to lobby Democratic congressional leaders for help in overcoming existing obstacles. Commentary surrounding the visit of a delegation led by Speaker of the House Thomas O'Neill from 27 March to 3 April 1983—the largest congressional delegation ever to visit China—appealed to Congress to play a role in furthering the process of reducing and removing obstacles to better relations.[58] This lobbying effort seemed more open than that directed at Senate Majority Leader Robert Byrd in 1980 and Senate Majority Leader Howard Baker in 1982. In each case, the visitors received high-level treatment. The O'Neill delegation saw Deng Xiaoping, Zhao Ziyang, Foreign Minister Wu Xueqian, and ranking officials of the National People's Congress (NPC). While claiming to be optimistic about the long-term prospects of Sino-American relations, Zhao Ziyang observed that the relationship was not satisfactory at present and had not improved since the 17 August 1982 communiqué on Taiwan arms sales and Secretary George Shultz's February 1983 visit to China. Foreign Minister Wu even stated that obstacles had increased.

Beijing's efforts to enlist congressional involvement in removing these obstacles included the following:

- Following up on NPC Standing Committee member Liao Chengzhi's more general remarks at the welcoming banquet, senior NPC Vice-Chairman Peng Zhen the next day expressed the hope that "the legislative bodies of the two countries will work together to get rid of" the Taiwan issue, "the crux of the matter" in developing the Sino-American relationship.[59]

- In their meetings with the delegation, Premier Zhao and Deng Xiaoping called on the congressmen to take action to resolve differences between the two countries. Zhao was especially explicit in hoping that "the U.S. legislative bodies" would "play a more positive role and make more efforts" to promote Sino-American relations, and Deng urged the visitors to work to build mutual trust.[60]

- Foreign Minister Wu complained about recent resolutions in both houses of Congress concerning "the future of Taiwan, which is part of China." *Xinhua*'s account of this meeting played up a theme prominent in Beijing's coverage of the visit when it quoted Speaker O'Neill as saying he had acquired a better understanding of the strong feelings of the Chinese people on the Taiwan issue. Similarly, a 1 April account in *People's Daily* of the speaker's press conference two days earlier quoted him as saying he had been unaware that the PRC "had adopted such a strong attitude" on the issue, but that from talks with the Chinese leaders, he had come to "really understand" the problems in the relationship. According to *People's Daily*, the speaker said he would like to improve relations and make better ties with China a matter of "first priority."[61]

SINO-SOVIET THAW

The Chinese campaign to push for U.S. concessions and to put some distance between China and the Reagan administration was accompanied by complementary initiatives toward the USSR and the third world. Although Beijing had halted the formal dialogue with the Soviet Union following the Soviet invasion of Afghanistan in December 1979, Soviet leaders continued efforts to improve the atmosphere in Sino-Soviet relations. The three annual visits of Soviet Foreign Ministry China expert

Mikhail Kapitsa, which began in March 1980, were presumably made with an eye toward detecting an opening in China's anti-Soviet stance. Though Moscow appeared to have no intention of compromising basic security or political issues with China, it had been prepared since the mid-1960s to offer expanded diplomatic, economic, and technical exchanges, and to sign agreements regarding nonaggression or nonuse of force. Typically, an authoritative *Pravda* article on 7 April 1980 called on China to reopen talks on Sino-Soviet border issues or on improving Sino-Soviet relations.[62]

Moscow seemed to judge that its interests would be well served by an improvement in Sino-Soviet relations, even though basic compromises between the two antagonists appeared unlikely. The USSR had seen itself at a disadvantage in the U.S.-Soviet-Chinese triangular relationship since the Sino-American reconciliation began in the late 1960s, and it presumably judged that a Sino-Soviet thaw would improve its leverage in dealings with the United States. Moreover, as Sino-American strategic cooperation had appeared to grow after the normalization of relations in 1979, Moscow had become more concerned about a possible close Sino-American military alignment; it wished to improve relations with China both to lessen China's incentive to move closer to the United States, and to insert an element of distrust in U.S. calculations of China's reliability as a supporter of U.S. interests against the USSR. The emerging Sino-American differences over Taiwan and other issues provided an opening for accelerated Soviet efforts to promote improvement, at least on the margins, in Sino-Soviet relations.

As a result, Chinese leaders were well aware that they could easily improve Sino-Soviet relations by responding positively to some of the many outstanding Soviet offers for improved contacts, exchanges, and talks. Thus, as part of its more independent stance in foreign affairs, Beijing moved in 1981 to respond positively to a few of the Soviet offers—resulting in an improved dialogue between the two powers. Benchmarks in the Sino-Soviet relationship included the following:

- On 23 February 1981, Brezhnev spoke at the CPSU Congress and was generally conciliatory toward China.

- In April, the two sides negotiated a bilateral railway protocol—the first time such an accord had been reached since 1963.[63]

- In August, an article in the Soviet journal *Kommunist* complained that China had "deadlocked" the talks on normalizing Sino-Soviet relations and on the border issue, and that Beijing "shows no desire to reconvene them." Nevertheless, Moscow put a new item among its array of offers to China on 10 August when the USSR officially proposed to the Chinese Foreign Ministry the adoption of "confidence building measures" in the Far East.

- On 25 September, the Soviets privately asked that China agree to resuming the Sino-Soviet border talks.[64]

- On 20 November, the first increase in bilateral exchanges in recent years was noted when Chinese gymnasts performing in the USSR were feted by the Sino-Soviet Friendship Society—the first such reported festivities in over a decade.[65]

- On 16 December, the Soviets privately proposed regular scientific and technological exchanges with China, and on the 25th, China reportedly agreed in principle to resume such exchanges.

- On 19 January 1982, a Sino-Soviet agreement on exchanging books was initialed.

- In February, the Soviets again proposed a resumption of the Sino-Soviet border talks and exchanges of language students and teachers.

- In March, Chinese economists and gymnasts were reported visiting the USSR, while Beijing put a more positive gloss on the annual meeting of the Sino-Soviet Border River Navigation Commission by noting that a "larger area of agreement" was reached in the talks ending 9 March.[66]

The Sino-Soviet dialogue began to gather momentum when Soviet President Brezhnev made a conciliatory gesture to China during a review of Soviet Asian policy in a speech at Tashkent in March 1982.[67] Emphasizing the common ground between Beijing and Moscow, instead of focusing on customary allegations of China's alignment with the West, Brezhnev affirmed that a "socialist social system" existed in China, reiterated Moscow's support for the PRC claim to sovereignty over Taiwan, and used language designed to portray new flexibility in the Soviet position on bilateral disputes with China, although the substance of his proposals contained no dramatic departures. He proposed reopening Sino-Soviet border negotiations, stalled since June 1978, asserting that the Soviet Union "is ready at any moment to continue talks on existing border questions." In the only deviation from past offers, the Soviet president issued the first public proposal to discuss "confidence building measures" in the specific context of the Soviet-Chinese frontier. In 1981, Brezhnev had proposed confidence-building measures—such as advance notice of military exercises and troop movements—as a subject for collective discussion by nations in the Far East.

Following the speech, both sides accelerated efforts to improve the relationship. Authoritative Soviet statements generally avoided direct criticism of Chinese policies on occasions that in the past would have required such statements. At the conclusion of the annual Sino-Soviet trade talks on 9 March 1982, Beijing noted that the two sides "exchanged notes on frontier trade" the first time frontier trade had been mentioned since the 1960s. In June, *Pravda* reported on a Soviet trade team's visit to China—the first reference in the Soviet central press to such revived exchanges. And in August, China reciprocated the trips of Mikhail Kapitsa to China by sending its senior Foreign Ministry Soviet specialist, Yu Hongliang, to Moscow for consultations.[68]

In September, Brezhnev was again conciliatory toward China in a major address at Baku. He claimed that the Soviet objective was normalization and gradual improvement in Sino-Soviet relations. Meanwhile, Soviet media cut back sharply on criticism of China.

A breakthrough was reached in October, when China finally responded positively to repeated Soviet calls for resumption of bilateral negotiations and allowed Soviet Deputy Foreign Minister Leonid Ilichev and Chinese Vice-Foreign Minister Qian Qichen to begin discussions in Beijing. After 6 formal sessions over 17 days, the talks produced an agreement that the two nations would continue what were called preliminary consultations on an alternating basis in Beijing and Moscow, with the next round of discussions in Moscow and the details to be set through diplomatic channels.

Speaking to Western reporters in Beijing on a backgroung basis, Chinese officials warned against expecting any quick breakthrough, saying that the Soviet Union seemed unlikely to meet Chinese conditions (involving demands for withdrawal from along China's northern borders and pullback from Afghanistan and Indochina) for improved relations. Brezhnev indicated that Moscow also felt that conditions for a breakthrough remained unfulfilled, although he said he remained watchful for "new things" appearing in Chinese foreign policy. In a speech on 27 October to a gathering of Soviet generals in the Kremlin, he said that the Soviet Union "sincerely" sought a normalization of relations, and was "doing everything in our power toward this end." He added that "no radical changes" in the foreign policy of the People's Republic of China had been seen so far.[69]

INITIATIVES IN THE THIRD WORLD

As China adopted a more sanguine view of the international balance against Soviet expansion, began efforts to ease bilateral tension with the USSR, and distanced itself from the United States over Taiwan and other questions, Beijing was in a better position to develop and broaden its relations with the third world. China had already started in 1979 to move away from the strong anti-Soviet, pro-Western public orientation that had characterized its third world policy, and it continued this trend through the 1980s. Thus, Beijing showed more concern over, and active interest in, third world issues through propaganda coverage, international exchanges, leadership meetings, and actions in international organizations. China's increased attention to Asian, African, and Latin American issues stopped short of increased outlays of aid, however. Beijing tried to enhance its image and influence at little cost. Its economic interchange tended to be very hardheaded and focused on areas that made economic, as well as political, profits for China.

Beijing had long associated itself with the developing countries of Asia, Africa, and Latin America. Like them, China was poor and nonwhite, and shared a common anti-imperialist, anti-colonialist outlook. At times, the Chinese had so played up the importance of the third world that it appeared to be the key element in Chinese foreign policy—although it never was. For example, during the mid-1970s, Beijing media repeatedly hailed the third world as "the main force" opposing superpower aggression and guaranteeing world peace—even though China's actual policy to secure peace for its interests was to practice a differentiated approach toward the superpowers, playing one off against the other. Typically, Mao Zedong's "three worlds" theory, enunciated in April 1974, gave pride of place to the struggle of the third world against U.S. and Soviet "hegemonism." In discussing ties with the third world, China usually soft-pedaled those aspects of its power (such as nuclear weapons, massive armed forces, global political role) that distinguished it from most of the developing countries. Of course, Beijing almost certainly was aware that these features of its power established China in a strong leadership position in this group of nations.

Chinese leaders, especially those with long experience in dealing with the third world, such as foreign affairs specialists Ji Pengfei, Wu Xueqian, and Ho Ying, were well aware of the costs China was paying in relations with many developing countries as a result of its earlier tilt toward the United States and the West, and strident opposition to the Soviet Union and its associates. As China brought its policy toward the superpowers more into balance and began to assert its "independence" in foreign affairs, these officials took the lead in reestablishing and broadening Chinese influence in the developing countries. They had several immediate reasons for pushing ahead:

- Criticism of China in the third world was on the rise. In particular, China was seen as unreasonably antagonistic toward third world countries that received extensive aid and political support from the Soviet bloc, but it was also seen as unwilling to offer compensating aid in its own right.[70] Beijing had now become an active member of international financial institutions and was competing with developing countries for development funds.[71]

- Beijing was demanding a greater share of the markets of developed countries—a demand that would be met largely by cutting back on the market share in other third world states.[72]

- China was vulnerable to charges that it served as a stalking horse for U.S. and Western interests against the Soviet Union in the third world.

- Beijing's image suffered as a result of Chinese racial discrimination against African students, publicized by repeated incidents.[73]

- Beijing had been heavily involved in political support and economic aid in many third world countries in the past. Without careful nurturing, this long-term investment could be lost.

- Stronger ties with the developing world would increase China's support in the United Nations and other international forums on issues important to its security and other interests (such as Afghanistan and Kampuchea).

- A stronger Chinese emphasis on the third world, including greater criticism of U.S. policies, not only enhanced China's image among developing countries but also drew the attention of U.S. policymakers to one of the "costs" of a deteriorating U.S.-Chinese relationship.

- By winning the confidence of third world governments through a more independent international posture and greater political support and interchange, Beijing would be able to exert influence more effectively against the USSR, when needed. Thus, by reestablishing contacts with such previously shunned "pro-Soviet" states as Angola, Libya, Mozambique, South Yemen, Syria, and Ethiopia, China was better positioned to watch for openings that would allow a reduction in these countries' dependence on the USSR.

- Improved Chinese political relations allowed an opening of favorable trade relations. In the Middle East and Africa, for example, Chinese trade grew as new markets were opened; it remained highly favorable for China, resulting in a trade surplus of over $1 billion in 1982.[74] China also used good political ties to open markets for its arms sales and to send tens of thousands of contract workers to the Middle East—the two together provided over $1 billion of foreign exchange for China each year during the early 1980s.[75]

In meetings with third world leaders during 1981, Chinese officials began to reaffirm—after a hiatus of several years—China's identity with the Maoist "three worlds" theory. The prominent journal *Liaowang* in August 1981 reiterated the "three worlds" theory as the basis of Chinese foreign policy. The article's stress agreed with the June 1981 11th CCP Central Committee Sixth Plenum which had offered a positive assessment of Mao Zedong's contributions to Chinese foreign policy.[76]

Subsequently, Chinese leaders softpedaled any Maoist ideological rationale for Chinese foreign policy, but Beijing asserted its identity with the third world through other means. Later in 1981, for instance, China became more critical of alleged U.S. "hegemonist" actions in Central America. The Chinese stance contrasted with its position earlier in the year, when it supported U.S. actions in the region against potential Soviet expansion. Beijing also worked hard to identify with the third world against the United States and the Soviet Union when it repeatedly blocked the U.S. supported candidate for U.N. secretary-general, during Security Council deliberations in late 1981, and when it strongly sided with Argentina over the Falkland Islands war with Great Britain in 1982.[77] At the Cancun summit meeting of October 1981, meanwhile, Premier Zhao stressed China's strong support for developing countries' demands for establishment of a new economic order, opposed by the United States and other developed countries.[78]

Zhao's trip to Mexico coincided with a series of high-level Chinese visits to previously slighted third world areas. Huang Hua, who accompanied Zhao, had traveled earlier in 1981 to several Latin American countries.[79] Huang Hua and Vice-Foreign Minister Gong Dafei also visited five African countries during this period. Their trips followed the extensive journeys to the region made by Chinese Communist Party delegations led by Wu Xueqian and Ji Pengfei in late 1979 and mid-1980, respectively.[80]

The capstone of this effort was Zhao's 1982-83 tour of 11 African countries. Throughout the visit, Beijing was at pains to underline China's strong reassertion of its third world credentials and its pullback from close public association with the developed countries—the United States in particular—and its more balanced posture toward both superpowers.[81]

The Zhao trip—the first of its kind since Premier Zhou Enlai's swing through Africa in 1963-64—included polite, low-key discussions with African leaders of varying political views. As Zhao refused to commit China to many new aid programs or outlays, the trip epitomized Beijing's low-cost effort to improve its standing among developed countries. At most stops, Zhao charged that superpower rivalry was the main source of political and economic instability in Africa and the rest of the third world. In an effort to eliminate African and other third world countries' tendencies to associate Chinese policy with the United States and the West, Zhao singled out unpopular U.S. policy in the Middle East and southern Africa for criticism. At the same time, he avoided caustic references to either the United States or the Soviet Union in public— presumably out of deference to his hosts' sensibilities.

Zhao's meetings with PLO chief Yasir Arafat, with representatives of the South West African People's Organization (SWAPO), and with the leaders of the African National Congress (ANC) and the Pan-African Congress enabled him to demonstrate Beijing's support for "liberation" groups that enjoyed broad support in the region.[82] This was done even though SWAPO and ANC had heretofore been kept at a distance because of their close ties with the USSR.

China's more ecumenical approach was complemented by Zhao's refusal to be drawn into controversy over issues that divided the region, including the civil war in Chad, the West Sahara dispute among Morocco, Algeria, and Libya, the Iran-Iraq war, and the disagreement between Ethiopia and Somalia over their border. Beijing thus carefully tailored its statements of support with an eye toward maximizing political gain and minimizing the risk of alienating important regional actors.

At most of his stops, Zhao offered to conclude trade and economic cooperation agreements as China's contribution to the economic development of third world nations. These and other agreements emphasized joint investment in small projects that would have a fairly rapid and relatively high political impact, and a low cost. In this regard, the most common Chinese assistance projects in Africa came to be sports stadiums and medical teams. Zhao, meanwhile, was careful to counsel his hosts against mechanically following the past Chinese model of self-reliant economic development.

Trips by Chinese officials established closer ties between Chinese and third world leaders with diverse interests and specialties. Beijing sent senior trade union, military, economic, trade, women's group, National People's Congress, and other officials abroad to establish new contacts with their third world counterparts.[83] Meanwhile, third world specialists like Ho Ying were sent on troubleshooting missions to reestablish closer ties with important developing governments heretofore considered pro-Soviet by China—these included Libya, Syria, Iraq, South Yemen, Ethiopia, and Angola.[84]

Beijing's more flexible and economically pragmatic approach to the third world allowed China to garner major economic benefits—for instance, in the oil-rich Middle East. Trade in the region ran heavily in China's favor, as it did throughout most of the third world. In 1981, China recorded a $6.1 billion trade surplus with the developing countries.[85] Beijing also began to send tens of thousands of contract workers, especially to Iraq and other Middle Eastern countries—earning considerable foreign exchange in the process.[86]

Perhaps the most lucrative source of foreign earnings at this time was in Chinese arms sales to the region, especially Iraq.[87] The start of the Iran-Iraq war in September 1980 caused an enormous loss of Iraqi

Soviet-made weapons and ammunition, and Moscow was reluctant to replenish the depleted Iraqi arsenals. This predicament pushed Iraq into the arms of the Chinese, who had the type of equipment Baghdad needed.

The first Sino-Iraqi arms deal was signed a few months after the war started, probably in early 1981. But it was only in November that information about the deal emerged publicly. Some reports said that China would supply Iraq with an unspecified number of T-59 tanks, the Chinese version of the Soviet T-54. The value of the deal was not noted, but it was said to have been financed in part by a $7 billion Kuwaiti loan. The size of the deal was known a year later. According to reports citing U.S. officials, China became a major arms supplier to Iraq—a quarter of Iraq's military purchases were said to have come from China and half of Chinese military sales were to Baghdad. Assuming that Iraq was spending about $12 billion a year on foreign supplies for the war effort, the Chinese share would have been about $3 billion.

An arms deal of such size almost certainly was not limited to T-59 tanks. There were reports that it covered light arms, field artillery and large amounts of ammunition, and spare parts. Moreover, in December 1982, it was disclosed that about 100 Chinese F-6 fighters had been delivered to Iraq. And in January 1983, sources in East Asia revealed that, under a deal estimated at more than $1 billion in value, China was supplying Iraq with a substantial number (over 200) of T-69 tanks. These were said to be China's most sophisticated tanks, equipped with Chinese-manufactured laser range finders, infrared equipment, and an improved engine.

The Chinese of course consistently denied these news accounts of arms sales to Iraq, stating that "China has not sold any weapons to Iraq because this is incompatible with our principled stand on the war between Iraq and Iran," which was based on "strict neutrality." China's denials aside, evidence strongly suggested that Chinese arms reached Iraq, though apparently they did so indirectly, having been shipped first to Jordan or Saudi Arabia. In order not to jeopardize Chinese claims of strict neutrality, these countries may have been the actual signatories of contracts concerning arms being transmitted to Iraq.

Iran, too, was reported to be receiving some Chinese weapons through North Korea. The Chinese also continued their military sales relationship with Egypt, Sudan, and Somalia. In total, China was estimated by some to have sold about $5 billion in arms from 1979 to 1983. This represented several times the total value of all Chinese arms sent to its long-standing ally Pakistan, and the largest arms transfer arrangements ever undertaken by the PRC.

SINO-KOREAN RELATIONS

China's newly independent foreign policy posture in the third world had perhaps its most important impact regarding relations with North Korea. Downplaying its past emphasis on relations with Washington and Tokyo, Beijing was able to reestablish more common ground with Pyongyang through a series of high-level visits in 1981 and 1982. Premier Zhao Ziyang and Defense Minister Geng Biao visited North Korea in December 1981 and June 1982, respectively. Deng Xiaoping and Hu Yaobang secretly traveled there in April 1982—a visit disclosed during Kim Il-song's trip to China in September 1982.[88]

The Chinese premier's visit in December 1981 reflected efforts by Beijing to improve relations after a period of strain following the normalization of U.S.-PRC relations and the signing of the Sino-Japanese peace treaty in 1978. Both sides used the 20-24 December visit, billed as reciprocating North Korean Premier Yi Chong-ok's January 1981 visit to China, to celebrate improving relations. The respective party papers published editorials to mark the occasion; the atmosphere during the visit was portrayed as warm; and the Chinese were more effusive than their hosts in describing the visit. Beijing's report of Zhao's meeting with Kim Il-song seemed designed to put the Korean leader's imprimatur on the relationship, quoting Kim as saying, "We are of one and the same family and we don't anticipate any differences among us." As was customary, North Korean media did not report Kim's remarks to the guest.[89]

Zhao voiced the routine Chinese line calling for withdrawal of U.S. troops from Korea without expressing a sense of urgency. He went beyond the usual formulations in criticizing Washington's Korea policy, however, when he declared at the welcoming banquet on the 20th that the U.S. troop presence was "a major factor in the instability in Northeast Asia." Beijing's standard charge in the past had been that U.S. troops presented the "major obstacle" to Korean reunification.

No new ground was broken on the subject of Washington-Pyongyang talks. Zhao repeated his call, made during Yi's visit to China, for a U.S.-North Korean dialogue to reduce tension in the region. The two sides also followed standard lines on reunification, the Sino-Soviet rivalry, and Kim Il-song's succession. On reunification, each side expressed strong support for the other's plans to end the division of the country. Beijing's support for Kim's October 1980 confederation proposal had grown stronger and more specific during 1981—coincident with the more critical Chinese approach toward the United States over a variety of third world questions. Meanwhile, Pyongyang's praise for Beijing's overture to Taiwan in September 1981 contrasted with the slight attention North

Korea gave to a similar Chinese proposal on reunification issued shortly after Sino-American normalization in 1979.

In the customary manner, Zhao used "hegemonism" as the code word for the Soviet Union while welcoming Pyongyang's opposition to "dominationism"—the term used by the North Koreans to condemn big powers' attempts to dictate to smaller countries. And, as they had done during Yi's visit to China, both sides skirted the North Korean succession issue. Unlike most other recent foreign visitors to North Korea, Zhao was not quoted as having lauded Kim Il-song's son, Kim Chong-il, and Pyongyang refrained from mentioning the "party center," the code phrase for the younger Kim, during Zhao's visit.

Geng Biao's visit to North Korea was unusual in that it was the first delegation led by a Chinese defense minister in two decades, and because of his more critical tone in characterizing the United States. Geng notably made a gesture to Pyongyang in calling for an immediate U.S. withdrawal from Korea, although Chinese media coverage of the visit carefully avoided citing that demand.[90]

During his 14-22 June visit, Geng Biao received the customary treatment accorded foreign guests of his rank. He was received by Kim Il-song, and his visit was marked by a *Nodong Sinmun* editorial. Geng Biao's talks with his counterpart, O Chin-u, were said to have reached "a complete unanimity of views."

The visit evoked the usual formulations that characterized Sino-Korean relations—including the pledge to fight "shoulder to shoulder" in the future—and prompted several references to the Korean War. Geng stressed the importance of close Sino-Korean relations in view of the "very tense" international situation and the "increasing" danger of war. As in previous visits by military delegations, there was no report of any military aid agreement, but subsequent reports from South Korea indicated that the Chinese had agreed to provide additional fighter aircraft for the North Korean air force.

The Chinese showed unusually lavish hospitality to Kim Il-song during his 15-26 September 1982 visit to China, thereby dramatizing the special relationship between Beijing and Pyongyang. Each side expressed support for the other's basic policies and took indirect but repeated note of the political succession arrangements under way in both countries by stating that their friendship would last from "generation to generation." Beijing seemed to take care to signal that its close relationship with North Korea would not pose a threat to the stability of East Asia.[91]

The welcome Kim received in Beijing was even more lavish than that given in April 1982 to Romanian Communist Party chief Nicolae Ceausescu, another fraternal party and state leader. In addition to attention from Hu Yaobang and Zhao Ziyang, Deng Xiaoping spent an unusual amount of time with Kim, accompanying him on a visit to Deng's home province of Sichuan.

Neither side shed much light on the substantive nature of the "cordial and friendly" talks held during the visit. At the farewell banquet on the 24th, Kim and Hu stated that they had reached "identical views" and were "fully unanimous in our views on all the issues discussed." Kim revealed only that they had "wide ranging" talks on relations between the two countries and "other issues of common interest." Hu said that the talks included "the international situation and major international issues of common interest."

The special Sino-Korean relationship was underlined by Hu's disclosure at the 16 September welcoming banquet that he and Deng Xiaoping had visited North Korea in April 1982.[92] There had been no other publicity on that trip. Hu merely noted that it had taken place four and a half months prior to Kim's arrival in Beijing, a time frame that would put it shortly after the massive celebrations of Kim's 70th birthday on 15 April. Ceausescu had gone on to Pyongyang after his 13-17 April visit to China. Hu and Deng may have visited North Korea within the period 26-30 April, when both failed to appear publicly in China.

Statements by both sides during Kim's visit to China generally hewed to standard lines on the Korean question, but the Chinese balanced a bow to Pyongyang's position on the U.S. presence with an apparent concern not to fuel a sense of insecurity on the peninsula. Thus, both the *People's Daily* editorial marking North Korea's 9 September anniversary and the editorial welcoming Kim's arrival supported Pyongyang's demand for an "immediate" withdrawal of U.S. troops. But Hu's speech on the 16th was more typical of past Chinese practice when he said that U.S. withdrawal and Korean reunification would be achieved "eventually" in accordance with the "inevitable trend of history."

12th PARTY CONGRESS, SEPTEMBER 1982

The formal enunciation of China's newly independent posture in foreign affairs came during the 12th Congress of the CCP, held in Beijing on 1-11 September 1982. The congress underscored the still mixed results of reform efforts fostered by Deng Xiaoping and like-minded leaders since the last party congress five years earlier. It suggested such leaders' preoccupation with domestic affairs and their unwillingness to disrupt Beijing leadership unity over foreign policy concerns.

Significant progress was seen in the reformers' steadily advancing efforts to consolidate political power, formulate pragmatic development policies, and ensure their continuity. But the process of leadership change—widely seen as the linchpin of the reform efforts—was slow, reflecting persistent resistance from cadres at various levels of the 40-million-member party. Deng and his younger associates were compelled to backtrack on some of their earlier calls for more sweeping party organizational reforms and leadership retirements, in favor of more gradual approaches to leadership change that were not expected to be completed until sometime in the latter half of the 1980s. As a result, it was highly likely that the 78-year-old Deng would be unable soon to follow his stated desire to retreat to the "second line" and pass full leadership responsibility to his younger protégés so they could more firmly establish their own bases of political power; because of continued pressing and conflicting political interests, Deng remained heavily involved in managing Chinese leadership affairs.

The discussion of foreign affairs in the authoritative party pronouncements at the congress underscored Beijing's emphasis on independence in foreign affairs, support for third world issues, and a more balanced assessment in criticizing the "superpowers"—an allusion to both the Soviet Union and the United States. Beijing dropped harsh invective against the USSR that had appeared during the last congress, but still saw major obstacles to improved relations with Moscow. Its assessment of relations with the United States was less critical, though relations were subject to what the Chinese saw as the "cloud" of U.S.-PRC differences over Taiwan. China reiterated interest in carefully planned imports of foreign technology and in growth of foreign trade, while reaffirming its basic stance of economic self-reliance and warning against the "corrosive" influence of capitalist ideas.

The main themes of the congress were set forth by Party Chairman Hu Yaobang in his 34,000-word report to the congress on 1 September.[93] In general, Hu strove to legitimize the more pragmatic programs and policies followed by the party since he and other reformers led by Deng had managed to gain the upper hand in leadership councils following the Third Plenum of the 11th CCP Congress in December 1978; to discredit the policies—associated with Maoist loyalists, such as former Party Chairman Hua Guofeng, and some other conservative leaders, such as party elders Ye Jianying and Li Xiannian—that had been followed prior to that time; and to offer a firm justification for continuing relatively pragmatic economic, political, and foreign policies over the next five years.

The Economy

Focusing on economic development as China's top priority for the foreseeable future, Hu optimistically predicted that China would quadruple the value of its industrial and agricultural production by the year 2000, in what was otherwise a more sober assessment of the problems and prospects of China's economy. He gave a strong rationale for the pragmatic and sometimes experimental economic policies and programs Beijing had followed since the Third Plenum in late 1978, indicating that post-Mao economic developments were likely to continue to reflect trial-and-error search for the correct path to sustained growth—a process that had encountered, and was likely to continue to encounter, problems and to undergo adjustments.

Hu confirmed earlier reports that Chinese planners would focus in the main on economic retrenchment and reorganization during the 1980s, in an effort to ease critical bottlenecks and shortcomings in agricultural production, energy, transportation, and education, which had "piled up over a long period." As a result, he noted, "it will not be possible for the national economy to develop very fast in this decade;" but he predicted that following the readjustment in the 1980s, "an all-round upsurge" in China's economy would follow in the 1990s.

Hu also laid special stress on the need for stringent population control in order to avoid serious problems in resource allocation and in living standards; he reaffirmed that recent use of more decentralized economic decision making and of market forces in the Chinese economy would continue to supplement the "leading role" of the planned economy; and he said that China remained interested in carefully thought-out imports of foreign technology—but not most consumer goods—within an overall context of economic self-reliance and aversion to the "corrosion of capitalist ideas" and "worship of things foreign."

Party Reform

Hu's report and other congressional documents stressed the need for improvement in the sometimes lax discipline and dedication of some party members; promotion of younger, "more revolutionary," and more "professionally competent" cadres, and retirement of veteran leaders; and the removal of disruptive cadres who had risen to power by means of "rebellion" during the Cultural Revolution, engaged in "factional" political activities, were unwilling to follow the more pragmatic policies formulated since the Third Plenum, were technically incompetent, or engaged in corrupt practices.

In contrast with comment associated with Deng Xiaoping and other reform-minded officials in the previous year, predicting more sweeping changes in party organization and large-scale retirements, the congress pronouncements made it clear that party reforms would take place slowly, "step-by-step." Thus, although the positions of party chairman and vice-chairman, as expected, were abolished, power did not automatically gravitate, as predicted, into the hands of the party Secretariat under the leadership of General Secretary Hu Yaobang. Rather, the Politburo was retained as the senior party body, and its six-member standing committee still represented the focal point of political power in the country. That body was also headed by Hu and included a younger reformer, Premier Zhao Ziyang, as well as Deng Xiaoping; but it also contained two veteran conservative leaders, Ye Jianying and Li Xiannian, along with the independent-minded veteran Chen Yun. The latter three, along with Deng, had been expected to retire from an active role in party affairs.

Meanwhile, little progress was made in the predicted transfer of jurisdiction over the military from the party to the state as the party's Military Affairs Commission was not abolished. Deng was retained as chairman of the commission, and Ye and two other old marshals kept their vice-chairman posts.

Below the top levels of the party, however, the reformers made major gains in adding many like-minded officials to the Politburo, the party Secretariat, and the Central Committee. And a considerable number of party veterans, including a few Politburo members, retired, many taking up responsibilities in the newly established Central Advisory Commission—a body of elder leaders that was to advise the Central Committee.

Regarding the Herculean task of making the 40-million-member party more responsive to central directives and policies, Hu indicated in his report that the party would eschew abrupt or sweeping changes in favor of a gradual, three-year effort, beginning in 1983. He indicated that the program was designed to give all cadres, including the more than half of the party members who entered after the start of the Cultural Revolution, a chance to show their loyalty to current policies and to improve their technical skills prior to the required reregistration of all members scheduled for late 1986.

Hu's report also put great stress on the need for instilling basic ideological principles, especially the "four truths" (adherence to the socialist road, to the people's democratic dictatorship, to the leadership of the Communist Party, and to Marxism-Leninism and Mao Zedong thought) among all party cadres; and he emphasized the importance of establishing firm laws and political institutions in order to guarantee that an individual's legitimate political rights would be protected under "socialist democracy."

Chinese-U.S.-Soviet Relations

The congress devoted comparatively less attention to foreign affairs. Hu's report expressed hope for forward movement in Sino-American relations, but added that this would require strict adherence to the 17 August 1982 U.S.-PRC communiqué concerning U.S. arms sales to Taiwan. He saw the Taiwan issue as a "cloud" hanging over otherwise beneficial U.S.-PRC relations, criticizing in particular the continued U.S. sale of arms to Taiwan and the Taiwan Relations Act, which, he said, "contravenes the principles embodied in the joint communiqué on the establishment of diplomatic relations."

More critically, Hu portrayed China as directly threatened by the Soviet "hegemonist" policies seen particularly in massed Soviet forces along the Sino-Soviet and Sino-Mongolian frontiers; Soviet support for Vietnam's invasion and occupation of Kampuchea, and its "constant provocations" along China's border; and the Soviet invasion and occupation of Afghanistan.

Hu averred that Sino-Soviet relations could move toward normalization on condition that the USSR took certain unspecified "practical steps to lift their threat to the security of China." Notably, Hu did not repeat the vivid portrayal of Soviet expansion as the main danger to world peace that had been presented in the keynote address at the 11th CCP Congress in 1977. He made a more general reference to "imperialism, hegemonism and colonialism" as the "main forces" jeopardizing peace, and said that the two superpowers' rivalry had become the "main source of instability and turmoil in the world." He also strongly reaffirmed China's identification with the third world against the superpowers, and he repeatedly stressed China's "independent" foreign policy, in which Beijing "never attaches itself to any big power or group of powers, and never yields to pressure from any big power."

NATIONAL PEOPLE'S CONGRESS, JUNE 1983

The evolution of China's independent foreign policy was reflected notably in Premier Zhao Ziyang's detailed survey of China's foreign relations at the opening session of the Sixth National People's Congress (NPC) on 6 June 1983. Zhao expressed Beijing's continuing wariness on relations with the United States, urged the Soviet Union to remove its threat to China's security in order to open the way to improved Sino-Soviet relations, and adopted an unusually upbeat approach to Soviet bloc countries in Eastern Europe.[94]

In laying out the guiding principles of Beijing's approach to foreign affairs, Zhao reaffirmed three elements that had been cited by other leaders as the basis of Chinese foreign policy over the previous year. Zhao called "opposition to hegemonism and safeguarding world peace" China's "basic point of departure," reaffirmed China's readiness to develop relations with all states on the basis of the five principles of peaceful coexistence, and cited "solidarity and cooperation" with the third world as China's "basic stand" in foreign affairs. As Chinese statements had done since 1981, Zhao identified "superpower contention for world hegemony" as the "main source" of tensions in the world.

Zhao's cool assessment of the evolution of recent Sino-American relations was in keeping with similar authoritative Chinese expressions of wariness that had appeared in recent years. Zhao acknowledged that there had been "some development" in Sino-American relations since normalization, but he added that what progress there had been "falls short of what could have been achieved." Zhao cited Washington's commitment to the Taiwan Relations Act and continued arms sales to Taipei as "flagrant violations" of commitments incorporated into standing PRC-U.S. joint communiqués. He sounded the plaintive theme heard from China recently in asking Washington to "stop doing anything" that harms the relationship and "hurts the Chinese people's feelings."

Regarding Taiwan, *Xinhua* reported Zhao's pledge to continue efforts to "end as soon as possible the artificial barrier" that separated the people of Taiwan from the mainland and his expression of gratitude to all Chinese who had contributed to efforts promoting China's "peaceful reunification."[95]

Zhao's comments on Sino-Soviet relations amounted to a message that Moscow must make a serious move toward meeting Beijing's demands before real progress could be achieved. He highlighted Beijing's longstanding demand that Moscow remove the "real threat to China's security"—a reference to Soviet troops along the Sino-Soviet and Sino-Mongolian borders, Soviet intervention in Afghanistan, and Moscow's support for Vietnam in Kampuchea—as the "first step" toward improving ties. At the same time, however, he avoided clouding the atmosphere surrounding the dialogue. Thus, he did not specifically place blame on Moscow. Instead, he observed that relations had been strained for a long time, and he struck a positive note in adding that such a situation was "not to the advantage of either party" and that the peoples of both countries were interested in normalizing ties.[96]

Zhao's comments on the loyalist Soviet bloc countries in Eastern Europe were notably upbeat. In keeping with the warm atmosphere reflected in Chinese treatment of Vice-Foreign minister Qian Qichen's visits to Budapest, Berlin, and Warsaw in May 1983, Zhao observed that the Chinese people held "friendly feelings" for the people of the East European countries, and he predicted that Chinese relations with those states would continue to improve. China's special relationships with Romania and Yugoslavia were duly noted, but Zhao went on to state Chinese interest in the "accomplishments and experience in socialist construction" of East European countries other than these two. He also pointed to these countries' "socialist" character.[97]

Zhao's overture clearly implied greater Chinese interest in fostering relations with the loyalist ruling parties of Eastern Europe and represented a significant broadening of efforts to increase Chinese influence in the international Communist movement. The Chinese had followed the restoration of party ties with Yugoslavia during Tito's visit to China in 1977 with exploratory contacts with some of the major West European Communist parties, resulting notably in the restoration of party relations with the Italian Communist Party in 1980 and with the French Communist Party in 1982. China's more ecumenical approach to interparty relations also achieved substantial success in the third world. In April 1983, for example, the CCP announced it had restored relations with the Communist Party of India-Marxist, a party Beijing had previously reviled as revisionist. As in the case of Chinese contacts with European parties, Beijing made it clear that it still had differences of opinion with the Indians, but it soft-pedaled these concerns for the sake of renewed relations on the basis of the principle of "independence"—a precept with implicit anti-Soviet overtones.[98]

Regarding developing contacts with the East European loyalist parties, China slowly built contacts with the East German party from 1982, and to a lesser degree with the Hungarian party. On 11 March 1984, for instance, both East German and Chinese media reported that Chinese Party Secretary-General Hu Yaobang conveyed greetings via the Chinese ambassador to East Germany's General Secretary Erich Honecker, and that Honecker reciprocated with greetings to the Chinese party leader.[99] Other developments in Chinese-East German party relations included the following:

- In June 1983, Honecker broke with past practice and used both his party and his state titles in a congratulatory message to the new Chinese president.

- In August 1983, a delegation from the Chinese party newpaper was received in East Germany by representatives of the party Central Committee.

- In October 1983, an East German party politburo member and party secretary attended a Chinese embassy reception.

- Also in October 1983, Chinese media reported that the East German ambassador briefed journalists in Beijing on his country's "socialist revolution and socialist construction in the past 34 years."

- In December 1983, Chinese Vice-Premier Wan Li—meeting an East German Minister in what the Chinese media called the "highest contact between the two countries in 20 years"—affirmed the view that China and East Germany are both "socialist countries."

Meanwhile, Chinese contacts with the Hungarian party were beginning to develop. In particular, during 1983 the foreign editor of the Hungarian party newspaper visited Beijing; a Chinese news delegation visited the offices of the Hungarian party paper in Budapest; and a representative of the Chinese Youth League journal met with Hungarian counterparts in Budapest.[100]

It seemed likely that in the contacts both sides were pursuing sharply different objectives. China appeared to want to broaden its influence in the international Communist movement, burnish its "independent" image in international affairs, and encourage whatever loosening of Moscow's grip on these parties might be possible. Beijing also may have calculated that improving contacts with the loyalist parties would implicitly but clearly hold out the possibility to Moscow of eventually restoring party-to-party ties, although such movement would almost certainly have involved substantial Soviet compromises on the major geopolitical issues dividing them. At the same time, Beijing probably suspected that the loyalist parties were cooperating with China as part of Soviet efforts to woo China back into the socialist camp. As a result, the contacts developed slowly as each side examined each initiative for assurance that it would accord with its interests and not be turned against it.

China's ability to deal more pragmatically and effectively with these and other previously shunned political parties and groups was reinforced by Beijing's more flexible attitude to the role of ideology in foreign affairs—an approach that in effect removed past serious ideological obstacles to improved relations. In particular:

- Beijing's more pragmatic approach to economic development caused Chinese leaders to all but ignore past criteria regarding "revisionist" domestic policies in determining whether to establish and maintain political contacts. Even in the case of the USSR, Beijing leaders now avoided critiques of most Soviet internal policies—a major source of disagreement in the past. Beijing portrayed the major ideological obstacle in Sino-Soviet relations as Moscow's insistence on practicing "hegemony" in the international Communist movement and in its foreign policy in general.

- Beijing also gradually put aside its past insistence on basing its foreign policy on the Leninist thesis that so long as imperialism exists, war is inevitable. During the late 1970s and early 1980s, Chinese officials slowly shifted to an approach that held out first the possibility of "putting off" world war, and then the possibility of "preventing" such a conflict. In this context, Beijing was then able to adopt a more reasonable approach to international disarmament efforts, including superpower arms control talks, and to take a more positive approach to the international peace movement.

NOTES

1. *DR China*, 3 April 1981.
2. *DR China*, 9 April 1981.
3. Ibid.
4. For background, see Banning Garrett and Bonnie Glaser, *War and Peace: The Views from Moscow and Beijing* (Berkeley: University of California Press, 1984); and Harry Harding, and Jonathan Pollack's article in Harry Harding, ed., *China's Foreign Relations in the 1980s* (New Haven: Yale University Press, 1984).
5. See, for instance, FBIS, *Chinese Party Plenum: Movement Toward Succession, Rectification*, analysis report, (Washington D.C. 1980).
6. See the text of the indictment in *DR China*, 20 November 1980.
7. For background and analysis, see FBIS, *Political Instability in China Slows Progress on Reforms*, analysis report. (Washington D.C., FBIS, 1981).
8. For background and analysis, see article by Robert Dernberger in U.S. Congress, Joint Economic Committee, *China Under the Four Modernizations* (Washington, D.C.: U.S. Government Printing Office, 1982). See also his article in U. Alexis Johnson, ed., *China: Policy for the Next Decade* (Boston: Oelgeschlager, Gunn, and Hain, 1984).
9. See FBIS, *Political Instability*.
10. The 17 January editorial is in *DR China*, 19 January 1981.
11. In *DR China*, 9 February 1981.
12. *DR China*, 10 March 1981.
13. *DR China*, 11 March 1981.
14. *DR China*, 29 June 1981.
15. See Dernberger articles in Joint Economic Committee, . . . *Four Modernizations*; and Johnson, ed., *China: . . . Next Decade.*
16. *DR China*, 16 December 1981.
17. See Kenneth Lieberthal, "Domestic Politics and Foreign Policy," in Harry Harding, ed., *China's Foreign Relations in the 1980s*; Carol Hamrin, "Emergence of an 'Independent' Chinese Foreign Policy and Shifts in Sino-U.S. Relations," in James Hsiung, ed., *U.S.-Asian Relations* (New York: Praeger, 1983); Jonathan Pollack; *The Lessons of Coalition Politics* (Santa Monica, Calif.: Rand Corp., 1984).
18. Ibid. See also article by Carol Hamrin in *Asian Survey*, May 1984.
19. For good background and useful analysis, see A. Doak Barnett, *The FX Decision* (Washington, D.C.: Brookings Institution, 1981).
20. *DR China*, 16 June 1980.
21. *DR China*, 20 and 23 June 1980.
22. *DR China*, 28 August 1980.
23. *DR China*, 16 October 1980.
24. See background and analysis in FBIS, *Beijing, Moscow Apparaisals of Haig Visit*, analysis report (Washington, D.C. 1981).
25. *DR China*, 15 June 1981.
26. The only precedent for such an omission in recent years occurred during the visit of Secretary of State Vance in 1977, at a time of similar PRC concern that disagreement over Taiwan might impede the bilateral relationship with the United States. See FBIS, *Beijing, Moscow . . . .*
27. When former President Richard Nixon was in Beijing in late 1979, Deng was quoted as hailing the "flourishing friendship" between the two countries and as stressing its importance for "the cause of world peace and the struggle against hegemonism." During the Brown visit, Deng was cited at length as praising the "momentum" that had been maintained in the relationship since the normalization, and as stressing the "great significance"

of the visit and the urgent need for Sino-American strategic cooperation. Such sentiments also were publicized in reports on lower-level talks between Brown and Vice-Premier Geng Biao. This time, *Xinhua* on 15 June merely reported that Secretary Haig and Geng had discussed defense matters. See FBIS, *Beijing, Moscow*. . . .

28. *DR China*, 16 June 1981.

29. The Western press had reported that Deng Xiaoping proffered this invitation through former President Ford, who visited China in March 1980, but Chinese media did not publicize it. See FBIS, *Beijing, Moscow*. . . .

30. *DR China*, 17 June 1981.

31. *DR China*, 17 and 19 June 1981.

32. See Pollack's *The Lessons of Coalition Politics.*

33. See Ellen Frost's article in U. Alexis Johnson, ed., *China: Policy.*

34. For background, see articles by Michael Hunt and Harry Harding in Harry Harding, ed., *China's Foreign Relations.*

35. See Chinese coverage of the Lebanon crisis in *DR China*, May-June 1982.

36. See the assessments of Garrett and Glaser, *War and Peace*; and Pollack, *The Lessons of Coalition Politics.*

37. Both repeatedly made these points in testimony before the U.S. Congress in 1981 and 1982.

38. See, for instance, Chinese handling of the visit of U.S. Speaker of the House Tip O'Neill in 1983, analyzed below. See also *DR China* 29, 30 March 1983.

39. See article by Alfred D. Wilhelm in U. Alexis Johnson, ed., *China: Policy for the Next Decade*; and article by June Teufel Dreyer in *Current History*, September 1984.

40. Carol Hamrin, "Competing 'Policy Packages' and Chinese Foreign Policy," *Asian Survey*, May 1984; Allen Whiting, "Assertive Nationalism in Chinese Foreign Policy," *Asian Survey*, August 1983.

41. *DR China*, 1 July 1981.

42. *DR China*, 5 July 1981.

43. See analysis in *FBIS Trends*, 15 July 1981.

44. *DR China*, 9 October 1981.

45. See *Far Eastern Economic Review*, 20 November 1981. See also Pollack, *Lessons of Coalition Politics.*

46. *DR China*, 16 December 1981.

47. *DR China*, 17 December 1981.

48. *DR China*, 31 December 1981.

49. *DR China*, 25 January 1982.

50. See *FBIS Trends*, 12 May 1982. See also Pollack, *Lessons of Coalition Politics.*

51. *DR China*, 10 May 1982.

52. During Secretary Haig's June 1981 visit, his opening talks with Foreign Minister Huang Hua were described as "sincere and frank." Later Deng commented that these early talks had gone "very well," and his own talks with Haig—in which he conveyed his best wishes to President Reagan—were conducted in a "cordial and frank" atmosphere, according to *Xinhua*.

Moreover, whereas Huang Hua told Secretary Haig at the end of his trip in 1981 that its results were "positive," and "warmly" congratulated him on a "successful" visit, Vice-Premier Wan Li told Vice-President Bush at the close of his visit merely that the discussions had been "useful" in clarifying the "importance and urgency" of settling the Taiwan issue. In contrast with normal practice, Beijing did not issue a wrap-up report on the visit. See *DR China*, 10 May 1982.

53. *DR China*, 17 August 1982.

54. *DR China*, 8 October 1982.

55. *DR China*, 12 October 1982.

56. See *DR China*, 4 January, 18 January, 9 February, and 5 April 1983.

57. *DR China*, 25 February 1983.

58. *DR China*, 29 and 30 March 1983.

59. *DR China*, 29 March 1983.

60. *DR China*, 30 March 1983.

61. *DR China*, 1 April 1983.

62. For background, see article by Chi Su in Samuel Kim, ed., *Chinese Foreign Policy in the 1980s* (Boulder, Colo.: Westview Press, 1984); U.S. Information Agency, "Sino-Soviet Relations: A Review of Developments Since Afghanistan," research memorandum, 7 March 1984; *China Quarterly*, "Chronology," (issued each March, June, September, December 1979-85).

63. *DR China*, 30 April 1982.

64. See Griffith, "Sino-Soviet Rapprochement"; articles by "Yurkov" in *DR USSR*, 3, 4, and 10 March 1982; Zagoria, "Moscow-Beijing Detente"; Pollack, *The Sino-Soviet Rivalry*; Chi Su article in Kim, *Chinese Foreign Policy*; USIA, "Sino-Soviet Relations."

65. *DR China*, 24 November 1981.

66. *DR China*, 9 March 1982.

67. See *DR China*, 26 March 1982, for PRC reactions.

68. See Chi Su's article in Samuel Kim, ed., *Chinese Foreign Policy*.

69. *New York Times*, 28 October 1982.

70. See U.S. Congress, Joint Economic Committee, *Allocation of Resources in the Soviet Union and China—1983* (Washington, D.C.: U.S. Government Printing Office, 1984), pp. 159-61.

71. Ibid., pp. 162-64.

72. Ibid., pp. 164-67.

73. See, for instance, *China Quarterly* "chronology" dealing with Africa during this period. Note especially March 1982 edition. See also London *Observer*, 11 October 1981.

74. Trade figures from Central Intelligence Agency, *China: International Trade* (updated quarterly).

75. See U.S. Congress, Joint Economic Committee, *Allocation of Resources*, pp. 86, 181-82.

76. See in particular *DR China*, 29 June 1981.

77. See respectively *China Quarterly*, "Chronology," March 1982 and September 1982 for coverage of these developments.

78. *DR China*, 19 October 1981.

79. *DR China*, 3 and 10 August 1981.

80. The trips are noted in respectively *China Quarterly*, "chronology" March 1980 and September.

81. For coverage of Zhao's trip, see *China Quarterly*, "Chronology," and *DR China* covering December-January 1982-83.

82. See *DR China*, 27 December 1982, 7 and 28 January 1983.

83. The trips are noted in respectively *China Quarterly*, "chronology" March 1980 and September.

84. Ho Ying visited Syria and Libya in May 1982.

85. CIA, *China: International Trade* (updated quarterly).

86. See U.S. Congress, Joint Economic Committee, *Allocation of Resources*, pp. 86, 181-82.

87. The following is based on Yitzhak Shichor, "The Middle East in Chinese Defense Policy," in Gerald Segal and William Tow, eds., *Chinese Defence Policy* (London: Macmillan, 1984). See also U.S. Congress, Joint Economic Committee, *Allocation of Resources*, pp. 181-82.

88. This section is based on Robert Sutter, "U.S.-Soviet-PRC Relations and Their Implications for Korea," *Korea and World Affairs*, Winter 1983.

89. See *DR China*, 21–23 December 1981.

90. Chinese defense ministers were generally in poor health during the previous 20 years—perhaps accounting for their lack of foreign travel. Prior to being appointed defense minister, Geng Biao had visited the United States in his capacity as secretary-general of the Military Affairs Commission of the CCP; and while there was no record in recent years of previous visits by either Chinese or North Korean defense ministers, lower-level military exchanges were routine. China had sent one or more military delegations each year for the previous several years, and North Korea dispatched a military group about every two years. See *DR China*, 21 and 22 June 1982.

91. See *DR China*, 16–22 September 1982.

92. *DR China*, 17 September 1982.

93. Coverage of the congress is in *DR China*, 7–10 September 1982. Hu's report appears in *DR China*, 8 September 1982.

94. Zhao's report appeared in *DR China*, 23 June 1983.

95. Zhou Enlai's widow, Deng Yingchao, a CCP Politburo member, also reaffirmed Beijing's united front approach toward reunification in a speech to the Sixth CPPCC's opening session on 4 June, citing both the 1 January 1979 NPC message to Taiwan and Ye Jianying's 30 September 1981 nine-point proposal as the continuing basis of PRC policy. See *DR China*, 6 June 1983.

96. Zhao did, however, put the burden for improvement solely on Moscow, declaring that "positive proposals" put forward by Beijing during consultations still awaited a Soviet response. Previous Chinese statements had not asserted that Beijing had presented proposals in the two rounds of bilateral talks held thus far.

97. Although Chinese media in the previous two years had carried several articles favorably describing economic reform policies in Hungary, Czechoslovakia, and other East European bloc countries, the conciliatory gesture implied in Zhao's statement represented a notable departure from the way the Chinese had depicted East European bloc countries other than Romania since the 1960s. As recently as September 1982, Hu Yaobang had observed simply that China's relations with East European bloc countries had "seen some development" in recent years, and even this modest observation was separate from his discussion of relations with the "friendly socialist countries"—Korea, Romania, and Yugoslavia. See *DR China*, 8 September 1982.

98. *Xinhua*, 26 April 1983.

99. See *Xinhua*, 11 March 1984.

100. See *FBIS Trends* and *China Quarterly*, "Chronology," for these developments in Chinese-East European relations. In particular see *FBIS Trends*, 15 June 1983, 13 October 1983 and 14 March 1984.

9

CONSOLIDATING TIES WITH THE WEST AGAINST THE USSR, 1983-84

Changes in Chinese calculations, based largely on perceptions of shifts in the international balance of power affecting China, caused Beijing to adjust its independent approach to foreign affairs beginning in 1983. At bottom, Chinese leaders became increasingly concerned about the stability of the nation's surroundings in Asia at a time of unrelenting build-up of Soviet military and political pressure along China's periphery, and of serious and possibly prolonged decline in relations with the United States. They decided that the foreign policy tactics of the previous two years, designed to distance China from the policies of the United States and to moderate and improve relations with the Soviet Union, were less likely to safeguard the important Chinese security and development concerns affected by the stability of the Asian environment. They recognized in particular that Beijing would have to stop its pullback from the United States for fear of jeopardizing this link so important for maintaining its security and development interests in the face of persistent Soviet pressure in Asia. Thus, in 1983 Beijing began to retreat from some of the tactical changes made in the previous two years under the rubric of an independent approach to foreign affairs. The result was a substantial reduction in Chinese pressure on the United States over Taiwan and other issues; increased Chinese interest and flexibility in dealing with the Reagan administration and other Western countries across a broad range of economic, political, and security issues; and heightened Sino-Soviet antipathy. Beijing still attempted to nurture whenever possible the increased influence it had garnered by means of its independent posture in the third world and the international Communist movement, but it increasingly sided with the West against the USSR to secure basic strategic and economic interests.

CHINA'S CALCULUS IN THE GREAT-POWER TRIANGLE

The key element in China's decision to change tactics toward the United States was an altered view of the likely course of Sino-American-Soviet relations over the next several years. When China began its more independent approach to foreign affairs and its concurrent harder line toward the United States in 1981-82, it had hoped to elicit a more forthcoming U.S. attitude toward issues sensitive to Chinese interests, notably Taiwan. Beijing almost certainly judged that there were possibly serious risks of alienating the United States, which had provided an implicit but vital counterweight serving Chinese security interests against the USSR for over a decade and assisting more recent Chinese economic development concerns. But the Chinese seemed to have assessed that their room for maneuver had been increased because:

- The United States had reasserted a balance in East-West relations likely to lead to a continued major check on possible Soviet expansion.

- The Soviet ability to pressure China had appeared to be at least temporarily blocked by U.S. power as well as by Soviet domestic and international problems.

- At least some important U.S. leaders continued to consider preserving good U.S. relations with China an important element in U.S. efforts to confront and contain Soviet expansion.

By mid-1983, China saw these calculations upset. In particular, the United States adopted a new posture that publicly downgraded China's strategic importance. The change in U.S. position occurred after the resignation of Secretary of State Alexander Haig, perhaps the strongest high-level advocate in the Reagan administration of sustaining good relations with China as an important strategic means to counter the USSR. Secretary of State George Shultz and his new assistant secretary for East Asian affairs, Paul Wolfowitz, were less identified with this approach. Shultz held a series of meetings with government and nongovernment Asian specialists in Washington in early 1983, in order to review U.S. Asian policy in general and policy toward China in particular.[1] The results of this reassessment—implicitly but clearly downgrading China's importance to the United States—were reflected in speeches by Shultz and Wolfowitz later in the year.[2]

U.S. planners now appeared to judge that efforts to improve relations with China were less important than in the recent past because:

- China seemed unlikely to cooperate further with the United States (through military sales or security consultations, for instance against the Soviet Union) at a time when the PRC had publicly distanced itself from the United States and had reopened talks on normalization of relations with the USSR.

- At the same time, China's continued preoccupation with pragmatic economic modernization and internal development made it appear unlikely that the PRC would revert to a highly disruptive position in East Asia that would adversely affect U.S. interests in the stability of the region.

- China's demands on Taiwan and other bilateral disputes, and the accompanying threats to downgrade U.S.-Chinese relations if its demands were not met, appeared open-ended and excessive.

- U.S. ability to deal militarily and politically with the USSR had improved, particularly as a result of the large-scale Reagan administration military budget increases and perceived serious internal and international difficulties of the USSR.

- U.S. allies, for the first time in years, were working more closely with Washington in dealing with the Soviet military threat. This was notably true in Asia, where Prime Minister Nakasone took positions and initiatives underlining common Japanese-U.S. concerns against the Soviet danger.

- Japan and U.S. allies and friends in Southeast Asia—unlike China—appeared to be more immediately important to the United States in protecting against what was seen as the primary U.S. strategic concern in the region— safeguarding air and sea access to East Asia, the Indian Ocean, and the Persian Gulf from Soviet attack.[3] China appeared less important in dealing with this perceived Soviet danger.

Western press reports[4] quoting authoritative sources in Washington alerted China to the implications of this shift in the U.S. approach for PRC interests. In effect, the shift meant that Chinese ability to exploit U.S. interest in strategic relations with China, in order to compel the United States to meet Chinese demands on Taiwan and other questions, had been sharply reduced. Underlining this trend for China was the continued unwillingness of the United States throughout this period to accommodate high-level PRC pressure over Taiwan, the asylum case of Hu Na, the Chinese representation issue in the Asian Development Bank, and other questions. The Reagan administration publicly averred that U.S. policy on these questions would remain constant whether or not Beijing decided to retaliate or threatened to downgrade relations by withdrawing its ambassador from Washington or some other action.

Moreover, Beijing saw its perceived political leverage in the United States to be small. Chinese press reporting noted the strong revival in the U.S. economy in 1983 and the positive political implications this had for President Reagan's reelection campaign.[5] China also had to be aware, through contacts with leading Democrats, notably Speaker of the

House O'Neill, that Beijing could expect little change in U.S. policy toward Taiwan under a Democratic administration.[6] As 1983 wore on, the Chinese saw an alarming rise in the influence of U.S. advocates of self-determination for Taiwan among liberal Democrats. In particular Senator Claiborne Pell took the lead in gaining passage of a controversial resolution in the Senate Foreign Relations Committee that endorsed, among other things, the principle of self-determination for Taiwan—anathema to Beijing.[7]

Meanwhile, although Sino-Soviet trade, cultural, and technical contacts were increasing, Beijing saw little sign of Soviet willingness to compromise on basic political and security issues during the vice-foreign ministerial talks that began in October 1982. And the Soviet military buildup in Asia—including the deployment of highly accurate SS-20 intermediate-range missiles—continued.

In short, Beijing faced the prospect of a period of prolonged decline in Sino-American relations—possibly lasting until the end of Reagan's second presidential term—if it continued to follow the hard line of the previous two years in relations with the United States. This decline brought the risk of cutting off the implicit but vitally important Chinese strategic understanding with the United States in the face of a prolonged danger posed by the USSR.

The Chinese also recognized that a substantial decline in relations with the United States would have undercut their already limited leverage with Moscow; it likely would have substantially reduced any possible Soviet interest in accommodating China in order to preclude closer U.S.-Chinese security ties or collaboration against the USSR. It also would have run the risk of upsetting China's ability to gain greater access not only to U.S. markets and financial and technical assistance and expertise, but also to those of other important capitalist countries. Now that the Chinese economy was successfully emerging from the strict readjustments begun in 1980-81, the Western economic connection appeared more important to PRC planners. Yet many U.S. allies and friends, notably Japan, were more reluctant to undertake heavy economic involvement in China at a time of uncertain U.S.-Chinese political relations. The United States also exerted strong influence in international financial institutions that were expected to be the source of several billion dollars in aid for China in the 1980s.

China had to caluculate as well that a serious decline in U.S.-Chinese relations would likely result in a concurrent increase in U.S.-Taiwanese ties. As a result, Beijing's chances of using Taiwan's isolation to prompt Taipei to move toward reunification in accord with PRC interests would be set back seriously.

Domestically, any backing away from the hard line toward the

United States on Taiwan and other issues almost certainly represented a difficult compromise for those leaders who had pushed this approach. Deng Xiaoping had not been closely associated with this group, however, favoring instead the building of a relationship with the United States against the USSR. Deng and his political protégés showed considerable power in pursuing their domestic reform programs during this time, suggesting that their ability to shift foreign policy to a more accommodating approach toward Washington was not seriously complicated by internal political factors. Meanwhile, Deng may have felt that a consolidation of China's relations with the Reagan administration was needed at this juncture, particularly to assure that his successors—only recently exposed to international affairs—would have a stable security framework as they began to grapple with internal and international problems following Deng's likely demise in the next few years.

Reflecting these kinds of calculations, the Chinese responded quickly and positively to the latest in a series of Reagan administration efforts to ease technology transfer restrictions—announced by Commerce Secretary Malcolm Baldridge during a trip to China in May 1983. They followed up by agreeing to schedule a long-delayed visit by Secretary of Defense Caspar Weinberger in September, and to exchange visits by Premier Zhao and President Reagan at the turn of the year. Beijing media attempted to portray these moves as Chinese responses to U.S. concessions, and as consistent with China's avowed "independent" approach to foreign affairs and its firm stance on U.S.-Taiwanese relations. But, as time went on, it became clear just how much Beijing was prepared to moderate past public demands and threats of retaliation over Taiwan and other issues for the sake of consolidating Sino-American political, economic, and security ties:

- In 1981, Beijing had publicly disavowed any interest in military purchases from the United States until the United States satisfied China's position on the sale of arms to Taiwan.[8] It continued to note that it was dissatisfied with U.S. arms transfers to Taiwan—which continued at a pace of over $700 million a year; but it now was willing to negotiate with the United States over Chinese purchases of U.S. military equipment. Defense Minister Zhang Aiping disclosed that negotiations on arms sales were revived during Secretary Weinberger's visit to China in September 1983.[9]

- Beijing soft-pedaled past demands, threats, and accusations that the United States was not fulfilling the 1979 and 1982 Sino-American joint communiqués.

- Beijing backed away from previous demands that the United States repeal or amend the Taiwan Relations Act, or face a decline in relations.

- Beijing muffled previous demands that the United States alter its position regarding Taiwan's continued membership in the Asian Development Bank.

- China reduced criticism of official and unofficial U.S. contacts with Taiwan counterparts. It notably avoided criticism of U.S. officials being present at Taipei-sponsored functions in Washington. Beijing was even willing to turn a blind eye to the almost 30 members of Congress who traveled to Taiwan in various delegations in January 1984—coincident with Zhao Ziyang's trip to Washington. It even welcomed some of the members who traveled on to the mainland after visiting Taiwan.

- Beijing allowed Northwest Airlines to open service to China in 1984, even though the airline still served Taiwan. This was a marked contrast with the authoritative Chinese position adopted in 1983 in response to Pan American's decision to reenter the Taiwan market while also serving the mainland.

- China reduced complaints about the slowness of U.S. transfers of technology to China and about the continued inability of the administration to successfully push legislative changes that would have allowed the Chinese to receive American assistance.

China's greatest compromise was to give a warm welcome to President Reagan, despite his continued avowed determination to maintain close U.S. ties with "old friends" on Taiwan. Beijing almost certainly was well aware that the timing of the visit would serve to assist the president's reelection in the fall, as well as that the president was unlikely to accommodate Chinese interests over Taiwan and some other sensitive issues during the visit. Indeed, Chinese reportage made it clear that there was no change in the president's position on the Taiwan issue during the visit.[10] Thus, the best the Chinese could have hoped for in this regard was to try to consolidate U.S.-PRC relations to secure broader strategic and economic interests, while possibly expecting that such a closer relationship over time would reduce the president's firm position on Taiwan and other bilateral disputes.

The Reagan administration, meanwhile, attempted to add impetus to the relationship by accommodating Chinese concerns through the avoidance of strong rhetorical support for Taiwan that in the past had so inflamed U.S.-PRC tensions, and by moving ahead on military and technology transfers to the PRC. Nevertheless, when the U.S.-Chinese nuclear cooperation agreement, which had been initialed during the president's visit, became stalled because of opposition from nonproliferation advocates in the United States who were concerned about reports of China's support for Pakistan's alleged nuclear weapons program, China went along with administration explanations with only minor complaint. In short, by mid-1984 it appeared that at a minimum Beijing was determined to further strengthen military and economic ties with the United States and to soft-pedal bilateral difficulties. On the question of Taiwan, Beijing retreated to a position that asked for U.S. adherence to the joint communiqués and accelerated reduction of U.S. arms sales to Taiwan, but was not prepared to make a significant issue of the question prior to the presidential election, unless severely provoked.

China's incentive to accommodate the United States was reinforced by Beijing's somber view of Sino-Soviet relations. Disappointed with its inability to elicit substantial Soviet concessions—or even a slowing in the pace of Soviet military expansion in Asia—during the Andropov administration, Beijing saw the Chernenko government as even more rigid and uncompromising. In response, China hardened its line and highlighted public complaints against Soviet pressure and intimidation—an approach that had the added benefit of broadening common ground between China and the West, especially the Reagan administration.

The Sino-Soviet vice-foreign ministerial talks,[11] revived in October 1982, met semi-annually, alternating between Beijing and Moscow. The chief Chinese negotiator was Vice-Foreign Minister Qian Qichen; his Soviet counterpart was Vice-Foreign Minister Leonid Ilichev, a veteran of the Sino-Soviet border talks. Technically, the talks were not considered formal negotiations, which had been suspended by the Chinese after the Soviet invasion of Afghanistan. Although progress was made on some secondary issues, these talks were unable to bridge a major gap between the positions of the two sides on basic security and political issues. Beijing stuck to its preconditions for improved Sino-Soviet relations involving withdrawal of Soviet forces from along the Sino-Soviet border and from Mongolia (later China added specific reference to Soviet SS-20 missiles targeted against China); an end to Soviet support for Vietnam's occupation of Kampuchea; and withdrawal of Soviet forces from Afghanistan.

Beijing sometimes said that Soviet movement on only one of these questions would open the way to substantially improved Sino-Soviet relations. But Moscow remained unwilling to compromise, stating that the USSR would not discuss matters affecting third countries.

In part to get around this roadblock, a second forum of vice-foreign ministerial discussions was begun in September 1983, during the visit of Soviet Vice-Foreign Minister Mikhail Kapitsa to China. This was the fourth visit to China by Kapitsa, a leading Soviet China expert, in as many years; but it was the first time he came at the invitation of the Chinese government. The other times he had come at the request of the Soviet embassy in Beijing.

Kapitsa held two sessions of talks with his Chinese counterpart, Vice-

Foreign Minister Qian Qichen, and met with Chinese Foreign Minister Wu Xueqian. The discussions covered each side's views of recent developments in the Middle East, Central America, the Indian Ocean, Afghanistan, and Indochina; concerns over arms control—including the deployment of the SS-20 missiles in Asia; and other questions. No agreement was noted.[12]

Progress in both sets of talks came only in secondary areas of trade, technology transfers, and educational and cultural exchanges:

- They agreed to substantially increase Sino-Soviet trade over the minimal levels in recent years.

- They agreed to exchange language students and teachers.

- China agreed to consider Soviet offers to rehabilitate some of the Soviet-supplied factories in China.

- They were in accord on exchanges of tourist, friendship, technical, and other delegations.

Both sides attempted to give added impetus to progress in these areas coincident with the exchange of high-level Sino-American visits in early 1984. In particular, Moscow proposed, and Beijing accepted, a visit to China by Soviet First Deputy Prime Minister Arkhipov, reportedly to discuss longer-term economic and technical assistance to China. Arkhipov, who had been a senior Soviet economic adviser in China in the 1950s, would have been the highest-level Soviet official to visit China since 1969. The visit was timed to occur just after President Reagan's departure from China in early May 1984. Moscow presumably judged that the visit provided the USSR with a certain amount of leverage over China— Arkhipov could be forthcoming or not with economic assistance for China, depending on how close Sino-American relations became during President Reagan's visit. For Beijing, improved contacts with Moscow allowed it to preserve a semblance of balance in its relations with the two superpowers and thereby enhance its independent image in foreign affairs.[13]

Nevertheless, both sides proved willing to disrupt these contacts when more important strategic and political issues were at stake. Beijing in particular was disappointed with the meager results of its initial overture to the new Chernenko regime. China had sent its ranking vice-premier, Wan Li, as its representative to the funeral of Andropov in February 1984—marking a substantial upgrading from Beijing's dispatch of Foreign Minister Huang Hua to Brezhnev's funeral in 1982. But Wan received a cool welcome in Moscow. Moreover, the Soviets then appeared to go out of their way to publicize strong support for Mongolia and Vietnam against China, and they underlined Soviet unwillingness to make compromises with China at the expense of third countries.[14]

Beijing also saw Moscow as resorting to stronger military means in both Europe and Asia in order to assert Soviet power and determination at a time of leadership transition in the Kremlin. Chinese media portrayed Moscow as on the defensive on a whole range of international issues, particularly its failure to halt the deployment of U.S. Pershing and cruise missiles in Western Europe, or to exploit the peace movement in Europe as a way to disrupt the Western alliance over the deployments and other issues. They now saw Moscow—faced with ever growing Western military power and greater solidarity in the face of the Soviet threat—as lashing out with new demonstrations of its military power.[15] In Asia, this perceived Soviet approach directly affected Chinese security and appeared designed ultimately to bring China to heel. In February and March, the Soviet Union deployed two of its three aircraft carriers to the Western Pacific; one passed near China in late February, on its way to Vladivostok.[16] And in March, the USSR used an aircraft carrier task force to support its first joint amphibious exercise with Vietnam, which was conducted fairly close to China and near the Vietnamese port city of Haiphong. This followed the reported stationing of several Soviet medium bombers at Cam Ranh Bay, Vietnam, in late 1983—the first time such Soviet forces were reported to be stationed outside areas contiguous with the USSR.[17]

Meanwhile, the Chinese escalated their military pressure against the Vietnamese—taking their strongest action precisely at the time of President Reagan's visit to China in late April and early May. As it had done in 1978, and again in 1979, Beijing presumably felt more secure in confronting Moscow's Asian ally after it had consolidated relations with the United States. China's action against Vietnam also underlined an area of important strategic common ground between Beijing and the strongly anti-Soviet Reagan administration. Beijing at the same time escalated charges regarding the Soviet threat to Chinese security, especially via Vietnam, and attempted to establish publicly an identity of interests with both Japanese Prime Minister Nakasone, during a visit to China in March, and President Reagan in April, on the basis of opposition to Soviet expansion in Asia.[18]

The result was the most serious downturn in Sino-Soviet relations since the Soviet invasion of Afghanistan in late 1979:

- Both Moscow and Beijing revived polemical exchanges, trading particular charges over issues involving sensitive security issues in Asia, East-West arms control efforts in Europe, and the international Communist movement. There were still limits on the polemics, however. They did not exchange charges against each other's internal political-economic-social system, nor did they engage in personal invective directed at individual leaders.

• The bilateral diplomatic dialogue was disrupted for a time, as the USSR— presumably concerned about and irritated by China's closer relations with the United States and its tougher posture toward Vietnam—postponed for an indefinite time the visit of First Deputy Prime Minister Arkhipov to China.

• Sino-Vietnamese military confrontation along their common border continued into the summer of 1984, well beyond the usual period of fighting coincident with the annual Vietnamese dry season campaign against Chinese-supported resistance forces in Kampuchea. This heightened fighting prompted the USSR leaders, and Chernenko in particular, to publicly condemn China by name—the first such occurrence since before Brezhnev's death in 1982.

• Sino-Soviet political competition heated up in Korea as both sides maneuvered to improve relations with Kim Il-song and his successors. In particular, Moscow welcomed Kim Il-song in May—the Korean leader's first visit to the USSR since 1961.

• Beijing continued to move ahead in establishing closer economic and military ties with the United States, despite the absence of ostensibly balancing progress in Sino-Soviet relations. An article in the Chinese journal *Liaowang* on 16 July 1984 rationalized the now clear Chinese tilt in favor of the United States, asserting that while China continued to pursue an "independent" foreign policy, current international circumstances dictated that it would make much greater progress with the United States than in relations with the USSR.[19]

China was still anxious to manage the Soviet threat without recourse to force, however. It notably held out the option of resumed Sino-Soviet border talks, with Hu Yaobang reportedly telling visitors that a border settlement could be reached relatively easily.[20] And China agreed to remark frontier lines with the Soviet satellite Mongolia, and agreed to set up joint commissions to discuss economic exchanges with Moscow's close East European allies. Moscow of course had long proposed renewed border delineation agreements and the establishment of similar joint economic commissions. Beijing also said that it was willing to receive Arkhipov whenever the USSR would send him, and to conduct foreign ministerial consultations with the Soviets during the U.N. General Assembly session in September.

Moscow moved to respond to the Chinese gestures and to resume forward movement in the less sensitive economic and technical areas of Sino-Soviet relations. The Soviets timed Arkhipov's visit for late December, only two weeks prior to Foreign Minister Gromyko's meetings in Geneva with Secretary of State Shultz on U.S.-Soviet arms control. This suggested that Moscow in part wanted to induce some uncertainty in the minds of U.S. planners about possible future progress in Sino-Soviet relations, and thereby reduce the perceived leverage the United States had gained in regard to the USSR as a result of the growing Sino-American relationship.

Arkhipov was warmly received as "an old friend of China" by high-level Chinese leaders headed by Premier Zhao Ziyang and economic overseer Chen Yun. The visit saw the signing of three agreements that would provide for a broad array of economic cooperation, including the exchange of production technology, the construction and revamping of industrial enterprises, and technical training and exchange of experts and scientific data under the supervision of a new Sino-Soviet economic, trade, scientific, and technological cooperation committee. It was announced that the two countries had agreed to sign a five-year trade agreement in 1985 and that their trade level in 1985 would be 60 percent greater than the value of their trade in 1984.

The visit and agreements brought China's economic relationship with Moscow into line with the its expanding economic relations with other Soviet bloc countries. It apparently did little to ease the differences between the two sides on major political and security issues. Indeed, such differences were exacerbated by Soviet-backed Vietnam's strong military attacks against Chinese-supported insurgents in Kampuchea near the Thai border, actions that coincided with Arkhipov's stay in China.

SINO-JAPANESE RELATIONS[21]

The strategic and economic imperatives governing China's renewed interest in better ties with the United States, and the rising Chinese antipathy toward the USSR were mirrored in China's relations with Japan. Sino-Japanese relations had made great progress in the decade since formal diplomatic relations were established in 1972, but in 1982 had run up against a serious political controversy over revision of Japanese textbooks dealing with the history of imperial Japan's war against China in the 1930s and 1940s. Beijing also registered concern in 1983 about the reported shift in U.S. strategic emphasis in Asia, away from China and in favor of more reliance on Japan, now under the leadership of the more "hawkish" Prime Minister Nakasone, warning anew against possible revival of Japanese "militarism." By mid-1983, however, Beijing had decided—coincident with its decision to improve relations with the Reagan administration—to solidify ties with Japan. Party General Secretary

Hu Yaobang visited Japan in November 1983, and Prime Minister Naka-sone reciprocated by visiting China in March 1984.

The Chinese had long looked upon Japan—their chief trading partner—as a major source of assistance in promoting economic develop-ment in China. And the growth of Soviet military power in East Asia prompted the Chinese to consult on security issues more frequently and to pursue parallel foreign policies designed to check Soviet influence and promote regional stability. While the Japanese enthusiasm for exploit-ing the Chinese market waxed and waned over the previous decade, broad strategic considerations consistently held together Tokyo's policy toward Beijing. In fact, Japan's willingness to involve itself heavily in China's economic modernization efforts reflected in part a determina-tion to help keep China preoccupied with peaceful domestic develop-ment, to draw China into gradually expanding links with Japan and the West, to reduce China's interest in returning to its more provocative for-eign policies of the past, and to obstruct any sort of Sino-Soviet realign-ment against Japan.

Thus, common strategic concerns, as well as economic interests, played important roles in bringing the two sides together. Until the late 1970s, the Chinese appeared more alarmed than Japan about the Soviet military buildup in Asia. But as Moscow increasingly sought to impede the development of strategic cooperation among Japan, the United States,, and possibly China, in part by means of stepped-up intimidation focused on Japan, the Nakasone government became more concerned about the Soviet military buildup.

In many respects, Tokyo's concerns with the USSR duplicated Chi-nese worries:

- The increased deployment in East Asia of Soviet SS-20 missiles, Backfire bombers, and ballistic missile submarines

- The growth of the Soviet Pacific fleet

- The Soviet invasion of Afghanistan and the potential threat it posed to Per-sian Gulf oil supply routes.

- The development of closer Soviet military cooperation and increased mili-tary presence in Vietnam.[22]

In response, both Japan and China adopted strikingly complemen-tary foreign policies—designed to isolate the USSR and its allies politically and to promote regional stability:

- In Southeast Asia, both countries provided strong diplomatic backing for ASEAN's efforts to bring about a Vietnamese withdrawal from Kampuchea. Japan cut off all economic aid to Vietnam and provided substantial economic assistance to Thailand to help with resettling refugees. China, of course, was a key supporter of Thailand, as well as of the Kampuchean resistance groups.

- In Southwest Asia, Japan and China backed the condemnation of the Soviet occupation of Afghanistan, refused to recognize the Kabul regime, and sought through diplomatic and economic means to bolster Pakistan.

- In Northeast Asia, both states sought to exercise a moderating influence over their respective Korean partners to reduce tensions. Indeed, the evolution of Chinese policy toward Korea over the previous decade was shaped in considerable part by Biejing's recognition that instability in Korea probably would have hampered China's efforts to improve relations with the United States and Japan. Thus, the Chinese advised North Korea against seeking a military solution and encouraged Pyongyang to work toward "peaceful" reunification with South Korea. At the same time, Beijing encouraged Tokyo to take the lead in expanding contacts with North Korea, to help bring it out of isolation, arguing that China could not afford to alienate Pyongyang by initiating contacts with Seoul. Nevertheless, in 1983 the Chinese did begin some tentative contacts with South Korean officials. These took place through international organizations to which both nations belonged. Meanwhile, Sino-Korean trade was estimated at several hundred million dollars per year. The Chinese, however, still opposed the idea of cross-recognition, in part because they feared that their endorsement might provoke North Korea to move closer to the USSR.

- In 1983, both China and Japan strongly criticized the Soviet proposal to redeploy some of their European-based SS-20 missiles to Asia. At the Sino-Soviet vice-foreign ministerial talks, the Chinese demanded, as a precondition for normalizing Sino-Soviet relations, that Moscow reduce the present number of SS-20 missiles in Asia. The Chinese also began official exchanges with the Japanese on how the two sides should endeavor to preserve their common interests in the face of the Soviet strategic threat.[23]

Complementary economic interests also served to strengthen Sino-Japanese relations. Japan was a major source of capital, technology, and equipment for China's modernization drive. In fact, it had been China's largest trading partner since the mid-1960s, accounting for more than 20 percent of China's total trade. Bilateral trade virtually exploded in the 1970s and early 1980s, from $1 billion in the early 1970s to over $8 billion in 1982. Tokyo also became China's largest creditor. Of the estimated $30 billion in credit China lined up from 1979 to 1983, Japanese sources accounted for nearly half.[24]

Although its share of Japan's global trade was still small—a modest 3 percent in 1982—China became Japan's sixth largest trading partner.

Japan regarded China as a significant source of coal, oil, and strategic minerals such as tungsten and chromium, and as an important market for Japanese steel, machinery, plant equipment, chemical products, and synthetic textile fibers.

The optimism that marked the economic relationship in the late 1970s gave way to a greater degree of realism on both sides by the early 1980s. China's decision to curtail imports of heavy industrial goods in 1981-82, and its inability to meet its oil and coal commitments to Japan at that time, had a sobering effect on the Japanese. Business people in Japan came to have a better appreciation of the problems China faced, and expected economic ties to grow at a slower pace as the Chinese experimented with various economic policies. Still, the Japanese continued to hope they would profit from China's potentially huge domestic market, whenever its modernization drive began to pick up speed.

Japanese economic interest in China focused on developing energy resources and infrastructure, and on promoting commercial trade. As of 1983, the Overseas Economic Cooperation Fund, Tokyo's official aid organization, had agreed to grant $3.5 billion in loans to China for basic infrastructure projects—such as port and rail modernization. In addition, Japan's Export-Import Bank extended $2 billion for oil exploration and coal mining at a 6.25 percent annual interest rate—the lowest rate China had gained from any country at that time. The Japanese also were heavily involved in China's oil industry, with Japanese drilling in the Bohai Gulf appearing to be promising.

KOREA

As Beijing moved in 1983 to consolidate relations with both Japan and the United States, it had a difficult time managing relations with its very important Asian ally, North Korea. China's difficulty was compounded by the Soviet Union's increased interest in cultivating relations with Kim Il-song at this time. Chinese leaders continued effusive public treatment of North Korea in several exchanges of high-level visits. This was seen notably during the visit of Kim Il-song's son and heir apparent, Kim Chong-il, to China in mid-1983, and the visit of CCP General Secretary Hu Yaobang to North Korea in May 1984. But differences between the two sides emerged over North Korea's assassination of South Korean leaders in a bombing incident at Rangoon, Burma, in October 1983. Though Beijing subsequently showed strong support for Pyongyang's peace proposal announced in January 1984, calling for talks among North Korea, the United States, and South Korea, and it encouraged North Korea to adopt a more flexible economic and development approach that would use greater contacts with the West, the limits of Chinese influence were underlined in late May 1984 when Kim Il-song made his first visit to the USSR in two decades. China may have feared that Kim would attempt to establish common ground with Soviet officials in opposition to what Moscow saw as an emerging U.S.-Japanese-South Korean military bloc in Asia—a position in stark contrast with China's ongoing efforts to improve relations with both Washington and Tokyo on the basis of common opposition to Soviet expansion in East Asia.

A significant, if perhaps temporary, decline in Sino-Korean relations was signaled in media treatment in mid-1984 of the North Korean anniversary of its defense treaties with both Moscow and Beijing.[25] In contrast with past practice, Pyongyang sought to strike a semblance of balance in its treatment of the respective treaty anniversaries. For over a decade, the North Korean anniversaries of the treaties with the Soviet Union (6 July) and China (11 July) had consistently reflected Pyongyang's close ties with China and the relative coolness of Soviet-Korean relations. This was the case even during 1979-81, when Sino-Korean relations were troubled because of China's avowed interest in fostering a strategic international front with the United States and Japan against the Soviet Union. Pyongyang saw that Chinese effort as coming at the expense of active Chinese support for North Korean ambitions on the peninsula. Nevertheless, at that time, Pyongyang made it clear that North Korea regarded its relations with the Soviet Union as secondary to its ties to China.

Pyongyang's new, more balanced approach in mid-1984 appeared to be designed in part to capitalize on Kim Il-son's visit to the USSR and other Eastern European countries from 17 May to 1 July 1984. At the same time, its less effusive treatment of the Chinese anniversary underlined the fact that Hu Yaobang's visit to Pyongyang in May—just after President Reagan's trip to China and just before Kim's departure for Moscow—had failed to resolve differences in the foreign policy strategies of China and North Korea.

Moscow's treatment of Kim's visit and the anniversary demonstrated Soviet interest in establishing closer relations after almost two decades of cool relations. For the USSR, the occasions marked its first diplomatic success in Asia since its reputation had plummeted after a Soviet plane had shot down a South Korean airliner in September 1983. The Soviets were careful not to commit themselves too closely to the unpredictable Kim Il-song, and they refrained from endorsing his son as successor. Nonetheless, Soviet comment showed interest in stepped-up economic and technical exchanges; high-level military talks occurred during Kim's Moscow stay; and Moscow highlighted Soviet-North Korean common views on some international issues.[26]

Before Kim's visit, the Soviets had made modest political gestures to convince Pyongyang of Soviet interest in closer relations. These moves included higher-than-usual representation at North Korean celebrations and unusually warm official greetings on those occasions. The Soviets increased their blandishments to North Korea following the downing of the South Korean airliner; that incident severely curtailed Moscow's heretofore fairly active contacts with South Korea. Moscow also supported North Korea's position on the assassination of South Korean officials in Rangoon in October 1983, and it withdrew from the Interparliamentarian Union meeting held in Seoul that month.

Perhaps Moscow's greatest short-term gain from Kim's visit—and Beijing's greatest concern—was that it demonstrated to China, the United States, and Japan that Soviet interests could not be ignored in talks on the future of the Korean peninsula, and that Moscow was capable of playing a disruptive role on the peninsula that could severely complicate China's relations with the United States and Japan. In particular, under extreme circumstances, Moscow could encourage North Korean adventurism, leading to a rise in tensions on the peninsula that could force China to side with North Korea against South Korea backed by the United States and Japan. It seemed clear that China was anxious to encourage renewed dialogue between North Korea and the United States at this time in order to reduce the possibility of tension that could provide an opening for the USSR, and to reach an understanding among the two Korean parties and three of the four major outside powers that would undermine Soviet influence in Northeast Asia.

VIETNAM, KAMPUCHEA, ASEAN

In Southeast Asia, China's renewed tilt toward the West and stronger opposition to the USSR had only a small effect. Beijing's approach remained centered on confronting Vietnam's Soviet-backed occupation of Kampuchea and the growing Soviet presence in Indochina. Since the Vietnamese invasion and Chinese counterstrike of 1978-79, China had followed a fairly uniform strategy of military, diplomatic, and economic pressure designed to wear down the Vietnamese in a protracted conflict in Kampuchea, and to solidify regional resistance to the Vietnamese and their Soviet supporters.[27]

China's immediate objective, aside from wearing down the Vietnamese in Kampuchea, was to prevent them from consolidating their position in the country. The Chinese also tried to use their influence with the non-Communist Southeast Asian countries—members of ASEAN— and more broadly with the United States, Japan, and other countries to establish a balance of power in the region against further Soviet and Vietnamese gains.

In the longer run, China appeared to hope to force the Vietnamese to withdraw their armed forces from Kampuchea. Beijing almost certainly preferred to see a new Kampuchean government that would be susceptible to Chinese influence, and it seemed to be sustaining close ties with the Khmer Rouge in part to achieve this end. However, Chinese officials also recognized that such a prospect was a long way off, at best, and that being seen as favoring a return of the Khmer Rouge would be counterproductive, especially because of strong ASEAN resistance.

Beijing also had ambitions to increase friction between the Vietnamese and the Soviets, hoping to see their alliance come apart over time, thereby leading to the termination of the Soviet military presence in Southeast Asia. As Soviet and Vietnamese influence waned, the Chinese no doubt expected that Southeast Asia would become much more susceptible to China's influence.

China's strategy to achieve these objectives involved several elements, including applying military pressure on the Sino-Vietnamese border and in Kampuchea; improving its relations with ASEAN members, especially Thailand, which acted as a conduit of Chinese aid to Khmer resistance forces; promoting international efforts in the United Nations and elsewhere to ensure Vietnam's continued international isolation; and encouraging the United States and other Western countries to become more involved with the anti-Vietnamese resistance as a means to counter Soviet support for Vietnam and to encourage greater ASEAN resolve.

China directed military pressure against Vietnam on two fronts—northern Vietnam and Kampuchea. Its long experience with the tough, independent-minded Vietnamese almost certainly caused Beijing to believe that Hanoi would have to feel it was losing on the battlefield before it would negotiate seriously. China's threat to administer a "second lesson"—backed by periodic artillery shelling and shallow incursions into Vietnamese territory—tied down about half of Vietnam's ground forces. Beijing's pressure prevented Hanoi from diverting these forces—armed with Soviet-supplied weapons—for use against the insurgents in Kampuchea, and it placed a great burden on Vietnam's already very poor economy. China probably also calculated that its threats deepened Vietnam's dependence on the USSR—over the short term this seemed to improve Moscow's position in Indochina, but from one point of view, it provided the potential, over the longer term, for tension in Soviet relations with the independent-minded Vietnamese.

Beijing usually reacted to Vietnamese annual dry season military action in Kampuchea and incursions into Thailand with military action along Vietnam's northern border. But this reactive approach changed somewhat in 1984, when China was more active in support of the Kampuchean resistance and Thailand, launching attacks on the northern border well before the height of the Vietnamese dry season offensive in Kampuchea. This led to the longest and most serious period of fighting along the Sino-Vietnamese border since 1979.[28] The height of the Chinese attacks came during the visit of President Reagan to China, suggesting that China wished to use its actions both to solidify Sino-American common interests regarding this issue and to signal Vietnam and its Soviet backer that China had tacit U.S. support for its tougher stance. The stronger Chinese policy in Indochina also came in part as a response to the unprecedented Soviet joint amphibious exercise with Vietnamese forces near Haiphong in March—the first time Soviet naval forces had been reported operating in such a way so close to Chinese territory. The Soviet action posed a clear threat to Chinese ability to hold the Paracel Islands, taken by Chinese forces in 1974 but still claimed by Hanoi.

In Kampuchea, China remained the primary supplier of aid to the three Khmer resistance groups—the Communist Democratic Kampuchean (DK) fighters under Pol Pot, which represented by far the most important of the three, and the non-Communist Khmer People's National Liberation Front (KPNLF), under the leadership of Son Sann, and the National Army under Norodom Sihanouk. The Chinese also provided weapons to all three groups, but most went to the Khmer Rouge. They appeared likely to continue to give a much larger share to the Communist insurgents as Beijing remained wary of moves that could potentially undermine the DK's fighting ability. At least some Chinese officials appeared to judge that a substantial increase in assistance to the non-Communist resistance might hurt DK morale. China also urged that ASEAN and the United States should supply the non-Communist insurgents;[29] presumably the Chinese judged that such material support would build stronger ASEAN and U.S. political commitment to the resistance effort.

Beijing also reportedly supplied weapons and training to small, and thus far reportedly ineffective, resistance forces in Laos and Vietnam.[30] Chinese involvement with Vietnamese resistance went back at least to the defection of former Vietnamese Politburo member Hoang Van Hoan to China in 1979. Hoang became the head of the Vietnamese National Salvation Front, a de facto government in exile based in China. The Front was involved mainly with propaganda broadcasts directed against Hanoi, and had little known armed support inside Vietnam.

Toward the non-Communist countries of Southeast Asia, members of ASEAN, China attempted to foster better bilateral relations in order to build stronger regional resistance to the Vietnamese in Kampuchea. Good relations with Thailand were vital to Beijing's efforts to provide military assistance and sanctuary for the resistance forces. As the state along the front line facing Vietnamese forces in Indochina, and as the member of ASEAN most threatened by potential Vietnamese expansion, Thailand found itself closely associating with China as a necessary security guarantor. But Bangkok remained suspicious of China's longer-term intentions—concerns shared to a greater degree elsewhere in ASEAN, especially in Indonesia and Malaysia.

Beijing attempted to meet these concerns by supporting the ASEAN-fostered, ostensibly neutral coalition government in Kampuchea, by reducing to a bare minimum or ending ties with Communist insurgents in Southeast Asia, and by moderating ties to overseas Chinese communities there. China would not explicitly reject a role for the DK in a future compromise political settlement in Kampuchea, but it clearly stated its support for a future "neutral and nonaligned" Kampuchea that did not envisage the return of a pro-Chinese regime led by Pol Pot. In this regard Beijing was probably influential in Pol Pot's 1980 decision to step down, at least nominally, as head of the DK, and for the group's decision to abandon Communism as its official ideology.

The Chinese reportedly stopped aid to the Communist Party of Thailand in exchange for Bangkok's cooperation in supplying the resistance in Kampuchea. Similarly, aid to the Communist Party of Malaysia ended or was reduced to a bare minimum, and aid to the Philippines insurgents had ended earlier. Beijing also cut off propaganda broadcasts from China in support of the Thai and Malaysian insurgents in 1979 and 1981 respectively. Judging from the contents of those broadcasts prior to their going off the air, the Chinese were advising local party leaders to put aside past emphasis on armed struggle in favor of political action and united front tactics against the Soviets and the Vietnamese.[31]

Confirming its discreet handling of overseas Chinese, Beijing repeatedly affirmed its long-standing policy of denying dual nationality. It emphasized that it expected Chinese residing abroad to integrate themselves into local society and to obey local laws. China rarely protested unfair treatment of overseas Chinese by ASEAN governments.

China also used trade, diplomacy, and the development of personal contacts through the frequent exchange of high-level visitors to build its influence. For example, the Malaysian foreign minister held talks with Chinese leaders in Beijing in late May 1984. Although differences persisted between Beijing and Kuala Lumpur—especially over China's refusal to sever all ties with the Malaysian Communist Party—the fact that the visit took place at all was a sign of Malaysian interest in sustaining a working relationship with the PRC.

To isolate Vietnam diplomatically over Kampuchea, Beijing insisted that any solution must conform to provisions of the resolution adopted by the United Nations in 1980 and the International Conference of Kampuchea in 1981. These required a complete withdrawal of Vietnamese forces from Kampuchea; neutralization of Kampuchea under international guarantees; and free elections under international supervision. Barring Vietnamese approval, Beijing rebuffed Hanoi's calls for Sino-Vietnamese talks, opposed compromise efforts by third parties that might add legitimacy to Vietnam's hold on Kampuchea, and supported ASEAN-led efforts to preserve the coalition government's seat in the United Nations.

The Chinese were sometimes compelled to adjust their political position to offset Vietnamese efforts to sow dissension in ASEAN's ranks and to portray China as the aggressor. In 1983, for instance, Beijing publicized a five-point peace proposal for the solution of the Kampuchean issue that appeared to be designed to offset Vietnamese charges of Chinese intransigence.[32] However, it deviated from China's standard formula only in stating that if Vietnam agreed to a phased withdrawal of its forces, Beijing would resume the Sino-Vietnamese dialogue after the first installment of troops returned to Vietnam. Beijing had previously insisted on full Vietnamese withdrawal prior to resuming the talks.

Beijing publicly differed with ASEAN on Kampuchea only when it believed an ASEAN initiative would harm the resistance effort or result in less than a complete Vietnamese withdrawal. For example, Beijing at first was reluctant to support ASEAN proposals for the formation of a coalition government and the convening of an international conference on Kampuchea in 1981. And the Chinese refused to yield to ASEAN efforts to form a coalition government that would have put the DK in a disadvantageous position.

China expressed more strenuous opposition to third party efforts to find a solution to the Kampuchean issue that compromised on the U.N. formula. Chinese Premier Zhao Ziyang warned France and Australia when they put forth their proposals on Kampuchea in 1982 and 1983, respectively.[33]

Regarding the problems posed by ever closer Soviet-Vietnamese relations, Beijing appeared to believe that its hard policy would eventually exacerbate Soviet-Vietnamese tensions, although in the short run it obviously increased Hanoi's dependence on Soviet support. China's military pressure raised the economic costs of Moscow's special relationship with Hanoi and created new demands for Soviet military assistance. Moscow's support for Vietnamese expansion also reduced the USSR's opportunities to make inroads in the ASEAN countries. Beijing probably calculated that as it was able to increase these economic and political costs to Moscow, the Soviets would be more likely to increase their demands on the Vietnamese, perhaps to the point of irreparably damaging relations.

China also tried to use the Sino-Soviet vice-ministerial and other talks to create concern in Hanoi that Moscow might compromise its ties with Vietnam in favor of a deal with China. But, although Hanoi exhibited some nervousness when the talks began in October 1982, the Soviets apparently succeeded in reassuring their ally that Vietnamese interests would not be sacrificed.

China also seemed to believe that greater U.S. involvement in support of ASEAN and the resistance in Kampuchea would help counter Soviet support for Vietnam and bolster ASEAN resolve against Vietnam and the USSR. Closer Sino-American cooperation in Southeast Asia also could serve to reduce ASEAN suspicions of Chinese intentions by signaling U.S. approval of China's regional posture. As a result, Beijing publicly supported the U.S. military presence in Southeast Asia, called for American military support to the Kampuchean resistance, and emphasized the compatibility of U.S.-Chinese interests in the region.

OTHER FOREIGN POLICY CONCERNS

China's policy toward other developed and developing countries was less strongly pro-Western and anti-Soviet during this period. In general, Beijing's policy in these areas attempted to develop the advantages it had gained from the broadly "independent" foreign posture it had adopted against both superpowers, set forth in Hu Yaobang's report to the 12th CCP Congress in September 1982.

In most third world areas, for example, China continued to broaden political, economic, and other contacts; used these exchanges to work unobtrusively to gain a deeper understanding of, and greater influence in, particular developing countries; avoided substantial commitment of material resources; exploited third world targets of economic opportunity—for instance, through substantial commodity, service, and arms transfers to well-to-do countries of the Middle East; and sidestepped sensitive regional disputes while endorsing political proposals having the full support of third world regional blocs.[34]

In Europe, Chinese leaders sought to promote an easing of tensions in the East-West conflict; to broaden Chinese ties with newly prominent peace movements on the Continent; and to use greater political contacts with West European governments to facilitate greater Chinese access to their markets and technology. The major complication was with Great Britain over the issue of Hong Kong, which was dealt with by an agreement announced in September 1984.

Meanwhile, China adopted an increasingly low-keyed and more moderate approach to international organizations, especially over questions of arms control and disarmament. China attempted to capitalize wherever possible on aid and technical support available through U.N. and other international agencies, especially low-interest loans from the World Bank. It took a low political posture on most issues before the U.N. General Assembly, in part to avoid alienating countries that could prove useful in China's effort to broaden its international influence and economic support. Beijing attempted to adopt a markedly more reasonable posture on arms control questions, both to ease China's past reputation as an unpredictable nuclear power anticipating world war, and to build international support for East-West arms control arrangements that would lessen the danger China faced from the Soviet buildup in Asia.

Beijing presumably judged that adopting a stronger pro-Western, anti-Soviet policy in these areas would have been counterproductive. It particularly would have run the risk of alienating a good deal of opinion in the third world and in Europe, and would have had only a marginal impact on China's ability to consolidate relations with the Reagan administration. Moreover, such a strong stance was not deemed to be necessary to shore up an international balance favorable to China. Although Beijing sometimes complained about excesses in U.S. policy against the USSR, Chinese officials judged that the Reagan administration had basically readjusted the balance in East-West relations and had effectively taken the lead in checking potential Soviet expansion.

As a result, China could afford to sustain its low public posture against the USSR in these areas and could maneuver more freely to seek its advantage. For example, Chinese policy attempted on the one hand to foster good relations with some of the conservative West European leaders who supported the Reagan administration's strong posture against the USSR and, on the other hand, to build sympathetic ties with European and other international "progressives" who judged that Reagan's policies were bringing the world dangerously close to full-scale war. In particular, its criticism of Reagan administration foreign policy in certain areas opened the way for China to improve relations with various left-leaning governments, including Soviet clients such as Cuba. Of course, China's ambiguous stance toward the United States sometimes confused international opinion and ran the risk of alienating the United States, but Beijing tried to explain its posture as a means of wooing certain pro-Soviet states away from the USSR.[35] Whatever confusion arose in the United States as a result of China's ambiguous stance toward East-West relations and U.S. policy in the third world was evidently offset by its continued strong push to develop improved relations with the United States on the basis of common anti-Soviet interests, especially in Asia.

This differentiated Chinese approach to foreign affairs—trying to garner as much benefit as possible from a generally more pragmatic and flexible "independent" image in foreign policy, while sustaining a strongly anti-Soviet, pro-Western posture on security issues having a direct bearing on China's surroundings in Asia—was underlined in Foreign Minister Wu Xueqian's review of Chinese foreign policy at the U.N. General Assembly in September 1983. Wu avoided the harsh anti-Soviet stance of the past on issues where China's security interests were not directly at stake (as they were in Asia), and projected an image of China as a more mature and responsible participant in the international community. Wu's presentation was virtually devoid of the shrill rhetoric and alarm that once had characterized Chinese speeches on this occasion. Gone were warnings of the near danger of world war caused by the rapaciously expansionist imperialist and social-imperialist powers. Gone were demands that nations take sides in the life-or-death struggle against these powers, and the sharp critiques of governments that cooperated closely with the superpowers, especially the USSR.[36]

Wu affirmed China's "independent" foreign policy and close affiliation with the third world, and he put forth evenhanded criticism of both superpowers for promoting global tension and turmoil, and posing serious threats to global peace and security. He had a more sanguine outlook for the world situation than previous Chinese speakers on this occasion, underlining a sense of optimism that a prevailing East-West balance gave China more room to maneuver on international issues than in the past. He underlined China's recent interest in the European peace movements, stating that their aspirations were "completely understandable and deserve sympathy." Consistent with Beijing's less ideological approach to foreign affairs, Wu sidestepped past Chinese interpretations of Lenin's theory of imperialism when he avoided the question of the inevitability of war stemming from the continued existence of imperialism; he concluded optimistically that the prospects for preserving peace were good "so long as the people of the world become truly united" in opposing "all manifestations of hegemonism."

On Asian security issues having direct bearing on China, however, Wu strongly affirmed Beijing's anti-Soviet views. On Kampuchea and Afghanistan, he insisted on implementation of relevant U.N. General Assembly resolutions calling for the withdrawal of foreign troops from both of those countries and expressed skepticism about efforts to seek "political solutions" to those questions. Wu took Moscow to task for its "armed aggression" in Afghanistan and for its support for Vietnam's "military occupation" of Kampuchea. He dismissed Hanoi's allegations of a Chinese threat to Indochina as a pretext for Vietnamese involvement in Kampuchea, and reaffirmed Beijing's five-point proposal of 1 March 1983 as a basis for resolving the Kampuchean question.

Wu expressed sympathy for efforts by "some countries" to promote talks as a means to seek a political solution to the Afghanistan question, but attacked Soviet calls for international guarantees of noninterference in Afghanistan prior to the withdrawal of Soviet troops as "obviously putting the cart before the horse." As he had done during a visit to Pakistan in July 1983, Wu declared China's readiness to participate in an international guarantee on Afghanistan "only after, and not before" Moscow publicly undertook to withdraw its troops.[37]

On other questions not directly bearing on Chinese security concerns, the PRC foreign minister was more circumspect as he avoided taking positions that would complicate China's efforts to broaden its international influence or would alienate important segments of international opinion. Wu's treatment of the Middle East situation in general and of the Lebanon crisis in particular reflected this kind of wariness as well as Chinese uncertainty as to the likely outcome there. Wu repeated the stock Beijing view that Israel's aggression remained the crux of the Middle East conflict, and he was relatively mild in criticizing Washington's "partiality" toward Israel. He failed to repeat past endorsements of specific Middle East peace proposals. One obvious omission from Wu's remarks was his failure to reiterate Beijing's endorsement of the Palestine Liberation Organization as the "sole legitimate representative" of the Palestinian people, an affirmation routinely present in Chinese addresses in past years. This deletion of explicit support for the PLO probably reflected uncertainty over the state of affairs within the PLO at that time of intense factional fighting among the Palestinian groups in Lebanon. As it became clear that Arafat and his organization would survive and continue to receive broad support from important Middle Eastern countries, Beijing became less diffident about the PLO. Chinese leaders warmly welcomed Arafat to China in 1984.

On arms control, the foreign minister strove to adopt a less controversial position than in the past, attempting to minimize China's past poor international reputation and to make Beijing's stance appear reasonable and acceptable to a wider international audience. While upholding long-standing Chinese positions on disarmament in general, Wu put forward what he called a "further effort" by China to "promote progress" on disarmament issues. His proposal went further than those that Chinese spokesmen had put forward on previous occasions, particularly those elaborated by Huang Hua at the U.N. General Assembly's special session on disarmament in June 1982.[38] On that occasion Huang had proposed that both the United States and the USSR "stop testing, improving, manufacturing nuclear weapons and reduce by 50 percent all types of nuclear weapons and means of delivery." "After that," Huang had stated, the other nuclear powers should "join in efforts" to reduce their arsenals as well. Wu's comments modified this basic position by suggesting that once Moscow and Washington "take practical action" to stop testing and producing nuclear weapons and to reduce their arsenals by half, "a widely representative international conference" be convened to negotiate a reduction of weapons by all of the nuclear powers.

Latin America[39]

China's policy toward Latin America had come a long way from the 1960s, when the Chinese had greeted Fidel Castro's victory in Cuba as a vindication of their theory that revolution in the less developed world should have its roots in the countryside. Despite the emergence of the Sino-Soviet polemic, pro-Chinese and pro-Cuban groups continued to pursue revolutionary tactics in ideological association for several years; the break came in the mid-1960s, when the Cubans, presumably under Societ pressure, became more cautious in exporting revolution.

China went on giving financial aid and encouragement to revolutionary groups in Latin American in the 1960s, but most of them adopted strongly pro-Soviet, pro-Cuban orientations. Subsequently, the more pragmatic policies it adopted after the violent height of the Cultural Revolution in the late 1960s, which led to China's entry into the United Nations and its rapprochement with the United States, were reflected in policy toward Latin America. China's past advocacy of violent revolution was replaced by championing of the interests of the third world governments, including those of Latin America. At the U.N. Conference on Trade and Development meeting, held in Chile in 1972,[40] China assumed the role of spokesman for the developing world and chief opponent of both the USSR and the United States, in Latin America and elsewhere. Nevertheless, China had few interests that coincided with those of the countries in Latin America, and it had few resources to expend there.

During the mid-1970s, Beijing attempted to fit its Latin American policy into its dominant anti-Soviet mold, but the results led to egregious excesses, notably China's close relationship with the Pinochet government in Chile. Offers of Chinese aid to Latin America remained small, especially in comparison with their outlays in Africa. And apart from interest in particular commodities, such as grain from Argentina and copper from Chile, trade relations remained relatively unimportant.

As China began in 1979 to adopt a more flexible and activist approach in the third world, one that took into greater account the diversity of opinion on the USSR and other issues in the third world, and as Beijing formulated in 1982 its more independent image in foreign affairs, Chinese leaders strove to broaden their nation's influence in Latin

America as well. Foreign Minister Wu toured Venezuela, Argentina, and Brazil in August 1984, the first such high-level Chinese visit to Latin America since Foreign Minister Huang Hua toured Mexico, Colombia, and Venezuela in 1981; and Premier Zhao Ziyang traveled to Mexico for the Cancun summit meeting in 1981.

China's interest in the region now focused on expanding its political and economic ties, encouraging developments in the region that worked against the expansion of Soviet influence, and fostering U.S. policies that would sustain regional stability and block penetration by the USSR. Recognizing that U.S. influence in Latin America dwarfed that of other powers, Beijing sought to cooperate where possible with U.S. interests, but not to the point of supporting what it judged to be heavy-handed U.S. policies that alienated regional opinion and provided new openings for the Soviet Union. Beijing supported the development of more pluralistic and democratically based societies in Latin America and disavowed involvement in revolutionary or terrorist movements. Having made significant breakthroughs in establishing diplomatic relations in the region only in the last ten years, China also appeared to be keenly interested in gaining further diplomatic recognition, especially from the Central American countries that retained close ties with Taipei.

On the question of the East-West confrontation over El Salvador and Nicaragua, the Chinese generally favored a U.S. policy of nonmilitary intervention. They supported American efforts to use multilateral aid programs, backed by political initiatives, as the best means to achieve regional stability and keep out the USSR. Beijing was careful to caution that excessive U.S. force would polarize opinion in Central America, provide new opportunities for the USSR, and alienate considerable segments of Central American opinion. In line with this approach, China fully endorsed the so-called Contadora Group's initiative to settle Central American problems through peaceful negotiations. It was aware that this approach not only was widely popular among the major Latin American states, but also fit in nicely with Beijing's anti-superpower line in the third world.[41]

Chinese flexibility in fostering their influence and encouraging anti-superpower trends in Latin America was underlined by Assistant Foreign Minister Zhu Qichen's visit to Cuba in July 1984.[42] Zhu was the highest-level Chinese official known to have visited Cuba since the deterioration of bilateral relations in 1964.[43] His presence in Havana was confirmed by the Chinese Foreign Ministry's Information Department spokesman, who said that Zhu was on an "inspection tour" of the Chinese embassy but was also prepared to exchange views with Cuban counterparts on bilateral and international issues.

The Chinese media's low-key treatment of the visit comported with other signs in recent years that Cuba was not of greatest importance in China's efforts to improve relations with Moscow's close allies. Only Vietnam remained lower in China's order of priority. Thus, in the case of relations with Eastern bloc countries, Beijing used authoritative forums like the NPC and the United Nations to make known its plans to improve relations; and it gave those efforts, along with concurrent attempts to improve relations with Mongolia, a higher profile in its media.

Nevertheless, Zhu's trip had been foreshadowed by several developments in the preceding year:

- The Cuban minister of external trade paid an official visit to China in the fall of 1983, at the invitation of the minister in charge of foreign trade. According to the Chinese media, the Cuban guest was also received by a vice-premier, who expressed China's willingness to develop relations with Cuba.[44]

- China in 1984 upgraded its representation at the Cuban National Day celebrations at the Cuban embassy in Beijing, sending a full minister to lead the Chinese delegation—a contrast with the lower-level Chinese attending in past years.

- The Chinese ambassador in Havana had a meeting in May 1984 with high-level Cuban officials at which, Xinhua reported, both sides underscored their desire to improve and develop friendly relations.[45]

These measures came against the backdrop of a gradual reduction in Chinese attacks on Cuba's role in Latin America and Africa. In the past, Beijing had condemned Cuba as Moscow's agent in Latin America and Africa, interfering in the internal affairs of other countries to expand its own influence and that of its Soviet backer. Beijing's treatment of Cuba began to take on a somewhat less hostile tone by 1979. At that time, China's strident invective against Cuba as a Soviet "cat's-paw" became less frequent than in the previous year, when the "Cuba of the West" and the "Cuba of the East" (Vietnam) were seen by China as the cutting edge of Soviet efforts to expand in the third world. By the early 1980s, China's attitude toward Cuban troops in Africa had moderated to the point that Beijing was willing to begin efforts to improve relations with African countries such as Angola and Ethiopia, even though they still hosted large contingents of Cuban troops.[46]

Western Europe

The main elements of recent Chinese policy toward Western Europe were high-lighted during premier Zhao Ziyang's June 1984 visit there—the first by a Chinese leader at this high level since October-November 1979, when premier Hua Guofeng traveled to Great Britain, France, Italy, and West Germany to press China's then strong anti-Soviet line. Zhao traveled to France, Belgium, Sweden, Denmark, Norway, and Italy, in part to repay visits by West European leaders to China. He also met with the EEC Commission president and other EEC leaders while in Belgium.[47]

As Hua had done, Zhao focused his discussions on economic cooperation and strategic issues reflecting Chinese interest in limiting Soviet expansion and promoting its modernization drive. But, unlike Hua Guofeng in 1979, Zhao was much more sophisticated in fostering China's influence in Europe, avoiding the undiscriminating anti-Soviet rhetoric that had proved to be counterproductive in the past. He impressed the European leaders with his low-key, nondoctrinaire approach, especially to issues of common concern. His remarks and concurrent Chinese comment implicitly underscored China's continued support for a strong, unified NATO and Chinese understanding for the U.S. deployment of intermediate-range missiles in Western Europe.

Zhao also publicly expressed concern about Soviet countermeasures that might worsen the arms race and, over time, threaten China. He suggested that the intermediate-range missile deployments be stopped in order to encourage the Soviet Union and the United States to resume arms control negotiations. Zhao reiterated China's opposition to any arms control agreements, however, that would permit the Soviets to shift missiles from Europe to the Soviet Far East.

Other Chinese comment criticized the manner in which the United States dealt with its European partners. The Chinese believed that U.S. unilateral actions in countering the USSR worsened tensions in the Western alliance and lessened the pressure on the Soviet Union to negotiate weapons reductions. The Chinese suggested that the West Europeans should play a larger role in the alliance in seeking to moderate Soviet behavior.

In underlining the nation's implicit but unmistakable tilt toward the West in Europe, Chinese comment insisted that Beijing pursued an "independent" foreign policy, but it also pointed out that this did not mean that China sought a position of equidistance between the superpowers. Rather, the Chinese said they did not want to ally themselves formally with either the United States or the USSR. Zhao cited France as having this kind of policy, implying that China could pursue an "independent foreign policy" and still support the West. During his European trip, Zhao used support for West European independence, stability, and security as code words for support for the Western alliance.

During his trip, Premier Zhao publicly supported superpower disarmament and said the European peace movement had justifiable concerns. In so doing, Beijing appeared to be trying to win support from the politically important West European peace movement, as part of a broader effort to enhance contacts that would be useful in fostering West European trends contrary to Soviet expansion. In the case of the peace movement, the Chinese seemed to be trying to encourage the West Europeans to be as critical of the Soviet Union as they were of the United States, thereby helping to preclude Soviet efforts to use the movement to sow discord in the NATO alliance.

Regarding economic ties, Zhao used his trip to encourage the Europeans to become more active in the China market, hoping in turn to promote increased sales of Chinese products in Europe. European countries were not large traders with China, except for West Germany, which occupied fourth position in importance, with a total volume of $1.7 billion in 1983. Trade with France and Italy in 1983 amounted to only $826.7 million and $623.8 million, respectively. Chinese exports to Europe were hurt by the Western recession, having declined from a peak of $2.6 billion in 1981 to $2.4 billion in 1983.[48]

Chinese leaders attempted to persuade Western European countries to adopt a less restrictive policy than the United States on the export of technology. By encouraging European countries to compete more vigorously as sellers of technology, China tried to play off its suppliers and gain better terms.

Despite the fanfare surrounding Zhao's trip, the overall economic results were quite modest. China signed two minor investment and taxation agreements with the French government, and a minor investment agreement with the Belgian government. Almost no commercial deals were signed. The Europeans remained cautious about the potential for trade with China. The Chinese tended to look but not buy, or to string out negotiations interminably. The French, in particular, experienced delay after delay in negotiations for building a nuclear reactor in China while the Chinese sought a better deal from the United States.

Moreover, European companies were hurt when the Chinese in 1979 signed several large contracts and then canceled or suspended them shortly afterward during a period of internal economic readjustment. Overall, Western European exports to China peaked in 1979 at some $3.4 billion and had not completely recovered. In 1983 they amounted to $2.9 billion. In addition, the Europeans had considerable difficulty with Chinese bureaucratic, legal, and management obstacles, as well as stiff competition from the United States and Japan.

SINO-BRITISH RELATIONS OVER HONG KONG[49]

Zhao did not stop in either West Germany or Great Britain during his European tour. China's continued strong interest in West Germany was underlined by the visit there in early May 1984 of Vice Premier Li Peng. The visit resulted in the signing of an important Sino-West German nuclear accord. The absence of a London stop on Zhao's itinerary probably reflected Chinese sensitivities over the unsettled question of Hong Kong's future status.

Prompted by the fact that 90 percent of the colony's territory would revert to the PRC in 1997, British and Chinese representatives began secret discussions following Prime Minister Thatcher's visit to China in September 1982 in order to determine how soon and in what ways China would assert its claims to sovereignty over the territory. The start of the talks was accompanied by sharp Sino-British disagreement over Hong Kong's legal status and implied PRC warnings that China might assert control over the territory well before 1997. It also coincided with a serious decline in the territory's economy, prompted in part by worries in Hong Kong over possible future PRC rule. Subsequently, there were signs of economic rebound; a new phase in the Sino-British talks on Hong Kong began in July 1983; and both London and Beijing announced, following the visit of the British foreign secretary to China in April 1984, their intention to reach an agreement on Hong Kong's future by the end of the year. The British foreign secretary traveled to China in late July, amid signs of more rapid progress in the talks. The accord was initialed in September 1984.

Chinese policy toward Hong Kong was pulled in different directions by often conflicting political and economic interests. Politically, Beijing leaders were pushed by anti-imperialist ideological and political imperatives, stemming from the deep and bitter experience of China over the past century, to reassert strongly their sovereignty over the colony and to eliminate vestiges of British colonial rule. Moreover, Deng Xiaoping and other PRC leaders were doubtless aware that they could use a successful recovery of such "lost" territory as a way to build nationalistic support for their leading positions and other programs at home. A firm stand regarding sovereignty over Hong Kong also clarified to foreign leaders with an interest in other territories claimed by China (such as Taiwan, Vietnamese-held islands in the South China Sea, and Soviet-controlled territory along the Sino-Soviet frontier) that China was determined to reassert its right to rule lands it regarded as Chinese.

At the same time, however, Beijing appeared to have important political reasons to avoid a strong reassertion of authority that could disrupt the social and economic status quo in Hong Kong. In particular, any PRC actions that prompted a serious downturn in Hong Kong's economic prosperity or its social-political stability would probably have undermined Beijing's repeated pledges to the people on Taiwan that reunification of Taiwan with the mainland would not involve any change in the island's social or economic life. Moreover, Beijing's repeated efforts to establish a political dialogue with Taipei had borne little fruit. A serious disruption in Hong Kong would likely have gone far toward aborting chances for success in getting negotiations started with Taipei, and it might have increased support in Taiwan and abroad for a future status for the island independent of mainland control. Conversely, if China were to succeed in reasserting sovereignty over Hong Kong with minimal disruption to the social-economic order there, its promises of "peaceful reunification" of Taiwan could gain greater credibility both in Taiwan and elsewhere, especially the United States.

Economically, Beijing appeared to want to avoid impairing the rapid growth of free enterprise in Hong Kong because China had a large stake in the territory's economy. Hong Kong was China's third largest trading partner. The favorable balance in PRC trade with the colony, along with remittances by Hong Kong residents to relatives in the PRC, provided an estimated 30-40 percent of Chinese foreign exchange earnings. Hong Kong was also the major entrepôt for PRC trade, handling an estimated $2.3 billion of PRC exports (10.6 percent of all PRC exports) and $1.5 billion of imports (6.9 percent of all PRC imports) during 1981. It remained the major conduit for PRC trade, estimated at several hundred million dollars each year, with Taiwan, South Korea, and South Africa—areas with which the PRC had difficulty managing a formal trade relationship.

Hong Kong entrepreneurs, who provided the vast bulk of investment in Hong Kong, also were the major investors in the new Chinese Special Economic Zone that adjoined the colony in Shenzhen, and provided the major share of foreign investment in Guangdong Province. Hong Kong was a rear supply and operations base for the large-scale oil exploration and development effort then getting under way in the South China Sea. It had excellent modern transportation facilities, including the best deepwater port along the China coast, the third largest container terminal in the world, and a modern airport that handled 7 million passengers and 300,000 tons of cargo each year. Hong Kong also provided the PRC with easy access to modern financial, trade, and management institutions, where PRC representatives could learn—from Chinese people in Chinese language—the intricacies of modern Western business practices. In Hong Kong, this could be done at a safe distance, without jeopardizing Beijing's strong commitment to maintaining its socialist system as free as possible of the "corrupting" influences of the "bourgeois" ideas of the West.

Chinese leaders also were almost certainly aware that Western business leaders would take into account PRC handling of Hong Kong issues as they began consideration of possible larger-scale investment in the PRC itself. Thus, a PRC policy toward Hong Kong that served to undermine business confidence and led to economic decline there could serve to make Western investors more cautious in pursuing closer ties with China.

Despite these strong economic incentives encouraging a restrained PRC approach toward Hong Kong, there were economic factors that might have prompted China to adopt a more active and direct role in managing the territory's affairs. PRC leaders might have judged that they had built up sufficient expertise in working with Western business interests over the past few years that they could now effectively manage enterprises in Hong Kong more directly, just as they had managed Western-style enterprises in the Special Economic Zones that had been set up in China in recent years. They might also have judged that profits from enterprises in Hong Kong should be controlled and channeled more directly to the benefit of the Chinese state, rather than having the PRC benefit only indirectly from Hong Kong's prosperity. Meanwhile, if conditions in Hong Kong were to deteriorate despite Beijing's best efforts to reassure people of the Hong Kong of China's future intentions, Beijing might have judged that rapid assertion of Chinese control well before the 1997 deadline would provide the best means to preserve the territory's prosperity and value to China. .

Beijing was particularly aware that its relations with the United States, and to a lesser degree with Japan, could be affected by Chinese handling of the Hong Kong issue, since both capitalist powers had important interests in the continued stability and prosperity of Hong Kong. In recent years, the United States had remained Hong Kong's largest foreign investor and trading partner. By mid-1983, according to official U.S. statistics, U.S. investment in Hong Kong had reached $2.7 billion; the actual figure was thought to be much higher, estimated at around $4 billion. The United States was the major foreign direct investor in Hong Kong's manufacturing sector, with 47 percent of total investment, followed by Japan with 30 percent. Out of Hong Kong's total two-way trade of $44.5 billion in 1982, $8.6 billion was with the United States. The United States absorbed 38 percent of Hong Kong's domestically produced exports that year. In 1983, Hong Kong's trade value jumped by over 20 percent and the United States absorbed 42 percent of its exports. As a supplier, the United States ranked third, after China and Japan; the U.S. share of Hong Kong's import market was 11 percent in 1982 and 1983. U..S. business people in Asia had long used Hong Kong as a base of operations and a major transportation, communications, and financial support center. Hong Kong loomed larger in U.S. consideration as U.S. firms used the colony as a base for exploring the China market. The U.S. government used Hong Kong as an important center of operations for information, commercial, and recreational activities.

Americans interested in Beijing's future policy toward Taiwan also followed closely China's approach to Hong Kong for indications as to how Beijing intended to deal with Taiwan. Chinese officials explicitly linked Beijing's approach on the two issues, though some added that while Beijing wanted British administration to be replaced by a "Chinese" one representing the "people" of Hong Kong, in the case of Taiwan, the administration was already Chinese and therefore would not have to be replaced.

If Beijing managed to reassert its sovereignty over Hong Kong without disrupting the social and economic order there, it could add substantial credibility to its claim that China's reunification with Taiwan would have no negative effect on the way of life there, and could thereby ease concerns of some Americans about how U.S. interests in Taiwan would be affected by reunification with the mainland. Of course, if Beijing was seen as mishandling the situation in Hong Kong, leading to serious economic decline and social disorder there, it would reduce, in the eyes of many Americans, the credibility of PRC claims that Taiwan's reunification would not adversely affect U.S. interests on the island. It could also have prompted American business leaders to be more cautious in ventures in the PRC.

As a result of these conflicting interests, Beijing followed a policy in the negotiations with the British designed to obtain an agreement giving China as much leeway as possible in future policy toward Hong Kong, but without causing an irreparable setback in stability and prosperity in the territory. The impending end of the lease governing the New Territories began to affect individual property leases, mortgages (often made for 15 years), and other financial and real estate arrangements in Hong Kong during 1982, and prompted British authorities to raise the issue again in discussions with Chinese leaders at the time of British Prime Minister Thatcher's visit to China in September 1982. The visit produced agreement between China and Britain to "enter into talks through diplomatic channels with the common aim of maintaining stability and prosperity of Hong Hong." But the visit was also marked by pointed differences over the current legal status of the territory. In particular, the British prime minister emphasized at a press conference in Hong Kong, following her China stay, that the 19th-century treaties governing the status of the colony remained the basis of Britain's position, although she added that London would talk with Beijing in the hope that the treaties could be amended by mutual agreement. She was sharply criticized by a statement of the Chinese Foreign Ministry's Information Department spokesman who said that Beijing's "consistent position" was that "China is not bound by the unequal treaties and that the whole Hong Hong area will be recovered when conditions are ripe."

After months of secret diplomatic communications, the two sides issued a joint statement on 1 July 1983 announcing the start of formal negotiations on Hong Kong's future. The talks continued into 1984 and were supplemented in June 1984 by discussions of a working group of Chinese and British diplomats who were trying to come up with a draft agreement by Beijing's September 1984 deadline. Deng Xiaoping reportedly told Prime Minister Thatcher in September 1982 that a Sino-British agreement on Hong Kong had to be reached in two years. Beijing subsequently announced that if the agreement were not reached by that time, China would announce its plans for the territory unilaterally. This represented an implicit threat presumably designed to keep the British from dragging their feet in the negotiations.

The Chinese gradually released details of their plans for Hong Kong informally, mainly through reports from Hong Kong residents who met with senior Chinese leaders from 1982 to 1984. The highlights included the following:

- After China regained full sovereignty and administrative control of Hong Kong in 1997, the territory would become a special administrative region in China under Article 31 of the Chinese constitution.

- Hong Kong will enjoy a high degree of autonomy, with local people administering the city. Beijing raised the possibility of local elections to select senior local authorities.

- Hong Kong's present capitalist social-economic system will remain unchanged for at least 50 years after 1997.

- Hong Kong's legal structure will remain basically unchanged, except that the highest court of appeals will be in Hong Kong instead of London.

- Local and expatriate civil servants, including policemen and administrators, can retain their jobs.

- Hong Kong's status as a free port and international financial center will remain unchanged.

- The Hong Kong dollar will remain a separate and freely convertible currency.

- Residents will enjoy the rights of free speech, assembly, and press, and the freedom to travel.

- Beijing will be responsible for Hong Kong's foreign affairs, but Hong Kong will maintain its separate status in international organizations and in international agreements. It will be allowed to issue its own travel documents.

- The Hong Kong government will be responsible for the public security, maintained by the local police force.

- The economic interests of Great Britain will be respected.

The British were more reluctant to speak out on their intentions or on the content of the negotiations with China. British leaders emphasized London's "moral" commitment to secure the best possible future arrangements for the people of Hong Kong, but British press comment and some political leaders claimed that London had little leverage over China. They underlined the fact that Great Britain had only a small economic interest in Hong Kong—it trailed far behind the United States, China, and Japan as Hong Kong's leading trading partners and accounted for only a modest share of foreign investment in the territory. Moreover, officials in London clearly differentiated between the legal status of Hong Kong and other contested British territories (such as the Falkland Islands and Gibraltar), recognizing, in particular, the legality of the second convention of Beijing (1898), which called for the New Territories to revert to China in 1997. Without that land—90 percent of the territory of Hong Kong—the colony appeared not to be viable as a British possession.

Press reports and the limited Chinese and British disclosures about progress in the talks showed that London was forced repeatedly to give ground to firm Chinese demands during the course of the negotiations:

- Some observers in London and Hong Kong had hoped at first that China would accept a renewal of the lease on the New Territories or would allow the status quo to continue after 1997. But they quickly ran up against strong Chinese determination to recover complete sovereignty over all of Hong Kong by 1997.

- By late 1983, it was clear that the British had been compelled to accept in principle China's sovereignty and administrative control of Hong Kong after 1997, and had agreed to negotiate on the basis of China's general plan for the territory.

- During a visit to Beijing in April 1984, British Foreign Secretary Howe agreed to a timetable in accord with China's deadline, calling for a draft agreement by September 1984, a debate in the British Parliament in autumn, and ratification by year's end. Howe then went to Hong Kong, where he reported that it would be "unrealistic" to expect Britain to retain an administrative role in Hong Kong.

By mid-year, it was disclosed that London was under pressure to accept a Chinese proposal to establish a joint liaison group to oversee developments in Hong Kong prior to 1997, thereby giving China a vehicle to influence developments in the colony prior to formal takeover. Foreign Secretary Howe again traveled to Beijing and Hong Kong in late July, in an effort to bridge differences. He reported that he found the Chinese more accommodating than in the past. In particular, while Britain accepted China's proposal for a joint liaison group, both sides explicitly stated that the group was not to be an "organ of power," but would serve only as a consultative body between the Chinese and the British over Hong Kong issues.

Moreover, Howe indicated that Britain had obtained China's agreement that the proposed Sino-British accord would contain detailed provisions governing future administration in Hong Kong and would be considered an international agreement legally binding on both parties. The foreign secretary revealed that London wanted such an accord because China had a strong record of strict adherence to international agreements, and thus would remain bound by the proposed detailed provisions of the accord in future administration of Hong Kong, thereby reducing Beijing's ability to disrupt the status quo in the territory.

The agreement reached on 26 September 1984 was in accord with British expectations and paved the legal path for British withdrawal. It ended any remaining doubt as to whether Hong Kong would become Chinese territory. It would.

Observers interested in Hong Kong's future had been worried during the previous two years that any prolonged impasse in the Sino-British talks leading to the current agreement could have resulted in serious uncertainty in Hong Kong, possibly prompting economic decline and social instability. Indeed, strong Sino-British differences in talks over Hong Kong in September 1982, and again in September 1983, had a serious, if temporary, negative effect on economic development in the territory. With the initialing of the current Sino-British agreement on Hong Kong, the danger of such a prolonged decline was markedly reduced. Great Britain attempted to negotiate the best deal it could get from China regarding the future of Hong Kong. The agreement contained various specific commitments by the Chinese to preserve Hong Kong's British-style laws and institutions, and to allow Hong Kong to continue to prosper as an autonomous economic entity with its own freely convertible currency and its distinctive standing in international economic affairs. Nevertheless, British officials acknowledged that London had few contingency plans in the event China did not fully uphold the accord in the years ahead. Foreign Secretary Howe was reported to say that the agreement relied on trust between Britain and China, rather than on tangible guarantees of its implementation.

INTERNATIONAL ORGANIZATIONS, ARMS CONTROL

International Organizations

The evolution of China's policy toward international organizations and arms control issues graphically underlined the more sophisticated, development-oriented Chinese policies of the 1980s. During the previous decade, Beijing had used its membership and participation in the United Nations mainly as a propaganda platform to drum up political support for China's seemingly unrelenting drive against superpower, especially Soviet, expansion. While Beijing also attempted to balance its sharp attacks on Moscow with criticism of the United States, it was evident—as Soviet commentary charged—that Chinese officials merely used anti-American criticism as an "appetizer" for the "main course" of virulent invective against the USSR.[50]

China's heavy-handed propaganda crusade often alienated Beijing from broad segments of international opinion; third world leaders, by the late 1970s, often identified China closely with the West and saw it as not seriously interested in third world concerns. As China's view of the imminent danger of Soviet expansion subsided in the 1980s, and as Beijing's concern to improve its image in the developing and developed worlds rose, China opted for a lower-key posture that attempted to win as many friends as possible with as little cost as possible for Chinese interests.

Meanwhile, Beijing only slowly developed an interest in international financial institutions. Its ideology until the death of Mao encouraged China to be a significant donor of aid and opposed foreign assistance to China on grounds of national adherence to the cardinal principle of self-reliance in economic development. These impediments began to fall by the late 1970s, concurrent with China's increased interest in cooperating more closely with international financial institutions and enterprises to obtain the capital and technology now seen as needed for China to modernize successfully.

During the early 1980s, China used its growing involvement in international organizations to pursue economic modernization and to preserve important political equities. Since it had ended its policy of economic self-reliance in 1978, Beijing had begun seeking and receiving substantial development assistance from the World Bank, International Monetary Fund, and U.N. agencies. This effort of course brought it into increasing competition with other developing countries—a trend likely to increase the possibility of complicating Chinese efforts to win political influence among third world nations.

Clearly aware of the potentially troublesome implications for Chinese political interests of its new receptivity to international aid, Beijing tried to reduce third world concerns. It also built greater goodwill by pulling back from earlier abrasive efforts to rally third world support in a united front effort against Soviet "hegemonism." The Chinese now encouraged so-called South-South cooperation among the developing countries and served on the U.N. Security Council in particular as a champion for broadly supported third world issues. Even in debates over issues of direct relevance to China—such as Soviet occupation of Afghanistan and Vietnamese occupation of Kampuchea—the Chinese, whenever possible, allowed others to take the lead in the struggle against the Soviets and their Vietnamese allies. The Chinese preferred now to shield their anti-Soviet motives behind a facade of strong support for third world positions.

China also began to relax its pressure on Taiwan in international forums during the 1980s. Beijing had by this time won the China seat in most such organizations, and was anxious to show flexibility and conciliation toward Taiwan as a way to enhance prospects for talks leading to reconciliation. Beijing was also aware that Chinese moderation on this issue could help reduce the credibility of the argument of those in the United States and elsewhere who used the "danger" posed by mainland China to justify large-scale U.S. arms transfers to Taiwan.

China's economic modernization drive spurred Beijing to join a number of international organizations in order to obtain low-cost technical and financial assistance. After delaying membership during the 1970s, China joined the World Bank and IMF in 1980, and it stepped up its participation in such U.N. organizations as UNCTAD, UNICEF, and WHO. Beijing preferred to receive aid through these multilateral channels because there were few hidden political strings attached and because the World Bank and IMF offered much lower interest rates than private banks and foreign governments.

Beijing joined some organizations to acquire the credentials to pursue other development goals. For example, its decision to join the International Atomic Energy Agency in 1983 was designed in part to encourage foreign suppliers, such as the United States and Japan, to relax their restrictions on providing China with nuclear equipment. Beijing appeared to be moving closer to deciding to join the General Agreement on Tariffs and Trade, partly because this move would make China eligible for U.S. consideration of tariff reductions under the generalized system of preferences.

The World Bank was Beijing's primary international source of development funds as of 1984. When it joined in the spring of 1980, however, it was too late to be included in the sixth replenishment of the bank's credit subsidiary—the International Development Agency (IDA). Further reductions in IDA donor funds and a one-year delay until 1984 in the beginning of the next replenishment of IDA made it difficult for China to receive IDA funding. Nevertheless, Beijing had obtained over $1 billion in World Bank loans and credits by 1984, about half at IDA concessional rates. In 1984, it expected to receive an additional $1 billion from the bank and hoped to obtain even larger amounts in the years ahead. Beijing used these funds for projects in education, energy, argiculture, and transportation.

The World Bank was also a major source of advice and expertise. Its

1981 comprehensive study of China's economy was unprecedented as a source of information for foreign governments involved with that economy. Beijing apparently was so satisfied with this study that it commissioned the bank to prepare another one.

Less than a year after joining the IMF in April 1980, China made two reserve tranche drawings, received a trust fund loan, and borrowed against its credit tranche worth a total of 1.23 billion special drawing rights (SDR) (approximately $1.3 billion). China's subsequent balance-of-payments surplus led Beijing to announce in May 1983 that it was paying back its 450-million SDR first credit tranche ten months early.

In addition, China received $230 million in development grants from the United Nations between 1979 and 1983. These funds were used mainly to purchase computers to tabulate the 1982 census and to sponsor the June 1982 foreign investment promotion meeting under the auspices of the U.N. Industrial Development Organization.

China's efforts to gain a greater share of the already limited development aid available from these sources placed it in increasingly stiff competition with other third world countries, especially India. The Indians previously had received as much as 40 percent of the IDA's credits. As Beijing pressed for more, smaller developing countries became concerned that there would be little left for them.

To offset such concerns, the Chinese backed third world demands that the developed countries increase their contributions to the World Bank, and that the IMF raise its borrowing limits. In addition, China announced that it would contribute over $3 million during 1984 for nine U.N. programs. These contributions included technical assistance to other third world countries. For example, Africans were brought to China for U.N.-sponsored training in medical care. Beijing tried to milk as much political benefit as possible from these relatively negligible aid donations, and it used its position on the U.N. Security Council to build political capital with the third world that would reduce opposition to its competition for development funds. The Chinese nonetheless were well aware from past experience that too high a profile on sensitive issues could alienate as many nations as it could attract. As a result, Beijing tended to follow the consensus among third world states, letting others take the lead. The Chinese approach seemed designed to gain as much goodwill as possible by offending the smallest number of third world states. As a result, they appeared more passive; even on issues of direct and vital interest to China, such as Kampuchea and Afghanistan, they confined themselves to routine efforts. More frequently, Beijing relied on others to take the lead, such as ASEAN on matters related to Southeast Asia, thereby building the prestige of the latter while getting the anti-Soviet job done.

Beijing also seemed to judge that too close an association with the United States would hamper its efforts to sustain broadly based goodwill in the United Nations and keep up an image of policy independence. As a result, the Chinese only infrequently sided with the United States, and on several occasions they took positions egregiously at variance with U.S. interests. Most notably, in September 1983, China abstained from supporting the U.S.-supported resolution condemning the Soviet Union for shooting down a South Korean jet liner that had intruded into Soviet airspace. In 1981, China had used its Security Council seat to block U.S.-backed efforts to reappoint U.N. Secretary General Kurt Waldheim, holding out until a candidate from the third world eventually won the post.

One of Beijing's primary goals in joining international organizations—both intergovernmental and unofficial—in the 1970s was to wrest the "China seat" from Taiwan. With few exceptions, notably the Asian Development Bank, it had met this goal by 1984. As a result, since 1981, China showed a much more relaxed attitude toward Taiwan's rejoining some nonofficial international organizations as China, Taipei. In so doing, Beijing seemed to hope to expand contacts and eventually induce Taiwan to hold reunification talks in accord with China's nine-point proposal to Taipei, announced on 30 September 1981.

While welcoming the chance to participate in international activities again, Taipei continued to finesse Beijing's overtures. It tried to keep all contacts between Taiwan and mainland athletes, scholars, and other nonofficial personnel to a minimum. Taiwan's prime minister announced in 1984 that these meetings could take place as long as they were held on an equal footing, were not political, and did not take place on the mainland.[51]

With some modifications, the Olympic solution formulated in 1981 became the model for dual participation of Beijing and Taipei in nonofficial intergovernmental organizations. Under this arrangement, Taiwan remained in the Olympic movement by calling its Olympic organization the Chinese Taipei National Olympic Committee. Taiwan also agreed to submit a new flag and emblem to the International Olympic Committee for approval.

Arms Control

China also attempted to tailor its position on arms control issues in international forums to appeal to as wide an audience as possible. But these questions also had direct bearing on fundamental Chinese security concerns. Thus, the parameters of China's stance on arms control and disarmament remained governed by several important Chinese goals.[52]

Beijing wanted to maintain as free a hand as possible to expand China's nuclear capabilities against likely adversaries. For over 20 years, Chinese leaders had given high priority to nuclear weapons development in order to help deter outside aggression and intimidation, to secure a strategic retaliatory capability, and to demonstrate China's international importance. Since the early 1970s, China's deterrence and strategic retaliatory capability focused on the Soviet threat. Beijing deployed over 100 missiles capable of hitting Soviet targets with nuclear warheads, and was reasonably sure that the USSR remained unable to neutralize this force with a first strike against China.

China also wanted to exert influence on U.S.–Soviet arms talks. In the 1970s, Beijing worked hard to encourage Western resistance to Soviet détente in the SALT talks, in part to avoid a decline in U.S. military pressure on the USSR that would allow Moscow more military leeway to deal with its China problem. As Beijing became less worried about possible U.S.–Soviet collaboration at its expense in the 1980s, it took a different tack, attempting to endorse a more moderate stance that both enjoyed wider international support and fit in well with China's security interests in Asia. Beijing also saw disarmament and arms control forums as useful platforms from which to project China's image as the only developing country possessing nuclear weapons, thereby underlining its credentials as a leader of the third world.

Beginning in the 1960s, Beijing criticized most arms control negotiations as designed to maintain the superpowers' nuclear arms monopoly. As China emerged from its isolation during the 1970s, Beijing believed it was confronted with the possibility that U.S.-USSR détente would lead to a deal being struck between Moscow and Washington that would perpetuate China's inferior status. China was sharply critical of the SALT negotiations, for example, accusing the United States of attempting to "appease" the Soviets in order to divert the Soviet threat toward China.

During the late 1970s, China became even more concerned about Moscow's "unbridled" arms buildup, especially in Asia, claiming it threatened world peace and presented China with the problem of dealing alone with the USSR—which it believed constituted its major security threat. Beijing thus called for a global "united front" against the Soviet Union, and moved closer to the United States and the West.

As the United States began—in Beijing's view—to adopt stronger military measures to check the Soviet expansion in the 1980s, China put aside most concerns about U.S.–Soviet arms deals coming at Chinese expense. The main exception was Chinese concern during 1982-1983 that the two superpowers might strike a deal on intermediate force missiles that would have allowed Moscow to redeploy SS-20 missiles from Europe to Asia. As the Chinese were repeatedly reassured of U.S. intentions, and as the U.S.-Soviet talks on controlling such arms made no progress and eventually broke down, Beijing shifted its concerns to the negative implications for China of the escalating superpower arms race. Chinese media in 1983 and 1984 persistently highlighted the dangers of the buildup of nuclear forces by both the Soviet Union and the United States; Beijing backed away from earlier Chinese criticism of East-West arms control talks and called for renewed negotiations in order to slow and halt the arms race.

In part, China's altered stance was based on security concerns. The Chinese were worried over what they increasingly saw as a stepped-up U.S.–Soviet arms race that in East Asia had led to a steady buildup of Soviet forces and a widening in the gap between Soviet and Chinese military capabilities. China hoped to focus on economic modernization and to avoid the increased defense spending needed to keep pace with the Soviet advances. In the interim, to avoid domination by Moscow, Beijing increasingly found itself forced to compromise, and to establish closer military ties, with the United States. Thus, the Chinese saw the East-West arms race entering a new stage of development that would leave China militarily further behind the United States and the USSR and would reduce Chinese leverage with both powers. It threatened greater bipolarity in world politics, making it more difficult for China to steer an "independent" foreign policy course.

At the same time, a moderate anti-superpower line fit in well with contemporary Chinese image making in foreign affairs. Thus, Beijing's arms control proposal at the U.N. Conference on Disarmament in 1982, and at the U.N. General Assembly the following year, turned away from China's own nuclear ambitions and focused instead on calls for the two superpowers to stop all testing, research, and manufacture of new nuclear weapons, and to agree to cut their stockpiles in half. Once the latter pledge was made, Beijing said it would be willing to attend a world disarmament conference.

Beijing obviously had little expectation that its proposal would win approval, but it served to focus critical attention exclusively on the superpowers in a way that would please the broad ranks of the international peace movement. This line of reasoning was almost certainly behind Premier Zhao Ziyang's support for the European peace movement during his trip to Europe in mid-1984.

NOTES

1. See coverage in *Washington Post* and *New York Times* in the week prior to Shultz's late January departure for China. For background, see Jonathan Pollack, *The Lessons of Coalition Politics* (Santa Monica, Calif.: Rand Corp., 1984). See also Richard Nations' article in *Far Eastern Economic Review*, 21 April 1983.

2. See coverage in *Far Eastern Economic Review*, 21 April 1983.

3. See discussion in Robert Sutter and Larry Niksch, "China's Role in U.S. Security Policy," *Issues and Studies*, March 1984.

4. See coverage in *Far Eastern Economic Review*, 21 April 1983.

5. See *DR China*, April–May 1983.

6. See O'Neill's official report on the visit to China, U.S. Congress House, *The United States and China* (Washington: USGPO, 1983). He found no interest in the Congress in amending the Taiwan Relations Act.

7. See China's reaction to the resolution in *DR China*, 14 March and 21 November 1983.

8. *DR China*, 10 June 1981.

9. See press coverage in the *Washington Post* and the *New York Times* of Zhang Ai-ping's visit to the United States in June 1984.

10. See *DR China*, 26 April–1 May 1984.

11. See for background, *DR China*, 16 June 1981; article by Chi Su in Samuel Kim, ed., *Chinese Foreign Policy in the 1980s* (Boulder, Colo: Westview Press, 1984); U.S. Information Agency, "Sino-Soviet Relations: A Review of Developments Since Afghanistan," research memorandum, 7 March 1984; *China Quarterly*, "Chronology," (issued each March, June, September, December 1979–85). See also U.S. Information Agency, "Sino-Soviet Talks: Round Four," research memorandum, 5 April 1984.

12. *DR China*, 16 September 1983.

13. See for background, *DR China*, 16 June 1981; article by Chi Su in Samuel Kim, ed., *Chinese Foreign Policy in the 1980s* (Boulder, Colo: Westview press, 1984); U.S. Information Agency, "Sino-Soviet Relations: A Review of Developments Since Afghanistan," research memorandum, 7 March 1984; *China Quarterly*, "Chronology," (issued each March, June, September, December 1979–85). See also U.S. Information Agency, "Sino-Soviet Talks: Round Four," research memorandum, 5 April 1984. See also Chi Su, "China and the Soviet Union," *Current History*, September 1984.

14. See Soviet press coverage in *DR USSR* in the week following Chernenko's rise to power in February 1984. See also *Liaowang* article in *DR China*, 16 March 1984.

15. These themes were common in Chinese media coverage through March, April, and May.

16. These ship movements were disclosed in the Japanese press at this time. See *DR Asia and Pacific*, March 1984.

17. Beijing published U.S. and Japanese references to these Soviet actions during March, April, and May 1984.

18. See Chinese leaders' remarks to Prime Minister Nakasone in *DR China*, 26–28 March 1984, and with President Reagan, *DR China*, 27 April 1984.

19. *Liaowang* article in *DR China*, 16 July 1984.

20. *Washington Post*, 22 June 1984.

21. For background, see section on Japan in A. Doak Barnett, *China and the Major Powers in Asia* (Washington, D.C.: Brookings Institution, 1977). For coverage of Japan-China economic relations and figures on those relations, see Japan External Trade Organization, *China Newsletter* (bimonthly). See also articles on Japan-China relations in U.S. Congress, Joint Economic Committee, *China Under the Four Modernizatiions* (Washington, D.C.: U.S. Government Printing Office, 1982); and *The Chinese Economy in the 1980s* (Washington: USGPO, 1985).

22. See in particular the annual White Paper published by the Japanese Defense Agency.

23. For background on Sino-Japanese relations and their implications for the situation in Korea and for the Sino-Soviet rivalry, see U.S. Congress, House Committee on Foreign Affairs, *The Soviet Role in Asia* (Washington, D.C.: U.S. Government Printing Office, 1983), pp. 90–159, 343–64.

24. For more background on Sino-Japanese economic relations, see testimony in U.S. Congress, House Committee on Energy and Commerce, Special Subcommittee on Trade with China, *Hearing, October 4, 1984* (Washington, D.C.: U.S. Government Printing Office, 1985).

25. The anniversaries, on 6 July and 11 July, were covered by North Korean, Chinese, and Soviet media, and reprinted in *DR Asia and Pacific, DR China,* and *DR USSR,* respectively.

26. Coverage of Kim's visit appeared in *DR Asia and Pacific* and *DR USSR* in late May 1984.

27. For background, see Evelyn Colbert, "Standing Pat," *Foreign Policy,* Spring 1984; and U.S. Congress, House Committee on Foreign Affairs, *The Soviet Role in Asia,* pp. 160–235. For good weekly coverage of China-Indochina events, see *Far Eastern Economic Review.*

28. See periodic appraisals of the border fighting in *Far Eastern Economic Review,* 19 April 1984, 26 April 1984, 7 June 1984, and 21 June 1984.

29. Consultations with diplomats, Washington D.C., 1980–84.

30. See Vietnamese coverage of such support in article by Major General Le Thang Van in Vietnamese army journal, *Tap Chi Doi Nhan Dan,* July 1984.

31. See review of China's relations with these countries in *Far Eastern Economic Review, Asia Yearbook,* 1981, pp. 121–3; 1982, pp. 134–5; 1983, pp. 133–4; 1985.

32. *DR China,* 1 March 1983.

33. See Zhao Ziyang's remarks in Australia, reprinted in *DR China,* 20 April 1983; and his meeting with the French foreign minister, in *DR China,* 2 August 1982.

34. For background, see the review of Chinese interaction with various third world countries in *China Quarterly,* "Chronology," March, June, September, December 1982; March, June, September, December 1983; March, June, September, December 1984.

35. See testimony by Winston Lord in U.S. Congress, Senate Committee on Foreign Relations, *United States-China Relations: Today's Realities and Prospects for the Future* (Washington, D.C.: U.S. Government Printing Office, 1984).

36. Coverage of the Wu speech appears in *DR China,* 30 September 1983.

37. Coverage of Wu's visit to Pakistan appears in *DR China,* 28 July 1983.

38. Huang's speech is in *DR China,* 14 June 1982.

39. For background on China's policy toward Latin America, see articles by Robert Worden in *Asian Survey,* May 1983, and in Chun-tu Hsueh, ed., *China's Foreign Relations: New Perspectives* (New York: Praeger, 1982).

40. See *DR China,* 5 and 14 April 1984.

41. For manifestation of this approach, see Foreign Minister Wu's comments in Latin America, reported in *DR China,* 6–9 August 1984.

42. For coverage, see *DR China,* 1 August 1984.

43. For coverage of developments in China–Cuba relations, see *China Quarterly,* "Chronology," December 1984.

44. See in particular *DR China,* 20 October 1983.

45. See *China Quarterly,* "Chronology," September 1984.

46. The evolution of Beijing's attitude was seen in its positive treatment of the Cuban response to the Contadora initiative to end outside involvement and restore peace in Central America. A 1 September 1983 article in the international affairs journal *Shijie Zhishi* analyzing the situation in Central America argued that since Cuba wished to avoid a showdown with the United States over Nicaragua, and since it faced economic difficulties, Havana repeatedly expressed its welcome of the Contadora proposals and advised the Nicaraguan government and the Salvadoran guerrillas to participate in negotiations in order to relax the situation.

Subsequently, in reporting the U.S. military action in Grenada in October 1983, Chinese media strongly condemned the United States for its "hegemonist act" of "gunboat diplomacy" and dismissed U.S. allegations of a Cuban role on the island as a "pretext." Similarly, Chinese commentary in December, reviewing the past year's events in Central America, eschewed charges of Cuban responsibility for the tense situation there, arguing more generally against "all outside interference" and reserving harsh and direct criticism for the "superpowers." See *Shijie Zhishi*, 1 September 1983; *DR China*, 26 and 31 October 1983.

47. Coverage of Zhao's trip begins in *DR China*, 24 May 1984, and concludes in mid-June. See also *China Quarterly*, "Chronology," for this period.

48. Trade figures from Central Intelligence Agency, *China: International Trade* (updated quarterly).

49. For detailed background, see weekly coverage of the Hong Kong issue in *Far Eastern Economic Review*. See also Robert Sutter's article in U.S. Congress, Joint Economic Committee, *The Chinese Economy in the Eighties* (Washington, D.C.: U.S. Government Printing Office, 1985). See also U.S. Congress, House Committee on Energy and Commerce, Special Subcommitteee on Trade with China, *Hearing, 4 October 1984*.

50. For good background on Chinese policy toward international organizations and arms control, see articles by William Feeney, Shao-chun Leng, Hung-dah Chiu, and Samuel Kim in James Hsiung and Samuel Kim, eds., *China in the Global Community* (New York: Praeger, 1980). See also Samuel Kim (ed.) *China and the World*, (Boulder, Colo., Westview Press, 1984). For details on China's policy, see *China Quarterly*, "Chronology," March, June, September, December 1982, March, June, September, December 1983, March, June, September, December 1984.

51. Consultations with Taiwan representatives, Washington D.C., October 1984.

52. This section is based heavily on Robert Sutter, "Chinese Nuclear Weapons and American Interests," in U.S. Congress, Joint Economic Committee, *The Chinese Economy in the Eighties*. See also Sutter's "Developments in Chinese Nuclear Weapons and Attitudes Toward Arms Control," paper presented at the International Studies Association Conference, Colorado Springs, 25 October 1984.

10

PROSPECTS AND IMPLICATIONS FOR THE UNITED STATES

Short-term (one–two year) prospects for continuity in China's overall strategy in foreign affairs appear good. The reform-minded officials led by Deng Xiaoping have been successful in establishing an administrative regime whose political success or failure rests fundamentally on its ability to bring about economic development for China and a better material life for the Chinese people. Several consequences flow from this governing priority, including some having direct implications for China's foreign policy. Thus, the Chinese will likely remain unwilling—unless severely pressed—to reorient recent government spending priorities in a major way so that military spending, rather than economic development, receives much higher priority. Such high levels of defense spending otherwise could represent a serious drag on China's drive to accelerate economic modernization. Correspondingly, Beijing will probably remain anxious to avoid expanded military conflict around its periphery, or other costly involvement abroad that would seriously drain resources needed for faster economic modernization.

Nevertheless, the unrelenting Soviet effort to build military power and expand political influence in Asia will almost certainly continue to confront Chinese planners with difficult policy choices as they attempt to secure China's environment in Asia without a major increase in defense preparedness and expenditures. Moscow, under two successor leaderships, has shown little indication that it is prepared to moderate the military-political effort in Asia begun by the Brezhnev administration in the mid-1960s. It remains convinced that the military buildup has been the essential ingredient in securing Soviet territorial integrity and allowing Moscow to exploit targets of opportunity for expansion against the West and China. For China, this Soviet effort appears designed militarily to encircle the PRC, to reduce China's influence in Asian and world affairs, and to force China to subject its future to the wishes of the USSR.

Unwilling to be subordinate to Soviet ambitions but well aware of the potentially disastrous consequences involved in confronting the USSR on its own, Beijing is likely to continue to rely heavily on diplomacy, backed by a moderate defense buildup, to deal with this fundamental foreign policy concern. On the one hand, this probably will involve continued efforts to moderate tensions with the USSR and perhaps reach accomodation on the margins of the Sino-Soviet dispute as means to manage the Soviet pressure. On the other hand, it will doubtless involve continued reliance on the United States and the West—to maintain an international balance of influence that curbs Soviet ability to focus power against China, and to provide an implicit security understanding between the Chinese and the United States that would pose open-ended negative consequences for the USSR in the event that Moscow attempted markedly to increase military pressure and intimidation against China.

Meanwhile, China's stress on economic modernization will likely strengthen its need for closer economic ties with the United States and the West. Beijing's development efforts probably will continue to stress gaining greater access to Western markets, financial and technical assistance, and advanced technology and equipment as effective means of promoting internal development.

Thus, security and economic imperatives appear strongly to constrain—at least for the near term—the possible choices in Chinese foreign strategy, forcing Beijing into a posture that avoids direct military conflict with the USSR but nurtures ties with the West as a critical ingredient in China's security against the Soviet threat and in its economic modernization. Chinese nationalism and ideological imperatives could argue for a tougher posture toward the West, especially the United States, over such issues as Taiwan, the alleged "bourgeois" influences entering China as a result of closer economic interaction with the West, disputes over policy in the third world, and other questions. Indeed, the Taiwan issue, the so-called "spiritual pollution" entering China from the West, and others of these questions could become enmeshed in Chinese domestic political disputes, as they have in the past, and be used by dissidents in the leadership to criticize the recent tenure of Deng Xiaoping and his associates. Or it could be argued in Chinese ruling circles—as it was in the recent past—that Beijing would be better served in securing its environment and successful economic modernization by a more accommodating posture toward the USSR on basic security issues. However, the record of Chinese foreign policy since the mid-1970s shows that such approaches—while perhaps still favored by some leaders in China—have been tried and have been found wanting; Beijing has been compelled by international and domestic circumstances to rely on carefully maintained ties with the United States and the West in order to effectively modernize its economy and to sustain its security and independence in the face of unrelenting Soviet pressure.

Thus, while the broad outlines of China's near-term strategy in foreign affairs appear relatively clear-cut, outside observers and even officials in China cannot predict with assurance the kinds of tactics Beijing may employ to carry out its policy. Nor can they have great confidence in predicting the longer-term (five–ten year) prospects for China's strategy in foreign affairs. For example, this study has examined five episodes of change in Chinese tactics in foreign affairs during the recent tenure of Deng Xiaoping (1978–84). The implication is clear: Chinese leaders are capable of more such shifts in the future. Indeed, the ambiguity seen in China's consolidating ties with the United States while attempting to maintain an independent policy posture attractive to third world developing countries, the European peace movement, and pro-Soviet Communist parties and governments suggests a certain degree of fluidity in its current tactics in foreign affairs. And over the period until the mid-1990s, it is conceivable that tactical shifts and modifications could lead to basic changes in strategy under appropriate circumstances.

Both domestic and foreign pressures could give rise to tactical adjustments, and perhaps even major changes in Chinese foreign policy, over the longer term. Within China, Deng Xiaoping and his associates have achieved a large measure of success in reforming Chinese political, economic, and military institutions, in purging dissident and incompetent officials, and in establishing institutions and leadership mechanisms that will allow for a smooth political transition and leadership succession to his protégés Party General Secretary Hu Yaobang and Premier Zhao Ziyang. But sober analysis clearly shows that a political crisis of leadership succession remains a distinct possibility and could have unpredictable consequences for China's approach to foreign affairs. Deng's reform efforts are far from complete. China remains in the midst of a major party rectification campaign and has only begun the complicated task of reorganizing the urban economy. Chinese military and public security organs have not been subjected to the same kind of strong reforms as the rest of the polity, and are seen as strongholds of conservative leaders opposed to many of the consequences of recent reform efforts. At present, Deng's personal leadership is able to keep potential disagreement under control, but there is no guarantee that his successors have the power and prestige to carry out the sometimes controversial policy changes in the face of possibly growing resistance once the 80-year-old Deng passes from the scene.

Moreover, leadership unity could be severely affected by negative consequences from the major economic, social, and political reforms carried out in recent years. The record since 1978 shows that while Chinese leaders want more efficient administration in the interests of faster economic growth and overall modernization, they remain concerned that the economic growth not lead to inflation or other threats to economic stability, that China's cultural integrity remain intact as it absorbs knowledge and technology from the outside world, and that rewards for efficiency not lead to gross inequalities in the distribution of wealth and status in the Chinese society. At the same time, a major failure in the economic modernization strategy caused by circumstances beyond the government's control (such as poor weather for agriculture) or by poor choices in policy could sorely test Chinese leadership cohesion, especially if Deng were no longer in charge.

The consequences of political conflict or other leadership crisis on Chinese foreign policy could be wide-ranging. Perhaps of most immediate importance, it could reduce China's ability to pursue an effective, activist approach to foreign affairs. A successor Chinese leadership, without the strong control exerted by Deng Xiaoping, might prove to be more hesitant in foreign affairs, unwilling or unable to reach a strong consensus on sensitive issues involving the two superpowers and other questions. Or, alternatively, insecure leaders might choose to shore up their positions by adopting strongly nationalistic postures on sensitive foreign policy questions like Taiwan, the Sino-Soviet border, or other problems. Meanwhile, a significant failure in current economic policies might reduce the importance China attaches to economic outreach to the West, and strengthen the arguments of those Chinese officials who are deeply offended by the social and ideological "contamination" they see accompanying closer economic and other ties with the West.

Internationally, the future policies of the two superpowers and their allies and associates will have a major bearing on China's approach to foreign affairs. It is likely that there will be a substantial generational change in the Soviet leadership now that the aged Chernenko regime has passed from the scene. The new generation of Soviet officials can see Moscow's interests better served by the establishment of a modus vivendi that allows for some reduction in current levels of Soviet military pressure on the PRC. Of course, fundamental change in Soviet policy will not come easily. But if it does occur, it could prompt China to reexamine the basic framework that has guided its foreign and defense policy since the 1960s; Beijing might respond by easing tension and reaching accommodation with Moscow over major security issues, and thereby attempt to increase Chinese policy independence and room for maneuver in East Asia and the great-power triangle.

The U.S. management of sensitive issues in relations with China, notably those related to Taiwan, could alter Chinese international behavior. Seeing that Beijing has little alternative at present but to sustain a close relationship with the West against the USSR, Washington could attempt to use this perceived leverage in order to upgrade arms supplies to Taiwan or restore official contacts with the Taipei government. Any such fundamental challenge to Chinese nationalistic sensibilities could prompt PRC leaders to reassess the pros and cons of its relationship with the United States. In particular, Beijing might respond by taking greater risks in confronting the United States over Taiwan, even to the point of possibly alienating the U.S. counterweight to Soviet pressure on China, in order to maintain the political integrity of the Chinese leadership in the face of such a perceived U.S. challenge.

Meanwhile, Chinese leaders will almost certainly remain on the lookout for international developments that could increase their leverage with either superpower and improve their room for maneuver in Asian and world affairs. And Beijing might choose to adjust its foreign posture in reaction to such developments. For example, it might see a future U.S.-Soviet military confrontation in the Middle East or Southwest Asia as increasing U.S. need for Chinese cooperation in maintaining a tough stance vis-à-vis the USSR. Otherwise, the USSR might relax against China in order to focus more force westward, against the United States. Under these circumstances, China might make it clear to the United States that continued strong Chinese opposition to the USSR might require greater U.S. concessions of Taiwan or other questions.

By the same token, Beijing leaders clearly will be sensitive to international developments that could reduce their leverage against the superpowers. China has recently made clear its concern about the U.S.-Soviet arms race, especially in Asia. It presumably recognizes that such an increase in weaponry not only endangers Chinese security and leaves China further behind in the arms race with the USSR, but also diminishes China's role as a significant actor in Asian and international politics. Under these circumstances, Beijing might become more sensitive on bilateral issues with both the United States and the USSR, for fear that either power would come to take China for granted or consider it as the "junior" player in the triangular politics.

A continuation of China's recent approach to foreign affairs would appear to serve several important American objectives.

China would continue to act as an implicit counterweight to Soviet power in Asia. The USSR would remain uncertain of China's likely position in the event it became involved in a military conflict with the

United States. And Moscow would still be required to confront China along the Sino-Soviet border and, indirectly, through Vietnam in Indochina.

Chinese development strategy and concern for stability in Asia would continue to limit the chances of the PRC reverting to its disruptive policies of the past and upsetting the rapid economic development of the countries along Asia's periphery. This would have a particularly beneficial effect on South Korea, Taiwan, and the non-communist ASEAN states that in the past had faced Chinese-backed instability and threat.

China would become a market of growing, albeit still limited, importance to the United States and its allies and friends.

Some Americans seek greater benefit from relations with China, or fear that China may turn away from the United States in the future. They favor further reducing obstacles in U.S.-Chinese ties or otherwise providing U.S. incentives to China, so as to ensure continued progress toward closer Chinese collaboration with the United States or to ensure that China will remain on the U.S. "side" in the anticipated period of protracted U.S. confrontation with the USSR. Thus, they favor more liberal U.S. market access for Chinese goods and greater technology transfers to China as a means to promote trade; greater reduction in U.S. arms sales to Taiwan as a way to build U.S. credibility as a reliable friend of the Chinese; or direct U.S. military assistance and arms sales as a means of steeling China's resolve against the USSR and further impeding possible Soviet expansion in Asia.

But other Americans think that Beijing's current posture is about right for U.S. interests and judge that there is little likelihood that the PRC will turn away from the United States in the foreseeable future. Some of this group suggest that China will remain strongly dependent on U.S. support for its economic modernization and security against the USSR. Accordingly, in their judgment, Beijing will have little choice but to go along with U.S. efforts to upgrade defense supplies and other contacts with Taiwan or to adopt tougher policies on other sensitive U.S.-PRC issues. But others in this group see little to be gained from antagonizing the PRC over Taiwan or other sensitive questions, particularly at a time when Taipei's security and other U.S. interests appear to be well provided for through a combination of carefully measured arms sales and the maintenance of sound U.S. relations with China.

SELECTED READINGS

Barnett, A. Doak. *China and the Major Powers in East Asia.* Washington, D.C.: Brookings Institution, 1977.

——. *China's Economy in Global Perspective.* Washington, D.C.: Brookings Institution, 1981.

——. *U.S. Arms Sales: The China-Taiwan Tangle.* Washington, D.C.: Brookings Institution, 1982.

Cammilleri, Joseph. *Chinese Foreign Policy: The Maoist Era and Its Aftermath.* Seattle: University of Washington Press, 1980.

Copper, John F. *China's Global Role.* Stanford: Hoover Institution, 1980. *Current History,* September 1984.

Elliott, David W.P., ed. *The Third Indochina Conflict.* Boulder, Colo.: Westview Press, 1981.

Fingar, Thomas, ed. *China's Quest for Independence: Policy Evolution in the 1970s.* Boulder, Colo.: Westview Press, 1980.

Garrett, Banning, and Bonnie Glaser. *War and Peace: The Views from Moscow and Beijing.* Berkeley: University of California Press, 1984.

Gelman, Harry. *The Soviet Far East Buildup and Soviet Risk-Taking Against China.* Santa Monica, Calif.: Rand Corp., 1982.

Gottlieb, Thomas M. *Chinese Foreign Policy Factionalism and the Origins of the Strategic Triangle.* Santa Monica, Calif.: Rand Corp., 1977.

Griffith, William E. "Sino-Soviet Thaw?" *Problems of Communism,* March–April 1983, pp. 20–29.

Hamrin, Carol Lee. "Competing 'Policy Packages' and Chinese Foreign Policy." *Asian Survey,* May 1984.

Harding, Harry, ed. *China's Foreign Relations in the 1980s.* New Haven: Yale University Press, 1984.

Hsiung, James C., ed. *U.S.-Asian Relations: The National Security Paradox.* New York: Praeger, 1983.

Hsiung, James C., and Samuel S. Kim, eds., *China in the Global Community.* New York: Praeger, 1980.

Hsueh, Chun-tu, ed. *China's Foreign Relations: New Perspectives.* New York: Praeger, 1982.

Jencks, Harlan W. *From Muskets to Missiles: Politics and Professionalism in the Chinese Army, 1945–1981.* Boulder, Colo: Westview Press, 1982.

Johnson, U. Alexis, ed. *China: Policy for the Next Decade.* Boston: Oelgeschlager, Gunn, and Hain, 1984.

Kim, Samuel S. *China, the United Nations and World Order.* Princeton: Princeton University Press, 1979.

Lieberthal, Kenneth G. *Sino-Soviet Conflict in the 1970s: Its Evolution and Implications for the Strategic Triangle.* Santa Monica, Calif.: 1978.

Manning, Robert A. "Reagan's Chance Hit." *Foreign Policy,* Winter 1984, pp. 83–101.

Oksenberg, Michel. "A Decade of Sino-American Relations." *Foreign Affairs*, Fall 1982, pp. 175–95.

Pollack, Jonathan. *The Lessons of Coalition Politics: Sino-American Security Relations*. Santa Monica, Calif.: Rand Corp. 1984.

——. *The Sino-Soviet Rivalry and Chinese Security Debate*. Santa Monica, Calif.: Rand Corp., 1982.

Reardon-Anderson, James. *Yenan and the Great Powers*. New York: Columbia University Press, 1980.

Segal, Gerald, and William Tow, eds. *Chinese Defence Policy*. London: Macmillan, 1984.

Shichor, Yitzhak. *The Middle East in China's Foreign Policy, 1949–1977*. London: Cambridge University Press, 1979.

Solomon, Richard H., ed. *Asian Security in the 1980s*. Santa Monica, Calif.: Rand Corp., 1979.

——. *The China Factor: Sino-American Relations and the Global Scene*. Englewood Cliffs, N.J.: Prentice-Hall, 1981.

Whiting, Allen S. "Assertive Nationalism in Chinese Foreign Policy." *Asian Survey*, August 1983, pp. 913–33.

Worden, Robert L. "China's Balancing Act: Cancun, the Third World, Latin America." *Asian Survey*, May 1983, pp. 619–36.

Yahuda, Michael. *Towards the End of Isolationism: China's Foreign Policy After Mao*. New York: St. Martin's, 1983.

Zagoria, Donald. "The Moscow-Beijing Detente." *Foreign Affairs*, Spring 1983, pp. 853–73.

INDEX

Afghanistan, 73; Chinese reaction to Soviet invasion of, 114-127; Soviet invasion of, 7

Africa; Chinese officials' visits to, 70, 73, 159; Zhao Ziyang's tour of, 159-160

African National Congress (ANC), 160

Albania, 14, 105; carries on polemic with China over foreign policy, 1977, 57-58

Aleksandrov, I.; comments on China, 49

Algeria, 19

Angola, 56, 70

appeasement, see U.S.-Soviet relations

Arafat, Yasir, 199; meets Zhao Ziyang, 159

Argentina, 159

Arkhipov, Ivan; visit to China, 183-186

arms control, 6; Chinese policy towards, 2, 73, 199, 215-217. See also SALT

arms sales; by China, 106. See also Iraq, Iran, Egypt

Asia; China's efforts to preserve a favorable balance of power in, 38-39, 62-64; China's support for continued U.S. presence in, 38; China's view of the balance of power in, 4-7, 9-12, 36-39; China's view of Soviet expansion in, 63, 184; future Soviet policy in, 221-222

Asian collective security arrangement; Soviet proposal for, 40-41, 43

Asian Development Bank; an issue in U.S.-China relations, 142, 178

Association of Southeast Asian Nations (ASEAN); Chinese policy toward, 67, 127-128, 191-196

Backfire bombers, 54-56; deployed in Asia, 89, 188

Baldridge, Malcolm; visits China, 1983, 180

Bangladesh, 43

Barre, Mohamed Siad, 56

Berlinguer, Enrico; visits China, 1980, 107

Blumental, Michael; visits China, 1979, 90

Brest-Litovsk; treaty of, 27, 57

Brezhnev doctrine of limited sovereignty, 6, 15, 115; opposed by China and the United States, 20

Brezhnev, Leonid; attacked by China, 22; attacked by Zhou En-lai, 26; sends condolence message to China, 1976, 49; speeches conciliatory toward China, 154-156; tours Soviet Far East, 1978, 88

Brown, Harold; visit to China, 1980, 116-121, 140-142

Brzezinski, Zbigniew, 6, 53; visits China, 1978, 67, 82

Burma, 13, 14-15; Deng Xiaoping's visit to, 1978, 61

Burmese Communist Party, 15

Bush, George; Chinese reception of, 1980, 140; Chinese reception of, 1982, 143, 149

Cam Ranh Bay; Soviet use of, 89, 193

Cambodia, 13, 19; collapse of U.S.-backed government in, 37. See also Kampuchea.

Carrington, Lord; meeting with Deng Xiaoping, 1981, 131

Carter, Jimmy, 52; Chinese view of policy toward USSR, 52-56, 68, 118-121; normalization of relations with China, 67-69; policy toward Vietnam, 82-84

Castro, Fidel, 200

Central America; China criticizes U.S. policy toward, 1981, 148; China's stance on, 1980-1985, 201

Ceylon, 13

Chamberlain, Neville, 41

Chad, 106

Chai Zemin; calls of strong U.S. response to Soviet invasion of Afghanistan, 115

Chen I, 14

Chen Yun; receives Ivan Arkhipov, 186; speaks on economic issues, 1980, 135; views of foreign policy, 113

Chile; Chinese relations with, 67, 105, 106

China; adjustments in foreign policy, 1979-1980, 87-108; advocates united front against the USSR, 6, 10-11, 34, 39, 48-49, 56, 64-70, 131-132; defense policy, 1960s and 1970s, 22-23; differentiated approach to U.S. and USSR, 20, 22, 44, 51, 63; domestic determinants of foreign policy, 7-12, 48-49; domestic developments, 1976-1978, 44-48; domestic political difficulties, 1980-1983, 133-139; domestic political and economic issues, 1982, 165-167; domestic reforms, 1978, 61-62; foreign cultural and technical exchanges, 30; greater "independence" in foreign affairs, 1981-1983, 131-171; interest in greater economic ties with the West, 29-30; leadership differences and debate over foreign policy, 5, 6, 7-8, 10-12, 16-19, 25, 30-33, 48, 55, 63, 76-81, 92-93, 114, 136-137, 145-146, 114-126; leadership differences over domestic reforms and foreign policy, 1976-1978, 47-48; more assertive anti-Soviet diplomacy, 1978-1979, 60-86; more positive view of U.S., 1970s, 24-25, 38; motivating factors in foreign policy, 3-12; overture to the United States, 1968-1969, 16-19; policy toward the USSR, 1976-1978, 48-50; reacting to international pressures, 6-7, 9-12, 62, 131-132; reactive diplomacy, 1976-1978, 56-58; reasoning behind harder line to U.S., 1980-1982, 144-146; reasoning behind more moderate line to U.S., harder line to USSR, 1983-1984, 176-186; response to Soviet policy, 1976-1978, 44-45; renewed interest in strategic ties with the U.S., 1979-1980, 116-121; responses to Soviet gestures, 1969-1973, 22-23; role of ideology in foreign policy, 20; shifts in foreign policy, 3-12; view of Soviet threat, 15-19, 38-39, 143; view of U.S.-Soviet cooperation, 15, 22, 25

Chinese Communist Party; cuts back ties with Southeast Asian parties, 98; Eleventh Party Congress, 50-52, 61, 65; Fifth Plenum of the Eleventh Central Committee, 133; Sixth Plenum of the Eleventh Central Committee, 137; Tenth Party Congress, 24-27, 33, 34; Third Plenum of the Eleventh Central Committee, 46, 65-66; Twelfth Party Congress, 164-168

Chinese People's Political Consultative Conference; greetings to Taiwan, 1979, 99; letter to Taiwan, 1979, 100-101

Communist Parties; Chinese cutback in ties with Southeast Asian parties, 98, 194; Chinese policy toward, 107-108, 169-171; relations with China, 8, 63

Contadora Group, 201

cruise missiles; an issue in U.S.-Soviet relations, 54-56

Confucius; campaign against, 8, 32
Cuba, 14, 67, 105; China's relations with, 200-202; China's view of Cuban troops in Africa, 56-58, 70
Cultural Revolution, 4; Chinese assessment of, 66; impact on Chinese foreign policy, 13-15
Czechoslovakia; Soviet invasion of, 6, 15, 17

Defense issues; Chinese leaders views of, 1976-1978, 48. See also PLA
Deng Xiaoping, 3, 5, 33, 152, 166, 167; and China's consolidation of ties with the U.S., 1983-1984, 180; and domestic difficulties, 1978-1979, 91-93; anti-Soviet foreign policy of, 113, 146; criticized by gang of four, 32; criticizes U.S. policy in third world, 1981, 148; explains Mao Zedong's three worlds theory, 1974, 34, 44; hits Soviet threat to China, 1980, 121; hosts Kim Il-song, 1982, 164; hosts President Ford, 41-42; meets Alexander Haig, 1981, 141; meets Harold Brown, 118; meets Lord Carrington, 1981, 131; meets U.S. scientific delegation, 120; more assertive foreign policy of, 1978-1979, 60-86; remarks on Taiwan, 99, 101; role in Chinese confrontation with Vietnam, 73-84; speaks on economic, political policy, 1980, 135; tours Southeast Asia, 1978, 76; views on Vietnam, Kampuchea, 77-81; visit to the U.S., 83-84, 97; visits Japan 1978, 69-70
Deng Yingchao; visit to Kampuchea, 71

East-West Relations; Chinese concern over, 1977-1978, 52-56. See also U.S.-Soviet relations.
Economic Reform in China, 45-47,
61-62, 66, 91-93; readjustment program, 46; ten year plan, 46
Egypt, 56, 67, 106-107; Chinese arms sales to, 106. See also United Arab Republic.
El Salvador, 201
Ethiopia; Chinese support for revolutionary movements in, 25; Soviet influence in, 56
Ethiopia-Somalia border conflict, 106
Europe; Chinese economic accords with Eastern European countries, 185; Chinese relations with Western Europe, 1980-1985, 202-204; Chinese view of, 51, 53-54; Hua Guofeng visits Western Europe, 96, 109-110; Zhao Ziyang discusses relations with Eastern Europe, 1983, 169; Zhao Ziyang visits Western Europe, 1984, 202-204; Zhou Enlai supports unity of, 34-35
European Security Conference, 1975; Chinese view of, 39-40

Falkland Islands; Chinese view of, 159
Fang Min; comments on Carter administration's response to Soviet invasion of Afghanistan, 118-119
Ford, Gerald; dismisses James Schlesinger, 41; hosted by Deng Xiaoping, 41-42; policy in Asia, 39; policy toward USSR, 40-41
foreign aid; China's policy toward, 48, 56, 105-106
foreign economic relations; Chinese interest in, 45-46, 48, 62, 63, 91-93, 211-214, 222
four modernizations; China's drive for, 45, 48
four principles, 92, 167
France, 96; China's response to French policy after the Soviet invasion of Afghanistan, 126-127

French Communist Party; relations with China, 107-108
F-X fighter; proposed U.S. sale to Taiwan, 143

Gandhi, Indira; Chinese policy toward, 124-125
"Gang of Four," 8, 64; arrested, 33, 44, 46-47; criticism of, 64-65; opposition to contacts with the West, 32; opposition to greater trade with the West, 31-32; opposition to Zhou Enlai at the Tenth Party Congress, 25; opposition to Zhouist foreign policy, 31-32; policy toward USSR, 49; trial of, 133; views on foreign policy, 30-31
Geng Biao; fetes Harold Brown, 117; visits Caribbean states, 70; visits North Korea, 163; visits United States, 125-126
Germany; Chinese relations with East Germany, 170-171; Chinese relations with West Germany, 29, 54, 205
Giap, Vietnamese Defense Minister; visits China, 1977, 71; visits USSR, 71
Giscard, President of France; meeting with Hua Guofeng, 1979, 96
Gong Dafei; visits Africa, 159
Great Britain, 14; Hua Guofeng visits, 110; relations with China over the Hong Kong question, 204-211
Gromyko, Andrei, 68, 94, 95
Guinea, 14

Haig, Alexander; views China's role in East-West relations, 144; visits China, 1981, 140-142
Hamrin, Carol, 139
Heixiazi (Big Ussuri) Island, 21
Hill, E.F., 57
Hitler, Adolf, 41
Ho Ying, 157, 160

Hoang Van Hoan, 98, 193
Holdridge, John, 144
Honecker, Erich, 170
Hong Kong, 63, 101-102; Chinese objectives in, 205-208; Sino-British relations over, 204-211; U.S. interests in, 207-208
Howe, British Foreign Secretary, 210
Hu Kwang Railway bonds; an issue in U.S.-China relations, 152
Hu Na, 142, 152, 178
Hu Yaobang; appointed party chairman, 137; denies possibility of Sino-Soviet party ties, 121; discusses Sino-Soviet border, 185; greets East German leader, 170; hosts Kim Il-song, 164; reports at the Twelfth Party Congress, 164-168; speaks at the 70th anniversary of the 1911 revolution, 147; speaks at 1 July 1981 rally, 146; states principles on party-to-party relations, 108; visits North Korea, 189
Hua Guofeng, 49, 61, 104; hits Soviet threat to China, 1980, 121; in opposition to Deng Xiaoping, 65-66, 91-92; message to Indira Gandhi, 124; removed as premier, 133; removed as party chairman, 137; report to 11th party congress, 50-52; report to 5th National People's Congress, 50, 65; views on Kampuchea, Pol Pot, 77, 80; views on U.S.-China normalization, 83; visits Western Europe, 96, 109-110
Huang Hua; attacks U.S. policy in third world, 148; attends Indian reception, 124-125; calls for strong U.S. reaction to Soviet invasion of Afghanistan, 116; criticizes U.S., 67; meets Alexander Haig, 140-141; meets Ronald Reagan, 147; remarks in Great Britain, 110; visits Africa, 159; visits

Pakistan, 123-124; visits Zaire, 70
Hungary's relations with China, 170-171

Ieng Sary, 80
Ilichev, Leonid, 26, 49, 50, 156, 182-186
India, 43; China's policy toward, 124-125
International Atomic Energy Agency, 213
International Organizations; China's policy toward, 211-215. See also United Nations, World Bank, International Monetary Fund.
Indochina. See Vietnam, Kampuchea, Laos.
International Development Agency, 213
International Monetary Fund; China's policy toward, 211-215
Iran, 43; Chinese arms sales to, 161; Chinese ties with the Shah, 67
Iran-Iraq war, 106, 160-161
Iraq, 43. Chinese arms sales to, 160-161; Chinese workers in, 160
Israel, 106
Italian Communist Party; relations with China, 107-108

Japan, 1, 2, 29; anti-hegemony clause in peace treaty with China, 67, 69; Chinese support for self-defense efforts of, 67, 70; controversy with China over history textbooks, 186; peace treaty with China, 60, 67, 69-70; relations with China, 35, 186-189; visit of Deng Xiaoping, 69-70; visit of Hua Guofeng, 126
Japanese "formula" of recognizing China, 68-69
Japan-U.S. security treaty; Chinese view of, 67, 70
Ji Pengfei, 157; policy preference in foreign affairs, 113; receives

Spanish party delegation, 108; visits Middle East, Africa, 107
Jiang Qing, 18; opposition to Zhou Enlai's approach to foreign affairs, 18-19

Kampuchea, 60; Chinese policy toward, 97-98, 127, 191-196; government of Democratic Kampuchea, 98; pressured, attacked by Vietnam, 70-82. See also, Cambodia.
Kaohsiung incident, 100-101, 111
Kapitsa, Mikhail, 122, 153-154, 182-183
Kenya, 13
Khabarovsk, 21
Khieu Samphan, 98
Kim Chong-il, 163, 189
Kim Il-song, 13; receives Geng Biao, 163; receives Zhao Ziyang, 162; visits China, 163; visits the USSR, 185, 189-191
Kissinger, Henry, 41
Korea, 1; China's relations with North Korea, 16, 19, 29, 102-104, 162-164, 189-191. China's response to North Korea's assassination of South Korean leaders, 189; China's response to North Korean peace proposals, 189-190; Sino-Soviet competition over Korea, 185, 189-191
Kosygin, Aleksei; meets Zhou Enlai, 19, 36
Kuomintang (Nationalist Party), 100-102, 111
Laos, 73; China's policy toward, 193; curbed Chinese influence in, 87; relations with USSR and China, 39; visited by Le Duan, 71
Latin America; Chinese policy toward, 200-202
Le Duan; visits China, 71; visits Laos, 71; visits the USSR, 71, 76
Lenin, Vladimir Ilich, 57

Lenin's theory of imperialism, 4
Li Peng, 205
Li Xiannian, 52, 166-167; endorses closer economic ties with the United States, 69; tours Africa, 70; views on foreign policy, 113; views on national sovereignty, Taiwan, 148-149; views on Vietnam, Kampuchea, 76-81
Liao Chengzhi, 111
Lieberthal, Kenneth, 139
Lin Biao, 5, 6, 16, 18, 21, 30; assessment of the U.S., 27; campaign against, 8; defense policy of, 23; foreign policy of, 7-8, 18-19, 25; support of revolutionary movements, 25

Macao, 101-102
Malaysia, 194
Mali, 14
Mao Zedong, 5, 7, 17; death of, 44, 46-47; declining health of, 30; efforts to revise policies of, 66; endorses opening to U.S., 21; May 20, 1970 statement of, 26; statement on danger of war, 51; thought of, 15. See also three worlds theory.
Marxism-Leninism, 4; Albanian-Chinese polemic over, 57; "betrayed" by USSR, 35
Mobutu, President of Zaire, 56
Mondale, Walter, 96-97, 140-142
Mongolia; China demands Soviet troop withdrawal from, 50; China finishes border accord with, 185
Most-Favored-Nation tariff treatment; granted by the United States to China, 120
Mozambique, 105
Munich agreement, 1938, 41, 53

Nakasone, Yasuhiro, 186-189

National People's Congress; 1 January 1979 greetings to Taiwan, 98-101; fifth session, 50; fourth session, 33-36; sixth session, 168-171
Nepal, 13, 14, 61
Ne Win, 15
Nicaragua, 201
Nitze, Paul, 54
Nixon Doctrine, 10, 19, 30, 37
Nixon, Richard; and the Watergate crisis, 37; calls for ties with China, 19; visits China, 6, 23-24; withdraws U.S. forces from Asia, 19, 23, 37
Nonaligned Movement, 70
North Atlantic Treaty Organization (NATO), 64
nuclear weapons; Chinese deterrent to Soviet nuclear attack, 1, 29
Nyerere, Julius, 14

Oman, 25
O'Neill, Thomas, 152-153, 179
Overseas Chinese; Chinese policy toward, 72, 74-76, 194

Pacific doctrine of President Ford, 39
Pakistan, 14, 123-125
Pan-African Congress, 160
Paris peace agreement, 1973, 27
Pell, Claiborne, 179
Peng Zhen, 153
People's Liberation Army (PLA), 30, 61-62, 64-65, 99
People's War, 23, 32
Philippines, 1, 38
Pol Pot, 71, 193
Poland, 131
political reform in China, 46-47, 61-62, 64-70, 91-93, 135-138
Presidential Review Memorandum (PRM), 10, 53
Proletarian Internationalism, 35

Qian Qichen, 156, 182-186
Qiao Guanhua, 40-41, 43

Reagan, Ronald, 6. China's policy toward, 132, 139-153; visits China, 181-182
Red Guard diplomacy, 4, 13-15
Ren Gubing, 53, 95
revolutionary movements; Chinese policy toward, 20, 25, 31, 104-105
Romania, 16, 29, 73
SS-20 missiles, 89, 179, 187-188
Sadat, Anwar, 56, 106-107
Schlesinger, James, 41
Schultz, George, 177
second world nations, 11, 34
Senkaku Islands, 69
Shanghai communique of 1972, 23-24, 35, 37, 38, 51
Sihanouk, Norodom, 84, 97, 193
Sino-Soviet alliance, 94
Sino-Soviet border; Chinese demand for Soviet troop withdrawal from, 22, 26, 50, 52; clashes of 1969, 6, 17; "disputed territory" along, 22, 26, 94; Hu Yaobang discusses, 185; incidents and reaction, 1979-1980, 122; negotiations over, 19, 20-23, 26-27, 29, 35-36, 52; Soviet offers to resume talks over, 154-155; Soviet military exercises along, 122
Sino-Soviet economic exchanges, trade, 50, 183; railway accord signed, 154; frontier trade discussed, 155-156
Sino-Soviet educational, cultural exchanges, 155, 183
Sino-Soviet political exchanges, 156, 182-186
Somalia, 56
Son Sann, 193
Southwest African People's Organization (SWAPO), 159-160
Soviet Union; capture of Soviet spies and border guards by China, 1974, 32; China's more assertive diplomacy against, 1978-1979, 66-70; China's policy toward, 1976-1978, 48-50; competes with China in the third world, 104-107; discussed at the Sixth National People's Congress, 169; discussed at the Twelfth CCP Congress, 167-168; easing tensions with China, 1969-1975, 20-22, 26; easing tensions with China, 1980-1982, 153-156; invasion of Afghanistan and China's response, 114-127; military and other pressure against China, 20, 63; military deployments in Asia and their impact on Sino-Japanese relations, 187; moderation in China's policy and start of political talks, 93-96; party ties with China, 21, 108; proposed nonaggression pact with China, 21, 27, 36; proposed non-use-of-force accord with China, 21, 36; relations with China, 3, 4-12, 13; relations with Vietnam, 76-82; response to Mao's death, 49; strategic posture in Asia, 88-90; suspected objectives in Asia, 36-39; tougher Chinese policy toward, 1983-1984, 177-186; viewed as the main source of war, 41; viewed by the gang of four, 31, 32; viewed by Hua Guofeng, 51-52; Zhou Enlai criticism of, 25-26, 35-36; Zhou-Kosygin talks viewed by, 19, 36
South Africa, 106
Spanish Communist Party, 107-108
Stalin, Joseph, 57
Strategic Arms Limitation Talks (SALT); China's view of, 24, 40, 41, 52-56
Supreme Soviet of USSR; greetings to Chinese leaders, 50

Taiwan; an issue in Chinese leadership politics, 48; an issue in U.S.-China relations, 139-153, 180-181; Chinese criticism of U.S. arms deliveries to, 142-153; Chinese overtures for reunification, 29; Chinese policy toward, 1979-1980, 98-102, 111; communique on U.S. arms sales to Taiwan, 143, 149-151; competition with China in international organizations, 215; Deng Xiaoping's treatment of, 1975, 41; discussed at the Sixth National People's Congress, 169; Hua Guofeng treatment of, 1977, 51; more moderate Chinese approach toward, 1978-1979, 67; tougher Chinese line toward, 1974, 31; treated in the Shanghai communique, 23; treated in U.S.-China normalization agreement, 68-69; U.S. arms deliveries to, 69, 150; viewed by the gang of four, 31; Ye Jianying's proposal for peace talks with, 148; Zhou Enlai's treatment of, 27

Taiwan Democratic Self-Government League, 100-101

Taiwan Relations Act, 140, 141-153, 168

Taiwan-U.S. defense treaty, 51-52, 68, 69

Taiwan uprising of 1947, 32, 100

Tan-Zam Railway, 105

Tanzania, 14

terrorism; Chinese view of, 2

Tet offensive, 17

Thailand, 38, 194

Thatcher, Margaret, 96, 205

third world nations, 4, 10, 11; Chinese efforts to halt Soviet influence in, 56-57, 66-67; Chinese encourage relations with the West, 67; Chinese relations with, 104-107, 156-161; referred to by Zhou Enlai, 25-26

Three Worlds Theory, 34, 44, 51, 157; Sino-Albanian argument over, 57-58

Tibet, 102

Tito, Josip, 57

Trotsky, Leon, 57

Tunisia, 13

Ulanhu, 101

United Arab Republic, 13. See also Egypt

United Nations, 29, 159. See also international organizations.

United States; altered view of China's strategic importance, 1983, 177-178; ambassadorial discussions with China in Warsaw, 13-14, 16, 19; China's conditions on normalization with, 51-52, 68; closer strategic ties with China after Soviet invasion of Afghanistan, 116-121; compatibility of interests with China in Asia, 20, 37, 38, 63, 82-84; discussed at sixth National People's Congress, 169; discussed at twelfth CCP Congress, 167-168; economic recession in, 1974-1975, 37, 40; economic relations with China, 2, 143, 152, 180-181; Hua Guofeng's assessment of relations with, 51-52; more moderate Chinese policy toward, 1983-1984, 177-178; normalization of relations with China, 68-69, 83-84; nuclear cooperation accord with China, 181-182; policy toward China during Vietnam War, 17; policy in third world criticized by China, 1981, 148; reaction to China's "lesson" against Vietnam, 90; relations with China, 1-12, 13; technology transfers to China, 143, 152, 180-181; U.S.-China communique on arms sales to Taiwan, 143; view of China as counterweight to USSR, 63; viewed by gang of four, 31, 32; withdrawal from Vietnam, In-

dochina, 17, 36-37; Zhou Enlai assessment of, 27, 35
U.S.-Soviet relations, 27, 33-34, 39-42, 52, 56, 67
Ustinov, Soviet Defense Minister, 88

Vance, Cyrus, 6, 52, 68
Vietnam, 13, 105; China's more assertive policy toward, 1978, 73-84; China's policy toward, 1980, 127-128; China's policy toward, 1983-1984, 184-185, 191-196; China's relations with North Vietnam, 16, 19, 29; Chinese military "lesson" against, 1979, 87; Chinese policy of restraint, 1977, 70-72; collapse of U.S.-backed government in Saigon, 37; confrontation with China, 6-7, 70-84; dispute with China over ethnic Chinese in Vietnam, 72; internal conditions, 1978, 72; joins Council for Mutual Economic Assistance, 74; negotiations with China, 74, 75-76, 97-98; offensive in Kampuchea, 1984-1985, 186; Overseas Chinese present in, 74-76; pressures, invades Kampuchea, 60, 70-72; relations with USSR, 39, 73-74; signs friendship treaty with USSR, 76; Soviet amphibions exercise with and China's response, 1984, 193; Soviet bases in, 73-74, 89, 193

Wan Li, 170, 183-184
Wang Bingnan, 121
Wang Dongxing, 76
Wang Hongwen, 30
Wang Youping, 95
Watergate affair, 37, 40
Weinberger, Caspar, 180
Western Sahara, 106
Wolfowitz, Paul, 177

World Bank; China's relations with, 211-215
world war; China's view of the danger of, 33-34, 40-41, 51, 54, 171
Wu Xueqian, 157; addresses UN General Assembly, 1983, 198-200; meets Mikhail Kapitsa, 182-183; meets Thomas O'Neill, 153; tours Latin America, 201; views on foreign policy, 113; visit to Africa, 107

Xi Zhongxun, 101-102
Xu Ziangqian: announces end of shelling in Taiwan Straits, 99; hosts Harold Brown, 117

Yanan rectification campaign, 91
Yao Wenyuan, 30
Ye Jianying, 65, 166-167; attitude toward reform in China, 91-92, 137; defines revisionism, 108; proposes peace talks with Taiwan, 148
Yemen, South, 77, 105
Yi Chong-ok; visits China, 103-104
Young, Andrew, 56-57
Yugoslavia, 19, 57, 73

Zaire, 56, 67, 70
Zhang Chunqiao, 30
Zhang Haifeng, 114-115
Zhao Ziyang; at Cancun summit meeting, 1981, 159; becomes premier, 133; becomes party vice chairman, 137; meets Alexander Haig, 141; meets Ronald Reagan, 147; meets Thomas O'Neill, 152-153; 1 December 1981 report of, 137-138; receives Ivan Arkhipov, 186; report to sixth National People's Congress, 168-171; speeches for North Korean premier, 103-104; speeches for Swedish premier, 131-132; tours Africa, 159-

160; visits North Korea, 162;
visits United States, 180-182;
visits Western Europe, 202-204
Zhen Bao (Damansky) Island, 21
Zhou Enlai, 5, 6, 9, 62; criticized by
gang of four, 32; death of, 44;
declining health of, 30; foreign
policy of, 8, 17-27; meets Julius
Nyerere, 14; meeting with Aleksei Kosygin, 19, 36, 50; speech at
fourth National People's Congress, 33-36, 51; speech to the
tenth CCP Congress, 24-27, 51
Zhu Qichen, 201
Zumwalt, Elmo, 52
Zuo Zongdang, 78

ABOUT THE AUTHOR

ROBERT SUTTER has been a specialist in Asian affairs with the Congressional Research Service of the Library of Congress since 1977. Previously, he served for nine years as an analyst of Chinese foreign policy with the Central Intelligence Agency. Since 1980, he has also held special assignments dealing with U.S.-Asian relations with the Department of State, the Senate Foreign Relations Committee, and the Central Intelligence Agency.

Dr. Sutter received the Ph.D. in history and East Asian languages from Harvard University. He teaches regularly at Georgetown University and the University of Virginia, and has published several books and articles dealing with contemporary China and Japan, and their relations with the United States.